THE ARYA SAMAJ

THE ARYA SAMAJ

An Account of its Origin, Doctrines, and Activities, with A Biographical Sketch of the Founder

by

LAJPAT RAI

A PREFACE
Prof. SIDNEY WEBB, LL.B.

GYAN

Published by

GYAN

Gyan Publishing House
5, Ansari Road
Daryaganj, New Delhi-110002
Phone: 011-47034999, 9811692060
E-mail: books@gyanbooks.com

Distribution Network
gyanbooks.com
India, USA, Canada, UK, Australia, France

ISBN : 978-81-212-2631-8 (PB)
First Published, 1915

2nd Impression 2021

Printed at: Gyan Press, Delhi.

The Arya Samaj
Author: Lajpat Rai

THE ARYA SAMAJ

AN ACCOUNT OF ITS ORIGIN, DOCTRINES, AND ACTIVITIES, WITH A BIOGRAPHICAL SKETCH OF THE FOUNDER

BY

LAJPAT RAI

WITH A PREFACE BY

PROFESSOR SIDNEY WEBB, LL.B.

OF THE LONDON SCHOOL OF ECONOMICS AND POLITICAL SCIENCE UNIVERSITY OF LONDON

WITH TEN ILLUSTRATIONS.

LONGMANS, GREEN AND CO.

39 PATERNOSTER ROW, LONDON

FOURTH AVENUE & 30TH STREET, NEW YORK

BOMBAY, CALCUTTA, AND MADRAS

1915

SWAMI DAYANANDA SARASWATI
(From an oil painting)

IN MEMORY OF MY DEAREST SON

(*PYARE KRISHNA*)

WHO DIED FEBRUARY 23RD, 1911,

AT THE AGE OF 20.

THE AUTHOR.

CONTENTS

CONTENTS

PART III

THE ARYA SAMAJ (*continued*)

LIST OF ILLUSTRATIONS

PREFACE

I BELIEVE that this is the first book to be published in the United Kingdom dealing with what may possibly prove to be the most important religious movement in the whole of India. I have been very much impressed by what little I have seen of that movement, and I willingly respond to the request that I should give this book a few words of introduction.

To many persons, official and non-official, one of the surprises of the last Indian Census was its revelation that the newly established Arya Samaj—a movement in which some observers see, of Hinduism, the Protestant Reformation or the Puritan Revival—numbered as many as a quarter of a million adherents. And these adherents are of more than statistical importance. They are, for the most part, of what we should call, in this country, the professional classes, though some of the recent industrial development of the Punjab is in their hands, and one of their most striking achievements is the inclusion and uplifting of " the depressed classes." Throughout the Punjab and the United Provinces—to some extent also in Central India, Rajputana, and the Bombay Presidency—the discreet inquirer finds a large percentage, often a majority, of the minor civil servants, schoolmasters, local pleaders, medical practitioners, and other active citizens belonging to this modern movement. One British official told me that 90 per cent. of his Indian subordinates were in its ranks. Especially during the past decade have the "Aryas" penetrated to other parts of India, and spread, indeed, in ones and twos, all over the world.

The Arya Samaj is undoubtedly a potent spiritual ferment in the Punjab, combining what may be called a "Protestant" reformation of the secular abuses and legendary accretions of orthodox Hinduism—a reversion from "ecclesiasticism" to the (Vedic) "scriptures"—with a Puritan simplification of life and a "Roundhead" insistence on the development of an independent Indian intellectual life and thought. Mr. Lajpat Rai makes us realize something of the personality of the founder. Swami Dayananda was a Gujerati of Kathiawar, who never learned a word of English; a Brahmin by caste, and by unmistakable vocation a Sadhu or holy man, a wandering ascetic of the sternest and most uncompromising type, without knowledge of European civilization or languages, but learned in the Sanskrit scriptures, and expressing himself with eloquence and lucidity in Gujerati, and latterly also in Hindi. Wandering up and down Northern and Central India in the decade that followed the Franco-German War—just when English thought was rejoicing in the most scientific materialism and the most successful commercialism—Dayananda preached a monotheism of an exalted type, and the union of a spiritual asceticism with an elaborate ritual and strictly defined rules of conduct for every department of life. In form, as Mr. Lajpat Rai shows us, what he insisted on was a going back to the Vedas, in which, disregarding all subsequent commentaries or additions, he found the germs of all knowledge and all wisdom. What is accessible to us of his teaching—here Mr. Lajpat Rai's careful bibliography ought to be useful—seems to have remained unnoticed by English scholars and the English religious and philosophical journals. After Dayananda's death in 1883, which Mr. Lajpat Rai feelingly describes, the numerous small groups of those whom he had impressed, and whom he had already designated the "Society of the Aryan Race," came together in a closer bond of union, and have since developed into the steadily growing religious and social movement of which Mr. Lajpat Rai now gives such interesting particulars.

There are, we may say, always two factors in every new religion: the magnetic influence of its founder and the practical application of his teaching by the first generation of his followers. In the Arya Samaj, which is still only a third of a century old, we see developed two great qualities of personal character: self-effacement in the service of Hindu society, and self-reliance towards the outer world. No one who knows anything of the Punjab of the past decade can fail to be impressed, not only by the gentle grace and purity of life and spiritual elevation of motive of these tens of thousands of comparatively obscure folk, but also by the heroic self-sacrifice and devotion which they put, on the one hand, into the service of their movement, for which many have suffered persecution, and, on the other, into any piece of social duty—education of the depressed classes, plague work, famine relief—that needs to be done. And with this moral elevation go also an indomitable courage and an almost aggressive pugnacity in cutting loose from the conventions of caste and Brahminism, the conventions of European pedagogy, and, finally, as must be added, the conventions of British officialism.

One of the leading factors in the regeneration of the Hindu race, for which the Arya Samaj looks, is to be the development of an indigenous educational system. The first outcome was the establishment of the Dayananda Anglo-Vedic College at Lahore, with its grade after grade of boys' school, capped by its large and flourishing University college. This institution, now in its twenty-seventh year, is a monument not only of the devotion of the Aryas, but also of the organizing and administrative capacity of the Hindu race. It is, and always has been, governed exclusively by representatives of the Arya Samaj; it is staffed entirely by Hindus and Musulmans. Its first principal and real intellectual founder has spent his whole life in its service without fee or reward, and its extensive and highly qualified staff get only bare subsistence. Mr. Lajpat Rai, whose own share in the administration of the college has been considerable, hardly makes us adequately realize the size, the efficiency and the earnestness of spirit that distinguish this remarkable educational foundation, which carries off annually far more of the degrees conferred by the Government University of the Punjab than any other College.

From the standpoint of some of the most earnest

of Dayananda's followers, this highly successful College had one flaw. Its organizers, intent on attracting to it all types of Hindu youth, and on training them for the rough and tumble of the world's work, did not think it possible to adopt all the stern rules of ascetic discipline, the elaborate ritual, and the concentration on Sanskrit studies in which Dayananda had seen the way to create a new and virile Hinduism. Hence the subsequent foundation of the still more remarkable Gurukula, near Hardwar, perhaps the most fascinating educational experiment in the whole world, of which Mr. Lajpat Rai gives us an interesting account. Here amid the beautiful scenery of the Upper Ganges, within sight of the snow-clad Himalayas, there has been growing up, during the past twenty years, a new type of monasticism. The principal—a man of remarkable personality—and all the teachers give their services in return for maintenance. In fact, though nearly all of them husbands and fathers, they lead a self-chosen life of obedience and poverty. The boys are admitted at 7 years of age, and remain until 25; paying nothing for tuition, and only a trifle for board, never once visiting their homes or parents, allowed to see no woman or be seen by any (except occasional visits from their mothers); living continuously day and night in company with, and under the closest scrutiny of their devoted teachers. The European student can only wonder and wait to see what will be the result on personal character and independence of this prolonged novitiate. For the first seven years of their training the whole attention of the boys is concentrated on Sanskrit and the

Vedas, combined with the regular daily practice of religious rites and strenuous physical training. At 14 they are introduced to the literatures and sciences of European civilization, and from thenceforth the English language, laboratory work, and "Western culture," studied largely through the vernacular, take up most of their school hours. I found the library extremely well-supplied with English works, especially in philosophy and economics—much better supplied, I may observe, than some of the Government University Colleges. At 25 the students are assumed to be accomplished servants of India, and they then go out into the world and choose the particular vocation in which they will work. There is even an attempt made to provide them (but not before 25) with wives whose training has been as strenuous and nearly as elaborate as their own, and who must—on this Dayananda had laid stress—be of full age. Perhaps the most eccentric feature, from the Indian point of view, is the obliteration of all caste distinctions, a cardinal feature of the Arya Samaj. Among the three hundred boys in residence at the Gurukula there are members of nearly all castes, from the highest to the lowest, all leading a completely communal life.

These two remarkable institutions, the Dayananda Anglo-Vedic College at Lahore and the Gurukula at Hardwar, represent, as Mr. Lajpat Rai justly indicates, only a fraction of the educational work of the Arya Samaj. Throughout the Northern provinces of India its branches are engaged in every type of educational service, from propagandist lectures for adults down to special schools for the children of the low castes and criminal tribes whom orthodox Hinduism refuses to touch. I retain in memory the picture of a little wooden building in an obscure village of the State of Baroda. Here a Brahmin and his wife and children, with another Brahmin as assistant, both men of high intellectual attainments and social position, were living, day and night, with a score or two of children of the lowest and most despised castes. These children were not only being gratuitously supported, and physically and mentally trained, but were also being initiated into the Vedic rites, and invested with the sacred thread, for hundreds of years restricted to the "twice-born." This is only a sample of the educational work, and the educational work is only a small part of the social service that the Arya Samaj is doing in Northern India—to the perplexity of the average unimaginative and somewhat "unspiritual" British official, who cannot understand "what it is that these people are after!"

Of this movement, and in this social service, Mr. Lajpat Rai has been long a leader. He adds a new service to us all, and to the Arya Samaj by bringing its history, its aims, and its achievements to the notice of the ever-growing English-reading public, not only in the United Kingdom and America, but also in India and Japan.

SIDNEY WEBB.

41, Grosvenor Road, Westminster.

November, 1914.

INTRODUCTION

भूरि त इन्द्र वीर्यं तव स्मस्यस्य स्तोतुर्मघवन् काममा पृण ॥ २ ॥

ऋ० १ । ५७ । ५

Great is Thy power, O Indra! we are Thine. Grant, O Bounteous Lord, the prayer of this Thy adorer.

R. I., 57, 5.

It was in 1907 that the Arya Samaj first attracted notice outside India. Since then hardly a book has been published in the English language, dealing with Indian movements or with Indian conditions of life, which does not speak of the Arya Samaj. Liberal and Labour writers have spoken of it in terms of appreciation and sympathy, while a few Conservative Imperialists have condemned it as anti-British. Missionaries have also written of it, either as fair critics or in a spirit of rancour. Before 1907, the Arya Samaj had very few books in English dealing with its doctrines. With the exception of a few tracts by the late lamented Pandit Gurudatta Vidyarthi and a few tracts by Bawa Chhajju Singh, there was hardly anything which could be presented to a non-Indian student of the Arya Samaj. The founder had written in Sanskrit or Hindi only. The bulk of the literature produced by his followers was also either in Sanskrit, Hindi or Urdú. It is true that two English translations of the Sattyárath Prakásh —one by Master Durga Prasad, the other by Mr. Chiranjiva Bharadwaja—existed even before 1907, but both lacked absolute accuracy and were otherwise unsuitable for foreign students.

The translation of Indian ideas and Indian sentiments into an occidental language, indeed, is an extremely difficult task. High proficiency in both languages is essential to even moderate success ; and even then sometimes an exact rendering of Indian terms into English is well-nigh impossible. Take, for instance, the Sanskrit word, "Dharma." The English language possesses no word which can accurately convey to an English person the idea which "Dharma" conveys to an Indian. Under the circumstances, translation from Hindi into English is of doubtful utility.

In spite of this difficulty, the demand for the Arya Samaj literature in English has been growing, and more than once it has been suggested to me that I should do something to meet that demand. The kind friends who suggested this did not perhaps know that I lacked qualifications for the work even more than those did who had attempted to give English renderings of the Sattyárath Prakásh. There have been and are abler men in the Arya Samaj who could acquit themselves creditably at this task. Some of them, unfortunately, have been removed from among us by death ; others, though willing, are otherwise engaged and cannot find the time necessary to do justice to the work; still others have neither time nor inclination for the effort. The Gurukula section of the Arya Samaj have been trying to do something in the matter, but so far nothing tangible has resulted. The fact is that the Arya Samajes have so much to do for their own people that they have scarcely any time or funds to spare for those who do not know our language. For the present their hands are too full.

Until recently the Arya Samajes were quite content to continue their work of reform among their own people, and had no desire to attract the notice of the outside world. They have been drawn into the world arena much against their will. Circumstances have forced their hands, and they have learnt in the school of adversity and by bitter experience that quiet, unassuming work is liable to serious misconstruction and misrepresentation. In these days of world-movements, no organization, however modest in its aims, can afford to be misrepresented and misunderstood—much less a movement which in its conception is not modest, nor in its aims and ideals, nor in its scope. So long as the Arya Samaj was attacked in India alone, it could afford to ignore those attacks. The people among and for whom it worked knew its worth, and no amount of interested criticism or ignorant misrepresentation could do it any harm. The Arya Samaj cared not for the foreigner, neither for his conversion nor for his opinion. It was not seeking recognition, either by Government or by learned societies. But when, in 1907, it found that its exclusiveness and self-reliance were misunderstood and that it ran the risk of being condemned unheard, it raised its voice in protest, and invited Europeans to visit its institutions, stay in them, and see for themselves the truth. Since then, some of the quiet workers have even gone out of their way to put their case before the Government, the learned world, and the English Press in India and in England. In self-defence, some of the busiest of Arya Samaj workers have had to find time to write in the English language of its principles, its teachings, its aims and its work. Still later, Lala Munshi Rama, the leader of the Gurukula section of the Arya Samaj, has published several speeches and tracts in the English language explaining the aims and objects of the Samaj and the Gurukula, as also have some of his colleagues, notably Professors Ram Deva and Bal Krishna. Among others who have written in English on this subject may be mentioned Rai Thakar Datta and Lala Ralla Ram, besides Professor Diwan Chand, M.A., of the Dayananda Anglo-Vedic College. Nevertheless, the need of a work which would give a general idea of the movement, its history, and its activities, for use both in India and abroad, has been felt very keenly. At one time it was hoped that the late Lala Dwarka Dass, M.A., who combined in his person a profound knowledge of Western thought with an equally profound knowledge of Hindu thought, would supply the need; but, unfortunately, that hope was frustrated by his death in October, 1912.

The present work is an attempt to meet the need we have explained. No one is more conscious of its defects than the writer himself, who can lay no claim either to profound knowledge or to excellence in style. His sole claim for being heard on the subject is that he has been in the movement ever since he was a boy of eighteen (A.D. 1882); that he has given the best part of his leisure time to the movement; that he has taken the lead in organizing several of its activities; that he owes a great deal of what may be considered good in him to its influence; and that the Samaj has passed through a serious political crisis on account of his connection with it. In the absence of abler and better qualified hands, having time and inclination to devote to the work, he has tried to do it from a sense of duty to and love for the Arya Samaj.

For the work itself no claim to originality is made; in fact, it is more of the nature of a compilation. This explains the presence of so many lengthy quotations in the body of the book. The object of these is to state the position of the Samaj in the words of its leaders, who naturally are the best exponents of its doctrine and its views.

The chapters on the life of Swami Dayananda are based on *The Life and Teachings of Swami Dayananda*, by Bawa Chhajju Singh, who for fifteen years or more edited the official organ, in the English language, of the Samaj. In his turn he had drawn upon, among other sources, one of the biographies of Swami Dayananda, written by the present author himself, in 1898, in Hindustani. On the teachings of the Samaj, the following books, besides the *Life* aforementioned, have been consulted:—(1) *A Handbook of the Arya Samaj*, published by the Tract Department of the Provincial Assembly of the Arya Samajes in the United Provinces of Agra and Oude; (2) *Teachings of the Arya Samaj*, by Bawa Chhajju Singh; and (3) Printed Lectures of Lalas Hansraj and Munshi Rama, the leaders of the two sections. Invariably I have given in a footnote the reference to the work from which I have borrowed anything bodily. By good fortune I have been able to reproduce the original article which appeared in *The Christian Intelligencer* in 1870, giving an account of the disputation held at Benares, in November, 1869, between Swami Dayananda and the Kashi Pandits. Bawa Chhajju Singh had had to retranslate into English the vernacular translation given in my work in 1898. For this valuable contribution my best thanks are due to Mr. Porter, the Librarian of the Church Missionary Society, London, for having lent me the volume containing the article.

In giving an account of the various institutions managed and controlled by the Arya Samaj, I have endeavoured to use the language of the official reports or of the pamphlets issued under the authority of the managers, as in the case of the Gurukula at Kangri. My position in relation to the two colleges of the Arya Samaj, the Dayananda Anglo-Vedic College of Lahore and the Gurukula at Kangri, is perhaps unique. For the first I feel the love of a parent, for the second that of a lover. Yet I am not in full agreement with either scheme, and have had my differences with both. For this reason I have felt it advisable to give the account of these two institutions in the language of their founders, which course has necessitated giving somewhat lengthy quotations, the substance of which could be condensed into much smaller space. Similarly I have exercised scrupulous care in describing the politics of the Samaj and in giving the position of its critics, by quoting the original documents. With these exceptions I take sole responsibility for the opinions expressed in this work.

If the fact be considered that I have played some part in making the Samaj what it is, I shall perhaps be excused if I venture to recommend this book to those who, within a brief space, wish to make acquaintance with the society and its founders, and have a bird's-eye view of its activities in the past. This book is meant for circulation both in and outside India—a fact which has contributed not inconsiderably to its bulk. Certain matters have been dealt with in detail for the benefit of non-Indians which might well have been omitted from a book intended for the use of Indians only ; and vice versa. There is another matter which I should like to mention in connection with the preparation of this book : viz., that the whole of it was conceived, sketched and written in the course of not more than eight weeks, in London, far from the scene of the activities covered by it ; and without the inestimable advantage of consultation with the leaders of the Samaj. My constant endeavour has been to take a detached, unbiassed view of all things : but I do not know if I have been quite successful in doing so, since it must be admitted to be difficult to take a detached view of affairs in which one has been so intimately involved. This work is the first of its kind, and might be improved in subsequent editions, if it should be so fortunate as to find favour with those for whom it is meant.

The Veda-mantras scattered through the book have been selected from Lala Gokal Chand's *Message of the Vedas*, or from Bawa Chhajju Singh's *Teachings of the Arya Samaj.* In the absence of any qualifications for translating the mantras for myself, I have adopted their translations, which I believe to be correct and very near to the translations made by Western scholars.

My acknowledgments are due to the authors from whose works I have largely quoted, and also to the editors of the monthly and other periodicals which I have used. I am, besides, very grateful to Professor Sidney Webb, LL.D., for having read my manuscript and written for it a preface. It is to his learned wife and himself that I am indebted for the encouragement which has stimulated me to write this book, and it is they who impressed upon me the necessity for such a work in the interest of the Arya Samaj. My thanks in addition are due to my friend, Mr. W. F. Westbrook, for having read the manuscript and made valuable suggestions.

LAJPAT RAI.

London.

October 13th, 1914.

LAJPAT RAI
(1908)

PART I

SWAMI DAYANANDA SARASWATI

CHAPTER I

EARLY LIFE

अग्निस्तु विश्रवस्तमं तुविब्रह्माणमुत्तमम् ।
अतूर्तं श्रावयत्पतिं पुत्रं ददाति दाशुषे ॥ ६ ॥
ऋ० ५ । २५ । ५ ।

"Agni gives to the worshipper a son, the best, of the highest fame, of deep devotion, of an unconquerable spirit, and the bringer of glory to his parents."
—R. V., 25, 5.

1. *Parentage and Birth*

MORVI is a small, prosperous, wealthy town in Kathiawar, Gujerat, at a short distance from the North-Western coast of the Indian Peninsula, the headquarters of the native State of that name under the Kathiawar agency of the British Government of Bombay. Dayananda's family belonged to the State, and his father held a post of some respectability and position in the Government of the State. His family had lands of their own and were considered wealthy enough to engage in the business of money-lending. They were Brahmins of the highest order, learned in Vedic lore and held in great respect on that account.

Dayananda's father had the reputation of being a

rigid, austere Brahmin, thoroughly orthodox and uncompromising in his religious beliefs and practices. Nothing would induce him to tolerate even the slightest departure from the letter of the law as laid down in books or handed down by tradition, in the matter of ritual observances and religious practices. He was a man of strong faith, determined will, and dour temper. His mother, on the other hand, was the personification of sweetness, gentleness, and goodness. She was a typical Indian lady, unlettered and uneducated in the sense that she was never taught reading and writing, but possessed of all the qualities of a good mother and a strong sense of efficient domestic management. She was a generous-hearted, kindly woman, with broad sympathies and benevolent temper. We have no knowledge of how the couple lived and agreed together, but we have no reason to suppose that they were in any way unhappy : since in India, marriages like these, arranged by parents in the early childhood of the contracting parties, are not necessarily unhappy. It is not rare to find husband and wife forming a complete whole by the union of the different qualities and temperaments peculiar to each, in a way complementary to each other. Swami Dayananda thus had the advantage of inheriting a strong will from his father and a benevolent mind from his mother. He was born in A.D. 1824 (Hindu era, 1881 Bikram), in his parent's home.

2. *Education and the Dawn of Enlightenment*

We have it on the authority of Dayananda himself that his instruction commenced when he was five years of age, and that in his eighth year he was invested with the sacred thread.

This investiture is a species of baptism which it is the privilege of every Hindu child, born of "twice-born" parents, to receive. From this time begins his life as a *Brahmchari* (*i.e.*, Brahminical student). The most approved age for this ceremony is eight in the case of children born of Brahmin parents, and twelve for others. For Brahmins, the reading of the alphabet begins at five. He may be invested with the sacred thread then or afterwards, but not at a later age than eight. With the investiture of the sacred thread he is admitted into the formal life of a student and becomes himself "twice-born," entitled to wear the symbolic thread and to read the Vedas. The investiture imposes upon him the vow of chastity, purity, and poverty for the period of his student life, which generally lasts until the age of twenty-five, but may in exceptional cases be extended to the age of forty-eight. It also imposes the obligation to daily worship, daily recitation of the Vedas, daily performance of *Homa*, the service of the Guru or spiritual teacher, and the strictest purity of thought, word, and deed consistent with a life of strict simplicity, amounting almost to austerity. Like everything else Hindu, this institution has lost its soul and at the present day is more or less a dead form, a remnant of the olden time, and a reminder of ancient beliefs : yet it has a halo of great sanctity round it, and is considered to be a great event in the life of a Hindu child—more especially if he be a Brahmin, the highest of all castes. It is performed with more or less ceremony, according to the means of the parents, and is an occasion of great rejoicing and festival, attended with extensive charity.

According to the letter of the law, the investiture must be followed by the removal of the child from the home of his parents and his admission into the family of his teacher, where he must stay until his education is completed. His successful return from his teacher's home is his graduation, which entitles him to marry and become a householder.

In educated Brahmin families, the father, if qualified, becomes the teacher of his son and thereby avoids the violation of the law, but in other cases the law is observed in its breach. We have no means of telling what happened in the case of young Mul-shankar (that was the original name of Dayananda), but from the account we have received of the relations of Dayananda with his father, and of the latter's strict orthodoxy, we have reason to believe that the father assumed the rôle of the teacher, and thus gathered into his own hands the reins of the twofold authority of father and teacher. So far the case is similar to that of John Stuart Mill. But Dayananda was a born rebel, and it did not take him very long to revolt against the authority of his father, who tried to impose upon him his iron will in all matters, even those that concerned the soul of his son and pupil. Dayananda's father was a devout worshipper of Shiva—one of the three highest gods in the Hindu Pantheon. In different parts of India, Shiva is worshipped in different forms : in some places as a symbol of creation, and in others as a symbol of destruction.

Among other duties Hindu worship entails the

keeping of a certain number of fasts during the year on days considered to be sacred. *Shivaratri* is one of such days, when every pious Shiva-worshipper is expected to fast for about thirty-six hours, or even more. Dayananda was fourteen when his father insisted on his keeping the fast, in orthodox fashion. The mother did not like the idea, but had to submit when Dayananda himself expressed his willingness to follow his father's wish.

Who could have imagined that Dayananda's father's piously-intended insistence upon his son's earning religious merit at the tender age of fourteen by observing the fast of *Shivaratri*, was to result in so tremendous a change in the mind of Dayananda as to turn him into the most virulent and successful opponent of image-worship of his time? In the words of Dayananda's biographer, as the fateful evening set in, the father and the son repaired to the temple outside the village, where the rules in connection with the worship were duly explained to him. One of these required the devotee who kept the fast to stay awake the whole night, repeating forms of prayer before the image of the god, since otherwise the fast would bear no fruit. The worship began with the chanting of hymns, the whole congregation joining in the singing. The first quarter of the night passed off very well, the entire congregation displaying great fervour and enthusiasm, such as is born of deep (though blind) religious faith. In the second quarter the fervour began to wane, but still they kept on to the letter of the law. As soon, however, as the midnight hour was past, the worshippers began to feel that nature was rather too strong even for blind faith. Dayananda's father was one of the first to succumb, and the officiating priest followed suit. The boy of fourteen, however, was resolved not to be beaten. He did not want to lose the merit to be gained by keeping the fast in strict accordance with the letter of the law. He used all sorts of means to ward off sleep, and succeeded where his father had failed. His hard-won success, however, was fruitful indeed, though in quite a different way from the one desired and expected by his father.

He was still engaged in struggling with sleep and muttering his prayers, when there suddenly occurred a common and insignificant incident which changed the current of his life. A mouse crept on the body of the Shiva, and, having satisfied itself that the image was quite harmless, began to enjoy the offerings that had been placed before it by the devotees in token of their love for the god. This set the boy thinking earnestly. He had been told that the god was omnipotent and omniscient; that the image represented him in all his glory; that it was God Himself; and that it had the power of blessing or cursing men. What he saw, however, was quite inconsistent with these things. The image was evidently a helpless inanimate object which could not protect itself even from the impertinence of a mouse. This, then, could not be the right way to worship, and the image could not be Shiva himself, as was taught by the priesthood.

The boy had been gifted with a logical mind, and, though young, possessed the courage born of true enlightened scepticism. The thought struck him as a thunderbolt, and, with this scepticism obsessing his mind, he could no longer do homage to the image as before. He would not, however, go to sleep, nor steal away from the place, without awakening his father and making an attempt to have his doubts explained. The father was at first angry, both at being disturbed and at the boy's audacity. Dayananda was not to be put off so lightly, but persisted and eventually got the only answer which a thoughtful and intelligent image-worshipper has for this fateful question. He said that the image was not the god himself. It only represented him for the purposes of worship, and, "he being worshipped through it, he is as much pleased as though he were actually present in the image and were himself adored." Dayananda's father gave the explanation, but at the same time soundly rated his son for his habit of raising doubts and putting questions. He did not like it. He insisted on unquestioning obedience; but this the boy was not prepared to render. His father's explanation did not satisfy him, so he quietly asked permission to go home. This permission the father reluctantly accorded, being unable to keep his son there by force, but at the same time reminded Dayananda of the obligation not to break his fast before sunrise. Dayananda, however, had already decided this matter in his own mind for himself. He had finished with image worship and all its ritual. He went home, broke his fast, and went to sleep.

When the father returned home in the morning and found his son deep in slumber he remonstrated, and was angry with the mother. On the boy's getting up, he scolded him long and fiercely. Dayananda, however, was nothing the worse for the scolding, but quietly took to his studies, and went his own way without regard to the wishes of his father. Henceforth, naturally, his relations with his father became unhappy, and he had to fall back upon the goodwill and sympathy of an uncle who was better qualified to understand him and to sympathize with the bent of his mind.

We have related this incident at some length, as giving a forecast of the developed mind of Swami Dayananda, the reformer, and also as explaining the iconoclasm of his nature. A born rebel like Dayananda who at the age of fourteen set aside the authority of his father with a will and determination uncommon even in grown-up persons, was not likely, in years to come, to submit to the tyranny of society and custom, after he had made up his mind to play the man and to unloose the chains of religious prejudice and superstition which bound the minds and so detrimentally affected the character of his countrymen. The Arya Samajists, all over the country, celebrate the night of *Shivaratri* as the anniversary of Dayananda's enlightenment, and even the non-Arya Samajists join in the celebration with pride and pleasure.

To return to Dayananda's early years. The education which he received had not much in it of what is understood by that term in the West. Dayananda's father was a *Sam-Vedi* Brahmin, the very highest among the Brahmins. The highest Brahmins of the Deccan are distinguished by and named after the particular Veda which has been specially studied and honoured in their family for generations. The Vedas are four in number, corresponding to the four castes. Among them the *Sâma-Veda* ranks highest, corresponding to the Brahmin of *Varnas* (the caste system). The *Yajura* comes next, then the *Rig*, and lastly the *Atharva*. All the four Vedas are studied and preserved by the Brahmins of the Deccan, but families are honoured and respected according to the Veda which has received special attention from them. In the troublous times of Musulman rule and amid the disturbance caused by frequent political changes, it was considered safer to preserve the Vedas in memory than to incur the risk of their being lost to humanity. Dayananda's family was of the highest class, being *Sam-Vedis* ; but we do not know why, in the case of Dayananda himself, his education began with the *Yajur-Veda*. Before he was fourteen, he knew the whole *Yajur-Veda Samhita* by heart, and also portions of the other three Vedas, besides having studied some minor works on Sanskrit Grammar. Brahmins, not affected by modern systems of education, start with the text of the Vedas and the rules of Grammar, and these are committed to memory. Explanation of the rules of Grammar and their application follow later ; but, in the vast majority of cases, the Vedas remain stored in the memory without the scholar ever learning their meaning. Other works of Sanskrit literature, both in prose and poetry, are taught, however, followed later by standard works on logic, philosophy, philology, law, ethics, religion, ritual, rhetoric, etc.

On these well-established lines Dayananda continued his studies and made considerable progress. He was an intelligent, earnest, and hard-working student. But, unlike ordinary boys, he was something more than a student. He was a seeker after enlightenment.

He wished to penetrate to the bottom of things. The death of a beloved sister set him on an inquiry as to the nature of death. His grief for her loss was too deep for tears. It plunged him into meditation on death as distinguished from life, what it meant, and how it could be overcome.

The youthful inquirer went on with his studies, brooding over the problem of life and death ; but ere long he was destined to witness what tended still more to intensify his desire to fathom the great mystery. He was nineteen when his beloved uncle, who had so often rocked him in his lap, and who had, when he grew up, so often shared his confidence and exerted himself to assist him when he was in trouble, had an attack of the disease that had carried off his sister. The distemper was of a virulent type, and baffled the skill of the physician. While the expiring man lay on his deathbed, he was looking at Dayananda with all the fondness of the fondest parent, his eyes filled with tears. Dayananda could not meet the gaze of this angel among men, and withal a person of vast learning, without bursting into tears in return, and he wept so much that his eyes swelled with weeping. The end came at last, and the house was once more a house of mourning.

Dayananda went about distracted, asking his friends and the learned Pandits of his acquaintance if they could tell him how death was to be overcome. The reply was that *yogâbhyâs* (contemplation or communion) was the way to obtain it. Dayananda thought over the answer, and came to the conclusion that in order to learn *yoga* he must leave home. The world and its attractions were transient and of no value in comparison with the bliss of salvation. Souls living on the high plane of existence will think in this fashion and average humanity is apt to misconstrue their words and actions. The fact is, that they do not look upon this world as something discardable: no, the very reverse of it, but the world is not an *end* to them—it is a means of gaining what is higher than the world, what is of infinitely more value and glory. They think, as Dayananda thought, in the strain of the Divine verse:

सम्भूतिञ्च विनाशं च यस्तद्वेदोभयंसह । विनाशेन मृत्युन् तीर्त्वा सम्भूत्यामृतमश्नुते ॥ यजु ४० ॥ १४ ॥

"Whoever thoroughly understands the nature of the visible creation and of the imperishable atom from which the visible creation springs *at one and the same time*, the same shall, by virtue of his knowledge of the primal atom, triumph over death, and shall obtain beatitude by virtue of his knowledge of the visible creation and by reason of his virtuous activity in that creation."

The nature of the aspirations which now filled Dayananda's breast was not long in becoming known to his father and mother. They were alarmed, particularly the latter, and began to devise means for preventing their son from carrying out his purpose.

3. *Flight from Home*

The remedy that suggested itself to them was the usual one, known to mankind from of old, of creating nearer interests which would prevent him from leaving home, and weave a web of affection round his person.

Parents all over the world and in all ages have considered marriage to be the best remedy to wean young minds from ascetic lines of thought. The Buddha's parents tried the same remedy, so did the parents of Nanak. These, however, were gentler spirits than Dayananda. They could not resist the will of their parents, who consequently succeeded in their immediate object, though failing in the end. Dayananda resisted the plan of his parents and declined to be married. He was by this time a boy of nineteen, and by the intercession of friends the marriage was postponed for a year. This year of respite quickly passed, and his parents insisted on his being married. For a time he met their demands by a request to be sent to Benares for the completion of his studies.

Benares, the sacred *Kashi,* is the Rome of the Hindus. It is also their Oxford. It attracts earnest students of Sanskrit literature, of Hindu theology, and of Hindu philosophy, from all parts of India. In pre-British days its charm was even greater, since no Hindu considered his education complete, entitling him to be called a scholar, without a course of study at Benares.

Under ordinary circumstances, therefore, the idea proposed by Dayananda would appeal to the parents of a promising student, since a course of study at Benares raises the scholar to the dignity of an authority on Hindu *Shastras*, whose advice would be sought and respected by prince and people alike. Dayananda's parents, however, having reason to suspect the workings of their son's mind, and not wishing to lose him altogether, refused to entertain his request. A compromise was eventually made by which Dayananda was allowed to go to a neighbouring village to prosecute his studies with a learned theologian who lived there. In the course of his studies he confided his secret to the teacher, who in his turn thought it obligatory on him to inform Dayananda's parents. At this, they recalled him home, with the intention of putting an end to his procrastination by fastening upon him, once for all, the matrimonial bond.

But they had not fully gauged the determination of their son. Within a week or so of the day fixed for his wedding, he fled from home. His father pursued, but failed to come upon his traces. In less than three days after leaving home, Dayananda was stripped of all the valuables he had on his person, as well as the money in his pocket. He became a *Sadhu*, changed his name, assumed ochre-coloured garments, and began to search for a suitable *Guru* (a spiritual teacher), who could put him in the way of solving the mystery of life and death for himself and attaining *moksha* (*i.e.*, liberation or beatitude).

Not many days had elapsed before Dayananda's father obtained a clue to his son's whereabouts from an acquaintance who had met him in his new garb. This time the pursuer had better success and effected the desired capture. Dayananda was imprisoned for the night in a room, with a guard posted at the door. Dayananda, however, was determined to make his escape, and did so the same night. Before morning he had put several miles between himself and his father, whom he never saw again.

That was his final separation from home and all that word implies. It was his cutting himself adrift from worldly ties. He felt all a son's sorrow for his mother, who loved him intensely, but he had before him a mission: and even as early as 1903 Bikram (about A.D. 1845 or 1846) he could visualize it, though faintly, before his mental eyes. He was leaving his home to make All India his home. He was leaving his kindred to give himself up to Humanity and the cause of truth.

From all that we know of him he never regretted the step he had taken—a step which alone made it possible for him to serve his people, his country, and his God as grandly as he did. It was the logical consequence of the step taken seven years before in revolting against his father's misuse of parental authority by attempting to dictate in matters affecting the freedom of the soul. Dayananda was the last man to submit to tyranny, even from his own parents. Long before his adult years he gave evidence of his love of liberty—liberty of thought and liberty of conscience; and hardly had he passed his teens when he stood up for liberty of conduct for the individual. The Dayananda of 1845 was only the precursor of the Dayananda of 1875, in which year he formally started his mission and began regularly to preach liberty of thought, liberty of conscience, and also liberty of action, in relation to the individual, so far as it did not contravene the binding laws of the social organism.

4. *Pursuit of Knowledge and Truth*

For fully fifteen years, from 1845 to 1860, young Dayananda wandered North, South, East, and West, almost all over India, in pursuit of knowledge and truth. During these wanderings he tapped the highest and the purest sources of knowledge. He went from place to place inquiring after scholars of renown, men of wisdom and ascetics (*Sadhus*) of great religious merit. Whenever he came across one from whom he could learn anything, he stopped and sat at his feet. With some he studied philosophy, with others the Vedas. It was during these wanderings that he learned the theory and practice of *Yoga*. There was hardly a Hindu place of pilgrimage throughout India which he did not visit. Some, famous as centres of learning, he visited again and again. In search of teachers of fame and *yogis* of merit he penetrated into the innermost recesses of the Himalaya, the Vindhya, and the Aravali, the three important mountain ranges in India. He crossed and recrossed the valleys of the noblest of Indian rivers, the Ganges, the Jamuna (Jumna), and the Narbadda, and mounted the highest accessible tops of the hills near or in the vicinity of the sources of those rivers. It is a distinguishing feature of the Hindu religion that its holiest places should be famed for their natural beauty, for the grandeur of their scenery, and for the excellence and purity of their water. These include some, or rather most, of the sublimest and loftiest peaks of the Himalayas accessible to man, of which some can be approached at particular times only of the year, and are open at the most from a month to four or five months only. The valleys of noble rivers are the favourite resorts of Hindu scholars, saints, and holy men. Some of them live there all the year round, at times getting no cooked food for months. All these places were visited by Dayananda, and every nook and corner of them was as familiar to him as the lanes of his native village. He loved nature and drank deeply from her inexhaustible sources.

It was in these surroundings of pure ozone and sublime beauty that he practised *Yoga*. It was there in direct communion with nature that he lifted his thoughts to God, contemplated and meditated on the deepest problems of life and death, and spent hours, days, and months, in an atmosphere of pure bliss and highest contentment. It was there that he made the acquaintance of the best, the noblest, and the purest of Hindu saints, who led a life of uninterrupted meditation and discipline, having subordinated their senses to their intellect and their intellect to their spirit. For days he ate nothing but wild fruits ; for months he lived on milk only, and sometimes for years at a stretch he spoke no language but Sanskrit. He dived deep into the mysteries of nature and tapped all sources of knowledge. He despised none from whom he could learn anything, either in the way of book knowledge, religious insight, or spiritual exercises. He attended all religious conferences and took part in all the discussions and debates for which religious India and Hindu fraternities are famous. Sometimes he followed the rivers (particularly the Ganges in the North and the Narbadda in the South) up to their sources, braved every danger and disciplined himself to a life of hardship and privation.

Travelling in the high Himalayas, particularly along the banks of the rivers, is always dangerous, but in those days of no railways, no roads, no camping places, no rest-houses, and very scanty shelter even in the lower ranges of the hills, the difficulties and dangers of travelling may be better imagined than described. Swami Dayananda, however, was never checked by them; he was preparing for a life in which he was to face dangers and difficulties even in the midst of civilization. These were the years of probation and discipline which eminently fitted him for the life which was waiting for him in the years to come, but of which he could not then have had the slightest notion.

For some time after his flight from home he passed as a *Brahmchari* (student), the first stage of a Hindu's life, but within a few years he was formally initiated into the highest order of *Sannyasis.* According to the most approved authorities there are four stages of a Hindu's life. The first is that of *Brahmcharya* (*i.e.*, studentship); the second is that of *Grihastha* (*i.e.*, the life of a householder, or, say, married life); the third is that of *Banprastha* (*i.e.*, retirement from active life and meditation); the fourth is that of *Sannyas* (*i.e.*, complete renunciation and a life of service). The duties and obligations of the first three stages must be duly discharged before one can be qualified to enter the fourth and last stage, which places him in a position of the highest respect which society can show and the most implicit trust which society and state can repose in any one of its members. In the case of persons of extraordinary ability and character, the *shastras* allow admission into the fourth order directly the first stage closes, at any time they are considered fit for that honour by one or more members of the fraternity. None but a *Sannyasi* can admit another into that order, and the rules on this point are so strict that even in this age of laxity and degeneration Dayananda had great difficulty in being admitted into the order. He was refused more than once, but his perseverance was soon rewarded with success, and within a few years of leaving home he was admitted into the highest order of *Sannyasis*, such was the estimate of his high character formed by the man who officiated at his initiation.

A Hindu *Sannyasi* is prohibited from cooking food for himself. He is not allowed to have money or valuables with him. He is not allowed to possess more than the absolutely necessary apparel. He must not acquire money or engage in profitable business of any kind, but must confine himself to study, contemplation, or service. He must not embellish his person, and must lead a life of perfect self-denial and incessant spiritual discipline. He may make himself useful to others, but must not accept payment or compensation for his services. He is of no caste and is absolutely free from all the restrictions of caste. He must not eat meat, but vegetarian food he may accept from anyone, be he of any caste, creed, or colour. He must not enjoy the company of women longer than may be strictly necessary in the discharge of his duty as a religious preacher. He must not stay very long at one place, and must not make a home for himself. He may accept no gifts excepting those of food, necessary clothing, and boots.

It was this life to which young Dayananda dedicated himself by his free will before he was twenty-five years of age, and no one, not even his worst enemies (for of enemies he had enough and to spare), could say that he was in any way false to his oath. Opponents have criticized his teachings virulently; they have questioned his motives and called him names; but not a suspicion has ever been breathed against the purity of his life and character. We may summarize the special features of Dayananda's life, during the period of which we are writing, under three heads:

1. His unquenchable thirst for knowledge. Dayananda was not of that class which accepts knowledge easily from authority. He would take nothing which could not be verified or demonstrated. An incident which happened during this period of his life may serve as an illustration. One day, when wandering in the valley of the Ganges, he observed a corpse floating in the river. At that time he had with him some books dealing with anatomy and physiology. The sight of a dead human body at once suggested to him the idea of testing by actual observation the accuracy of the facts cited in those books. He was in a jungle, far from human habitation, and not likely to be disturbed. He got hold of the body, cut it open, and looked into it. On examination he found that what was taught in the books was not true. So into the river went the books along with the body.

2. The second fact is that never for a moment did he falter or look away from the ideal which he had set before himself. In India are numbers of religious shrines and temples, the heads of which live in a condition of state and luxury born of wealth. They have large endowments in land and revenues attached to their shrines and are in receipt of constant

offerings from their disciples and devotees. Being a handsome young man of good physique and prepossessing appearance, intelligent, well read, clever, and well versed in religious polemics, more than one *mahant* (as the heads of the institutions or fraternities are called) wished to make of him a *chela*, or spiritual son, and offered to nominate him as his successor, but on every such occasion Dayananda refused, saying that his goal was different and that he was not seeking wealth or power.

3. During this period, he met crowds of Sadhus and Pandits, some good, some bad, some noble, some ignoble. Some attracted him, others repelled him. He met a few for whom he entertained the highest respect, and at whose feet he sat for long in a spirit of perfect reverence and true homage; but he did not meet with one who came up to his ideal of a *Guru* (spiritual teacher). Born rebel as he was, he could not accept as his models the blind followers of authority or slaves of tradition; nor did he care for a life of mere renunciation or mere meditation. Surrounded by ignorance, prejudice, superstition, misery, and tyranny, he did not desire a life of soulless bliss and peace. He was a passionate lover of liberty. In his wanderings through that beautiful and noble land of his—land of the loftiest thoughts, the purest ethics, and the noblest traditions, land of the Vedas and the Upanishads, land of *Kapilas, Kanadas* and *Gautamas,* land of *Patanjalis* and *Vyasas,* land of *Yudhishtras* and *Ramas*, land of *Kumarals* and *Shankars*—he found everything upside down. Even the repositories of the sacred lore of the Aryas, the representatives of the authors of the

Upanishads and the *Darshanas*, the descendants of *Manu* and *Yajnyavalka*, were steeped in ignorance and superstition. The religion which once allowed liberty of thought and conscience to every human being; in which difference of opinion was not only tolerated but respected; which imposed on every one the duty of reading and understanding the Vedas for himself; which taught that everyone was master of his own soul, directly responsible for his thoughts and deeds to his God, and entitled to receive inspiration by direct communion with that exhaustless source of spiritual replenishment and uplift, the Maker of the Universe—this magnificent religion had been reduced to a soul-destroying system of blind faith in authority. Persons who had no mediators and who gloried in their freedom from spiritual or religious bondage, had created thirty millions of gods, and had accepted as their Saviours an equal number of Brahmins by caste. He found that in that land of eternal sunshine, physical, intellectual, and spiritual, everything was steeped in darkness. Light and knowledge had left the land. Even the best, the purest, and the loftiest among men were only moonlike. The sun had set, perhaps never to rise again. It made his heart bleed to observe that a land once distinguished by freshness and vigour of intellect and force of mind should be so stale, shallow, and feeble in its intellectual and mental products. It grieved his soul to find that his people should have lost all originality of thought, and that the descendants of the boldest intellectual pioneers that the world ever produced should stagnate in intellectual bondage and spiritual bankruptcy. He saw that the best of the Hindus had cultivated a morbid and ridiculous desire for peace ; that instead of fighting the passions and lower instincts and leading the way by their successes, they were flying from them out of sheer cowardice. He was for conquest, and he wished a guide, a friend and a teacher who would, by practice as well as precept, show him the way. He wished to conquer death by conquering ignorance and superstition and fear, and at the same time to put others in the way of doing the same. He wished to imitate nature, which was ever active, ever vigilant, ever conquering, even amid scenes that impressed the superficial observer with the peace of death and the calm of inactivity. He had conferred with the Himalayas, with their eternal snows and cloud-masked summits ; he had conversed with the Ganges and Narbadda ; he had penetrated the sanctuaries of the dense and almost inaccessible jungles and forests of the plains ; he had slept in the top of the loftiest Himalayan deodar ; he had enjoyed the embraces of the hardest of primeval rock and the caresses of the swiftest of waters : all these friends of his youth and companions of his wander-years had told him not to seek the peace of repose or the lassitude of an inactive life. They had inspired him with the desire for increasing activity ; they had given him the strength of their simple but unshaken faith in duty and in service ; they had added to the purity, loftiness, and strength of his soul, not to enable him to enjoy unearned peace, but to nerve him to play the man and to establish the reign of intellectual and religious freedom in Hindu India. The soil had been well-prepared. The seed had been sown. It required only to be watered by a careful gardener able to appreciate the capabilities of the soil and the strength of the seed. In due time he found the man he wanted, the *Guru* for whom he had searched all these years, the teacher, guide, and philosopher who was to water the seed already sown.

5. *Virjananda Saraswati*

Swami Virjananda Saraswati, at whose feet Dayananda completed his education, was a Sannyasi of the order to which Dayananda belonged. He had been bred in the school of adversity. Dayananda had left his home because his parents loved him too much and wished to save him from a life of poverty to which he was minded to dedicate himself in the pursuit of what they considered to be only a phantasy; he had left his home at the comparatively advanced age of twenty-one, by his own choice, to the great sorrow and disappointment of his parents. Poor Virjananda, on the other hand, was a child of only eleven when circumstances turned him adrift on the world, without anyone to care for him. He had lost both parents and was an orphan. Brothers are, as a rule, kinder in India, but in this case the biting tongue and the cruel temper of his brother's wife proved too strong even for the child of eleven. What added to the sadness of his orphanhood was the fact that he was totally blind, having lost his sight at the age of five in consequence of a virulent attack of smallpox. He was too spirited, however, in spite of his blindness and his orphanhood, to submit to the tyranny of his brother's wife. He left his brother's house with a heart full of sorrow ; for since his blindness he had been the object of special care and love on the part of his parents. The death of his parents had deprived him of the ties and associations which make home so attractive and sweet. All that was left him now was his own soul, his own mind, and his will to make the best of them by his own exertions. On leaving his brother's house he repaired to Haridwara, on the banks of the Ganges, one of the most beautiful spots in Northern India, where the Ganges issues from the hills and spreads itself in the plains. This is one of the most sacred places of the Hindus and a favourite resort of *Sadhus*, *Sannyasis*, and Pandits.

The Ganges, indeed, is an object of adoration and love to every Hindu. Hundreds and thousands of them visit it, year in, year out; a great number traversing thousands of miles barefoot and following the river to its source high in the Himalayas. The banks from the source downwards to where it enters the Bay of Bengal at the eastern extremity of India, for a distance of 1,500 miles, are set with temples and other places of study and contemplation ; but the part from the source down to Haridwara has a very high sanctity in the eyes of the Hindus. A Hindu who dies on its banks is supposed to enter heaven immediately, so great is the religious virtue of the river. The pious Hindu's reasons for this exaggerated notion of the sanctity of the Ganges are based on his love of nature, whose grandeur and beauty fill him with ecstatic love of and a boundless admiration for the Creator. They help him in his contemplation of the Universal Spirit, and carry him to the feet of the Almighty. Where on this earth does one come into contact, so immediate and vital, with nature, its grandeur, its purity, its all-embracing life, its beauty spread in multitudinous shapes and expressions, as in that part of the Himalayas which gives birth to the Ganges and provides an outlet for it in its progress towards the sea? The writer has seen this part of the Himalayas and has travelled along the banks of the Ganges for many miles. Never before had he fully realized the reasons for which the Hindu had selected this, of all the Indian rivers, as the special object of his love and adoration.

The water of the Ganges is perhaps unsurpassed in the world for its purity, its sweetness, and its wealth in salts. It can be kept for years without loss of freshness. Gallons of it are stored in Hindu households for use on occasions of religious celebration or even of worldly importance. People swear by it as they would swear by their gods. No Hindu dare tell a falsehood with the water of Ganges (*Gangá jalí*, as it is called) in the hollow of his hand. Scores of learned *Sadhus*, *Yogis*, and *Pandits* live on its banks for purposes of study and contemplation. Some of the best and most profound Sanskrit scholars have received their education there, and in their turn imparted it, free of cost, to all who came and asked for it. A Hindu charges no fee for teaching. Charging a fee for imparting knowledge, especially if it relates to the spirit, is a sin of the gravest kind. He can never sell knowledge. The giver and the recipient alike must give and receive in a religious spirit, and as performing an obligation both sacred and pleasant.

The teacher and the pupil, the *Guru* and the *Chela*,

are supported alike by private philanthropy. There are numerous feeding places, where cooked food is supplied twice a day for the mere asking to those who are engaged in the holy work of teaching and learning, or in religious contemplation and meditation. This flow of charity never fails, not even when millions are dying in other parts of India from famine due to failure of rains. Permanent endowments, landed and house properties of immense value, are attached to these institutions. If and when they fail, fresh donors come forward and guarantee their continuity.

Sadhus and *Sannyasis*, *Yogis* and teachers of sanctity, generally live in isolated huts made of straw, but the general body of students and pilgrims have large and commodious buildings of brick and mortar and stone made for their convenience by pious donors and benefactors.[1] This system has grown up from time immemorial and has existed without disturbance from generation to generation: and it is this system which explains why poor and needy students, as well as those who wish to drink deeply and profusely from the fountain of knowledge, flock to these places and spend years of their lives there, receiving education and enlightenment. But there are always some who come never to depart, unless it be a mere transference to another place of learning of equal or greater facilities. These are the life-long students, as well as teachers in their turn.

Such is the place to which Virjananda repaired when misfortune forced him to leave his home; and well may the country that gave him birth be proud

[1] The same may be said, more or less, of all the sacred places of the Hindus.

of the decision to which he came so early in life. He went never to return. In a few years he learned all that the best and most learned in Haridwara could teach him. He was an apt pupil and was gifted with a wonderful memory, to whose power his blindness had added considerably. The reputation and esteem which he gained by his scholarship and character were so high as to induce a *Sannyasi* of high ability and profound austerity to admit him into the highest order of his class, in spite of his blindness. Later in life Virjananda migrated to Mathura (Muttra), another holy place in the same province, famous as the birth-place of the Lord Krishna, one of the greatest and wisest of Hindu heroes, accorded the honours of Divinity. It was here that Dayananda met him.

It was a meeting of two kindred souls, brethren of the same mystic but scattered order. Virjananda had outgrown his education. His hatred of image-worship, of superstition, of the pettiness of current Hindu life, and of the traditional system of teaching, was a consuming fire. He had the intolerance of the true iconoclast. His soul was full of the purity and greatness of the past. By incessant labour and constant concentration of mind, he had acquired a mastery of Sanskrit language and literature, and of all the intellectual treasure therein, such as had no equal, no rival, in that part of India in his time. His vision was clear and his intellect of a very superior order. He had an intuitive faculty of separating the chaff from the grain. He dissected and analysed everything that fell within range of his observation and study, and had thereby acquired a special qualification to lay his finger on the weak points of current Hindu thought and Hindu religion. He could see clearly where the fault lay. Moreover, he was morally fearless. He expressed what he thought—he uttered what he believed. His denunciation of the popular gods, of the popular modes of worship, and of the popular method of teaching, was trenchant and merciless. He spared no one, and in consequence was in his turn intensely hated and denounced by the teachers of popular Hinduism and their patrons. Yet, such was the prestige of his character, his reputation and his learning, that, in spite of his blindness, students flocked to him for teaching, though few could stay long enough to receive the full benefit thereof, since his temper was rather sharp. Nor did he ever suffer privation. Hindus of wealth and position disliked him, but they attended to his wants and kept him well provided with the necessaries of life. He had a house to himself, and was regularly supplied with food and clothing.

Three ruling chiefs of Rajputana, at different times, became his pupils. One continued his studies for fully three years ; but when, one day, he absented himself, the Swami left him without notice and returned to Mathura. Another, the ruler of a first-class principality, asked him to compile for him an easy grammar—which the Swami refused to do, since he considered this would be a slur on the ancient Rishis who had left monumental works on the subject.

This was the man with whom Dayananda completed his education, and who charged him with the duty of inaugurating a mission to purge Hinduism of all the evils that had found admittance into it.

Dayananda had been studying for over thirty years already, and what he now required was only a finishing touch at the hands of a master spirit. For two years and a half he waited on Virjananda, served him with filial love, and learned all that Virjananda had to teach. Virjananda was a man of hot temper and sometimes treated his pupils harshly. Once he actually inflicted corporal punishment on Swami Dayananda ; yet the latter did not leave him, and duly finished the course laid down for him by the former. Then Virjananda told him that he had nothing more for him, and that he must now enter the world as an independent teacher.

The day of leave-taking was a memorable occasion for both pupil and teacher. It was on that day that Swami Virjananda demanded the customary fee which in old times every *Brahmchari* had to pay to his *Guru* on the day of leave-taking. Virjananda knew that Dayananda had nothing of worldly value to offer him, nor did he himself care for any such gift. What he asked of his pupil was a pledge to devote his life to the dissemination of truth, to the waging of incessant warfare against the falsehoods of the prevailing *Puranic* faith (faith based on the Puranas), and to establish the right method of education, as was in vogue in pre-Buddhist times.

This pledge Dayananda gave willingly, and with a solemn joy: and never was any human pledge kept more loyally and faithfully.

CHAPTER II

FIGHTING FOR TRUTH

अभयं मित्रादभयममित्रादभयं ज्ञातादभयं पुरोयः ।
अभयं नक्तमभयं दिवा नः सर्वा आशा मम मित्रं भवन्तु
॥ ६ ॥ अथ० १९ । १५ । ६ ।

"May we be fearless from friends and from the unfriendly, fearless from whom we know and whom we know not, fearless in the night and fearless in the daytime. May all the directions be friendly to us."

—Ath. XIX., 15, 6.

1. *First Years of Public Life*

THE first few years of Dayananda's public life were more or less years of preparation for the stupendous task to which he had set his hand. In these years he reviewed and revised what he had read, and disciplined himself in the methods of public life. He visited some of the most important towns of what was then known as the North-Western Province, but spent most of his time on the banks of the Ganges and in the vicinity thereof. Wherever he went he preached and taught. Everywhere his outspoken views, his bold utterances, his then novel exposition of the Hindu religion and his profound learning attracted hundreds and thousands of his countrymen to his discourses. Grammar and a knowledge of the Vedas were his strong points. Many came to cross swords with him, but stayed to admire and follow. He issued challenges broadcast and held numerous discussions with high and low, student and scholar, theologian and sceptic, Sadhu and Pandit. He spoke in Sanskrit, since Sanskrit was the language of the learned, and, the language of Upper India not being his mother tongue, he felt a certain amount of diffidence in using the latter for purposes of discourse and controversy. Wherever he went he made a commotion in the Hindu world. The Hindu theologians, with their myriad followers, whose deepest and most vital interests were so adversely touched by his teachings, were up in arms. They not only abused and threatened, but even more than once conspired to kill him. In the course of five years, no fewer than four or five attempts were made on his life. Yet there was a charm about his life, his ways and his manners, which secured for him friends and protectors. While the Brahmins, men of his own caste, hated and detested him, non-Brahmins admired and honoured him. He never stooped to prosecute his persecutors. Once, when a man who had tried to poison him was arrested by the police, he interceded and secured his release.

In orthodox circles he became famous in a very short time. High and low, rich and poor, from the rulers of the highest Native States down to the coolie, all classes flocked to him, drank in his discourses and gazed at him with mingled awe, respect, and admiration. In some places the public discussions were presided over by British officers of the highest rank in the district, this being considered the most effectual way of preserving order and preventing rioting and violence. In the first five years of his ministry he made numerous admirers but few adherents and followers. Yet among the latter were some of the most wealthy traders and landholders of the districts visited by him. For the first time since the days of the celebrated Shankara there had arisen a teacher of the highest order, a man worthy of the mantle of a prophet, a man who at least gave promise of being an *Acharya* (Professor), and who shone among other teachers as a sun among moon and stars.

It was true that he was very learned, and but few could venture to face him in controversy ; yet what surprised and at the same time attracted hearers to him were his boldness, his courage, his defiance of the conventions of theological controversy, and his attacks on popular beliefs and popular practices. Never before had they seen and heard such a man. In a part of the country hundreds of miles distant from his native province, the language of which he could not use with freedom and effect, to whose people he was a stranger, with no friends to fall back upon or to protect him at need, he went straight to his work and attacked some of the most cherished beliefs of the population with a scathing vehemence that itself—apart from the force of his arguments—struck terror to his opponents. People looked at this fiery teacher askance and with awe. He had dropped in their midst as a bolt from heaven, and threatened havoc to the beliefs they had held so unquestioningly The worst, or perhaps the best, of it was that he spoke with so much authority and directness, with so much erudition and confidence, with so much cogency of reasoning and force of logic, that the very first onslaught brought the opponent to his knees. The expounders of popular religions and the repositories of Hindu faith were struck with the suddenness and rapidity of lightning. The attack was so sudden and so furious that fortress after fortress fell without the assailant being made to feel any the worse for his exploits. He swept the country, with something of the effect of a mighty sheet of water descending the hills and carrying everything before it.

The orthodox leaders appealed to Kashi, the Rome of Hinduism. That was their last hope, and they had no doubt that there the invader would meet foes worthy of his steel and would be routed. Dayananda, too, well knew that unless he subdued Kashi and won a decisive battle there, all his victories so far achieved would be useless. So, before the sixth year of his public career was over, he reached Kashi, and, in his humble way, under the shade of a tree, started preaching and expressing his views on religion, philosophy, and grammar. Soon after this a public discussion was announced. It was attended by thousands of people. On one side were 300 of the leading Hindu scholars and theologians of Benares ; on the other, Dayananda, with but a few laymen to make show of support. The meeting was presided over by no less a personage than the Maharaja of Benares. At the close of the discussion both sides claimed victory; but what really happened may be gathered from the following account which was published in a Christian Missionary Journal, evidently written by a European Christian missionary:

"A HINDOO REFORMER[1]

"The fame of the reformer who lately put the whole city of Benares in commotion seems to have gone abroad. Some account, therefore, of him and his views, and the public disputation held with him, from one who was present at the disputation, and met and conversed with the reformer several times before and after that event, will perhaps be not uninteresting to the readers of the *Intelligencer*.

"The name of the reformer is Dayananda Saraswati Swami. He is a native of some village in Guzerat; the name of the place he will not disclose to any one, from a fear that his father, who declares him to be mad, will come and take him forcibly away, as he already once did on a previous occasion. He is a fine-looking man, large but well proportioned; his face, especially, expressive of much intelligence. His outward appearance is that of a Sanyasi or religious beggar: almost entirely naked and besmeared with the sacred bhasma (ashes of cow-dung). He speaks Sanskrit fluently, though not in very polished style, and in a few instances not quite correctly.[2] He is a good reasoner and pretty fair in controversy, at least so far that he generally allows his opponent to state his case without interruption;

[1] The spelling of this writer is preserved, but some of his accents are omitted.

"[2] For example, he denied that the verbal root *man*, to believe, may form the I. pers. plur. pres. *manmahe*, beside the forms *manumahe* and *manyamahe*.

but extremely authoritative in all his positions. His case and mind is made up, and, believing his acquaintance with the Vedas to be superior to that of any of his adversaries, he will listen with a kind of contemptuous courtesy to anything that they may have to bring forward, and often, especially in the case of inferior pandits, only answer by an authoritative assertion of the contrary. He is well versed in the Vedas, excepting the fourth or Atharva Veda, which he had read only in fragments, and which he saw for the first time in full when I lent him my own complete MS. copy. It should be remembered, however, that the Brahmans understand by the Vedas a great deal more than we do, namely, not only the hymns generally known as the four Vedas, but also the theological treatises in prose appended to the former, called the Brahmanas and Upanishads, etc. He devoted himself entirely to the study of the Vedas from his eleventh year, and thus he is more practically conversant with them than most if not all of the great pandits of Benares, who generally know them only at second-hand, or even less. At any rate, and this is the most remarkable feature distinguishing him from other pandits, he is an independent student of the Vedas, and free from the trammels of traditional interpretation. The standard commentary of the famous Sáyanácharya is held of little account by him. It can be no wonder, therefore, that his Vedic studies, conducted in that spirit, led him to the conviction that almost the whole of the (comparatively) modern Hinduism is in entire and irreconcilable contradiction with the Vedas and the Hinduism of Vedic times, about 2,000 years ago. Being of an active character, he determined not to keep his conviction to himself, but to impart it to his countrymen, and try to effect an entire reform of Hindu society. Briefly, his object is to replace Hindu society exactly into the same state as it was about 2,000 years ago, when, as yet, none of the six philosophical systems existed, nor any of the eighteen Puranas, the sources of modern Hinduism with its castes and idolatry; but when the Vedas and Vedic usages reigned supreme, and when one God only was adored, and the Vedas only were studied, and the sacrifice of the homa only, with its elaborate ceremonial, was performed by the priest for himself and the soldier and the peasant. At least, this is the fond dream of the reformer. But history never travels back in this manner; no nation, especially not one like the Hindus, can or ever will retrace its steps to live again in a state of things of 2,000 years ago. Hence this attempt at reform must fail. But he may prepare the way for another reform; he may possibly convince the Hindus that their modern Hinduism is altogether in opposition to the Vedas, a fact of which most of them are profoundly ignorant, and the few who know or suspect it find it convenient to shut their eyes to it. If once they become thoroughly convinced of this radical error, they will no doubt abandon Hinduism at once, for they cling to it only because they believe that it has the sanction of immemorial antiquity and of the earliest forefathers of their race, who are believed to have communed with the Eternal One Himself. They cannot go back to the Vedic state; that is dead and gone, and will never revive. Something more or less new must follow. We will hope it may be Christianity, but, whatever it may be, anything seems better than the present intellectually and morally monstrous idolatry and caste. I confess, however, that I am not sanguine that the efforts of the reformer will effect even this preparatory step to reform. He travels up and down the banks of the Ganges, and stops here and there in the large towns to disseminate his views, but, as far as I could ascertain, he seems to have met nowhere with much success except in Furruckabad, near Cawnpore, where, indeed, if report is to be trusted, his success has been complete. The Brahmins of that place in a body are said to have declared for him, and to have cleared the temples of all idols. It is certain that a very rich Mahajan of that place has become a convert to his views, and has established a school where the reformed Hinduism is taught; and there is not much doubt that his influence will have effected the conversion of all those needy Brahmins who depend on him for their sustenance. But beyond this probably the report is exaggeration. His appearance in Benares was certainly a failure. Nevertheless the commotion caused by it at first was great, and though it now, to outward appearance,[1] seems to have quite subsided, some of the ferment is still active under the surface; and, if it were judiciously worked by the Mission, and indirect support given to the cause of the reformer, it seems not improbable that the result, of which his attempt failed at first, might yet be accomplished.

"The date of his arrival in Benares I do not know.

[1] This evidently was written five or six months after the event. —*Author.*

It must have been in the beginning of October: I was then absent. I first saw him after my return in November. I went to see him in company with the Prince of Bhurtpore and one or two pandits. The excitement was then at its height. The whole of the Brahmanic and educated population of Benares seemed to flock to him. In the verandah of a small house at the end of a large garden near the monkey-tank, he was holding daily levees from early in the morning till late in the evening, for a continuous stream of people who came, eager to see and listen to, or dispute with the novel reformer. It does not appear, however, that the heads of the orthodox party or the pandits of the greatest repute ever visited him, unless they did it secretly. The intensity of the excitement at last induced the Raja of Benares, in concert with his court pandits and other men of influence, to take some notice of the reformer, and to arrange a public disputation between him and the orthodox party, in order to allay the excitement by a defeat of the reformer. They were quite sanguine as to his defeat; but I fear there was a determination from the beginning that they would win the day by any means, whether foul or fair. The disputation took place on the 17th of November, in the place where the reformer had taken up his abode; it lasted from about 3 to 7 o'clock p.m. The Raja himself was present and presided. Even the great Vedantist, the head it seems of the orthodox party, Vishudananda Gour Swami, who is said never to have left his dwelling before—of course an exaggeration—condescended to emerge for once from his place of meditation on the banks of the Ganges to assist with his learning the failing wits of the defenders of orthodoxy, and to give additional authority to the anticipated defeat of the reformer—a clear proof that the reformer was thought a formidable enemy. All the most reputed pandits were there, and a large concourse of other people, learned and unlearned, but all of the respectable class. A detachment of policemen also were present, who guarded the entrance to the garden against a dense crowd outside, which in vain strove to get admittance; but they were also intended, I suspect, to protect the lonely reformer in case any act of violence should be attempted against him by his enraged adversaries. But nothing of the kind occurred; all went off quietly, except that, at the last, when the assembly broke up, the orthodox party loudly jeered the poor reformer in token of their ill-gotten victory. But, whether gotten ill or well, their victory had certainly the result they desired. The change was very remarkable in the state of things before and after the disputation. As quickly as the excitement had arisen before, so quickly it subsided afterwards. Whereas, before, multitudes flocked to see him, those who came afterwards might be easily counted. The reformer himself was practically ex-communicated, and any one who would visit him after his refutation was threatened with the same measure. Immediately after the disputation, a written defence was sent by the reformer to his opponents, but I believe no notice was taken of it. Then an account of his doctrines was prepared by the reformer and printed about a month afterwards. At the same time also a public challenge to his opponents to answer his pamphlets was issued by him. But again no notice was taken of it by the orthodox party. The reformer still remained till towards the end of January. Then he left Benares to visit the *Mela* at Allahabad, and to try to influence the multitude assembled there. When I saw him for the last time, he had not made up his mind whether he should return to Benares after the *Mela* or visit some other place. Since his departure the orthodox party have also brought out a pamphlet on the disputation and the question between themselves and the reformer in general. The doctrines of the reformer may be referred chiefly to the following three heads: the extent of the Hindu Canon, the truth of idolatry, and the mythology and the question of caste; connected with these, however, there are many minor points.

"The first of the three forms the foundation of his whole reform. The only writings which he acknowledges as Shastras are the following twenty-one: 1-4, the four Vedas; 5-8, the four Upavedas; 9-14, the six Vedangas; 15, twelve Upanishads; 16, the Sarirakasutras; 17, the Katyayanasutras, etc.; 18, the Yogabhashya; 19, the Vakovakya; 20, the Manusmriti; and 21, the Mahabharata.[1] Of these

"[1] The four Vedas are the Rigveda, the Yajurveda, the Sámaveda, and the Atharvan Veda, including their respective Brahmanas. The four Upavedas are the Ayurveda on medical science, including two books; the Dhanurveda on military science; the Gándharvaveda on musical science; and the Arthaveda on mechanical science; the six Vedangas are the Siksha on pronunciation; the Kalpa on ceremonial; the Vyakarana or Grammar of Panini; the Commentary of Patanjali (Mahabhashya); the Nirukta or etymological vocabulary; the Chhanda on prosody; and the Jyotisha on astronomy and astrology, including only *one* book; the Bhrigu Sanhita. The twelve Upanishads are: Isa, Kena, Kathá, Prasna, Mundaka, Mándúkya, Taitareya, Aitereya, Chhándógya, Brihadáranyaka, Svetásvatara, and Kaivalya. There exist many more Upanishads which are acknowledged by orthodox pandits;

the Vedas are acknowledged on account of their being the utterance of God Himself, and the others as being directly founded on the Vedas or expressly mentioned in them. Whatever else is considered as shastras by the orthodox Hindus, notably the six Darsanas or philosophical systems and the eighteen Puranas, he repudiates as false, because their contents are contradicted by the Vedas or because they are not mentioned in them. Starting from this premise, he rejects everything in modern Hinduism which is either directly contradicted in the Vedas or not expressly sanctioned in them.

"It will be seen from this statement that there is no difference between him and the orthodox pandits as to the principle of the Canon; for both agree in this, that the Vedas only are authoritative, and that whatsoever is opposed to them is false; the difference really arises in the previous question: what are the Vedas? Dayananda acknowledges only the present Vedas, and what can be proved from them; the other pandits, on the contrary, believe and assert the previous existence of many other Vedic writings, which they say have perished, and which, they assume, contained the complete proof for every shastra and everything in Hinduism which cannot be supported by the now existing Vedas. Such a position, of course, is very difficult to be proved. But some European scholars think that the pandits

but they are all rejected by Dayananda. The Mahabharata is not acknowledged by him in its entirety; but many portions are declared by him spurious, among others, if I mistake not, the famous Bhagavadgitá. This list of shastras here given may be relied upon as correct, as the reformer wrote them down for me on a paper with his own hand.

are to be believed ; among them is Max Müller. His argument is shortly this[1]: the assertion of lost Vedas was first made during the Buddhistic controversy to vindicate a Vedic origin to some parts of Brahmanism ; now, as the assertion is incapable of proof, the Buddhists might easily have made use of it to support their own tenets : it is therefore a dangerous weapon, and, it is thought, would not have been used by the advocates of Brahmanism, unless it had been true. I doubt, however, whether this is a sound argument. As there was no proof for some things in the existing Vedas, there was only this alternative left to the advocates of Brahmanism, either to admit that there was no Vedic proof, which would have been suicidal, or to assert the previous existence of lost Vedic writings, whether or not there was any foundation for it, although this was dangerous. There can be no hesitation as to which of these alternatives they would choose. Dayananda denies altogether the possibility of a loss of Vedas.[2] But, however that may be, it must be clear to any unprejudiced inquirer, that even if other Vedic writings existed formerly, their general tenor must have been the same as that of those which still exist, and that they would in no wise have given support to modern Hinduism.

2. *Idolatry and Mythology*

"The former the reformer rejects entirely, not only as a harmless error, but as positively sinful. He

"[1] See his *Ancient Sanskrit Literature*, pp. 106-7.

[2] I am afraid this is not quite correct. Dayananda denied that any Vedas had been lost, but he maintained that much Vedic literature had been lost.—*Author*.

further rejects polytheism. There is only *one* God with all those attributes generally ascribed to Him by Monotheists. He is the creator first of the Vedas, then of the world, hence the Vedas are eternal as compared with the world; but non-eternal as compared with God. The names of God are manifold: He is named in the Vedas Vishnu, Atma, Agni, etc., according as one aspect of the Divine nature is prominently remembered. Though God is distinct from the world—for Dayananda rejects the Vedantic and ordinary Hindu pantheism—yet He is also immanent in the world as the principle of its life and existence. As such, God is to be viewed as Agni (life) and hence to be worshipped by means of Agni (fire). But he must not be misunderstood: when he says that God in the world is Agni, he does not mean by Agni fire, but something which may best be expressed by soul or vital principle, or principle of existence; again, he does not mean to say that the ordinary Agni (fire) is a representation of God, but, as being the clearest manifestation of God-Agni, it is the fittest ceremonial means of worshipping God; fire is not to be worshipped, but to be used as a means in the worship of God. The worship or service of God consists chiefly in the following three acts: first and foremost the study of the Vedas with a view to the knowledge of God; then the observance of the moral laws as the will of God; thirdly, the worship of God by fire or the homa-sacrifice. The observance of these is the means of salvation. Incarnations (avataras) for the salvation of mankind never took place, nor *can* they ever take place; it is incompatible with the nature of God to become incarnate. Hence Dayananda rejects the Hindu avataras as much as the Christian incarnation ; that is to say, he rejects them as avataras of God. If such avataras really took place, they were avataras of devatas, and not of God. Vishnu, Siva, Brahma, if there be such beings, are only devatas, *i.e.*, superior created beings or angels, not Divine beings. Thus he rejects also most, if not all, of the mythology of the Puranas, especially the fables about Krishna.

3. *Caste*

"This the reformer considers only as a political institution made by the rulers for the common good of society, and not a natural or religious distinction. It is not a natural distinction ; for the four castes were not created by God as distinct species of men ; but all men are of equal nature, of the same species, and brothers. It is not a religious institution, for the salvation of men and their fate in the other world does not depend upon its observance. The castes are simply different professions or guilds (adhikaras), established by the state to guard against confusion and mutual interference, and for the better accomplishment of the different works. Some men, specially fitted for the work, were set aside by the state for the prosecution of worship, science, and literature (the Brahmans) ; others to guard the outward peace and internal order of the state (the Kshattriyas) ; others to carry on trade and till the ground (the Vaisyas) ; again, others to do all the meaner kinds of labour (the Sudras). Each class was made up into a guild and furnished with its rights and privileges and made hereditary. But, as the whole classification is a creation of the state, any Sudra, who is deserving of the promotion, can be made by the state a Vaisya or Kshattriya or Brahmana, if he qualifies himself for the work of the respective class. Likewise any Brahmana, who deserves the degradation, can be made by the state a Sudra. In fact, any Brahmana who is disqualified for his work, becomes at once a Sudra *de jure*, and a Sudra, who qualifies himself for it, becomes at once a Brahmana *de jure* ; though neither can become so *de facto* also either by his own will or the will of others, as long as the state does not make him so. This last limitation obviously makes his theory impracticable. The state will not concern itself nowadays with the regulation of such guilds, to degrade a disreputable Brahmana into a Sudra, or reward a clever Sudra with Brahmanhood. He ought to leave that to the spontaneous action of society regulating itself.[1]

"The public disputation took place on November 17th in the house where the reformer was staying. As soon as the Raja of Benares arrived, the discussion commenced by Dayananda asking Pandit Taracharana, the Raja's court pandit, who had been appointed to defend the cause of orthodoxy, whether he admitted the Vedas as the authority. When this had been agreed to, he requested Taracharana to produce passages from the Vedas sanctioning idolatry, Pashanadipujanalit (worship of stones, etc.). Instead of doing this, Taracharana for some time tried to substitute proofs from the Puranas. At last Dayananda happening to say that he only admitted

[1] That he does. See his *Sattyarath Prakash*.—*Author*.

the Manusmriti, Sarirakasutras, etc., as authoritative because founded on the Vedas, Vishudananda the great Vedantist interfered, and, quoting a Vedanta Sutra from the Sarirakasutras, asked Dayananda to show that it was founded on the Vedas. After some hesitation Dayananda replied that he could do this only after referring to the Vedas, as he did not remember the whole of them. Vishudananda then tauntingly said, if he could not do that he should not set himself up as a teacher in Benares. Dayananda replied, that none of the pandits had the whole of the Vedas in his memory. Thereupon Vishudananda and several others asserted that they knew the whole of the Vedas by heart. Then followed several questions, quite unconnected with the subject of the discussion, but put by Dayananda to show that his opponents had asserted more than they could justify. They could answer none of his questions. At last some pandits took up the thread of the discussion again by asking Dayananda whether the terms pratima (likeness) and púrti (fulness) occurring in the Vedas did not sanction idolatry. He answered that, rightly interpreted, they did not do so. As none of his opponents objected to his interpretation, it is plain that they either perceived the correctness of it, or were too little acquainted with the Vedas to venture to contradict it. Then Madhavácharya, a pandit of no repute, produced two leaves of a Vedic MS., and, reading a passage[1] containing the word "Puranas," asked to what this term referred. Dayananda replied : it was there simply an adjective, meaning "ancient," and not the proper name.

" [1] *Bráhmana nitihásak puránáni.*

Vishudananda challenging this interpretation, some discussion followed as to its grammatical correctness; but at last all seemed to acquiesce in it. Then Madhavacharya produced again two other leaves of a Vedic MS., and read a passage[1] with this purport, that upon the completion of a yajna (sacrifice) on the tenth day the reading of the Puranas should be heard, and asked how the term " Purana " could be here an adjective. Dayananda took the MS. in his hands and began to meditate what answer he should give. His opponents waited about two minutes, and, as still no answer was forthcoming, they rose, jeering and calling out that he was unable to answer and was defeated, and went away. They might certainly have allowed him a little more time, but it is evident that he was puzzled as to an answer; and the answer which he afterwards published in his pamphlet— that to the word Purana was to be supplied vidya (science), meaning purani vidya, that is, the Veda— is not very satisfactory. There can hardly be much doubt that the eighteen Puranas are really referred to in that passage; but, as it is out of a Brahmana of the Samaveda, and that contains many modern additions, its value would after all be not much in the eyes of non-Hindus, and, I suspect, even of Dayananda; for he once admitted to me that the Brahmanas did contain modern interpolated portions, and that any passage sanctioning idolatry was to be considered, as such, a spurious portion.

"The reformer is not unacquainted with Christianity. He has read the Gospels, though I do not think very

" [1] *Yajnasanáptói satyán dasame divase puránánám páthain srinuyát.*

carefully. I had some conversation with him about it. But at present his mind is too much occupied with his own plans of reformation to give any serious thought to the investigation of the claim of another religion.—A.F.R.H.[1]"

For a long time a heated controversy was kept up in the Press, both Indian and Anglo-Indian, about the disputation.[2] The matter was so important and of such great interest from a public point of view that even the *Pioneer*, the leading semi-official Anglo-Indian paper of Allahabad, opened its columns to correspondence on the subject. The event was discussed throughout India, and aroused enormous interest.

From this date may be counted the effective beginning of Dayananda's mission for a reformed Hindu Church, free from cant, from superstition, and from popular error, and worthy of the intelligence, the genius, and the culture of that historic people.

From Benares the Swami continued to march eastward and presently reached Calcutta, the capital of India and the headquarters of British Government in India. The Brahmo Samaj accorded him a hearty welcome, and some of its leading members conferred with him with a view to win his co-operation for their movement; but the Swami could

[1] From *The Christian Intelligencer,* Calcutta, March, 1870, p. 79.

[2] A number of tracts were published by partisans and non-partisans giving their versions of what had actually happened and of the merits of the disputants. Partisans and non-partisans were all agreed that Dayananda was a great scholar and that his knowledge of Sanskrit was unique.

not give up his faith in the infallibility of the Vedas and the doctrine of transmigration of souls, the two cardinal principles which distinguish the Arya Samaj from the Brahmo Samaj. His visit to Calcutta, however, brought him into immediate contact and intimate touch with the leaders of the English educated community. Here he learned their points of view and benefited thereby. For instance, Babu Keshub Chunder Sen, the respected leader of the Brahmo Samaj, suggested to him the supreme importance of carrying on his propaganda in the language of the people, a practical suggestion that was readily and gratefully accepted by the Swami. It was put into operation at once. This single step made a mighty difference in favour of his mission, since it brought him into direct touch with the bulk of his countrymen, both educated and uneducated, who did not know Sanskrit and could not understand him except through translators and interpreters. In Calcutta he made the acquaintance of Maharishi Debendranath Tagore, the father of the now famous Rabindranath Tagore, whose Brahmoism had more in common with the faith of Dayananda than the religious beliefs of the other leaders of the Brahmo Samaj.

After spending another two years in the dissemination of his doctrines, Dayananda proceeded to Bombay, where eventually his mission was to take an organized shape.

CHAPTER III

FOUNDING OF THE ARYA SAMAJ AND DEATH

समानो मन्त्रः समितिः समानी समानं मनः सहचित्तमेषाम् ।
समानं मन्त्रमभि मन्त्रये वः समानेन वो हविषा जुहोमि ॥
२॥ ऋ० १०।१९१।३
समानी व आकूतिः समाना हृदयानि वः । समानमस्तु
वो मनो यथा वः सुसहासति ॥ ३ ॥ ऋ०१०।१९१।४

"Walk together, speak together, let your minds be all alike.

"May the purpose be common, common the assembly, common the mind: so be their thoughts united. I lay before you a common object, and worship with your common oblation.

"May your decisions be unanimous, your minds being of one accord. May the thoughts of all be united so that there may be a happy agreement among all."

—R. X., 191, 2—4.

1. *Constitution of the Arya Samaj*

THE first Arya Samaj was established at Bombay on April 10th, 1875, with the following principles and rules representing both its creed and its constitution :

" . . . 2. The (Arya) Samaj shall regard the Vedas alone as independently and absolutely authoritative. For purposes of testimony and for the understanding of the Vedas, as also for historical purposes, all the four Brahmanas—Shathpatha, etc., the six Vedangas, the four Upavedas, the six Darshanas, and 1,127 Shakhas or expositions of the Vedas, shall, by virtue of their being ancient and recognized works of Rishis, be also regarded as *secondarily* authoritative, in so far only as their teaching is in accord with that of the Vedas.

" 3. There shall be a *principal* Arya Samaj in each province, and the other Arya Samajes shall be its branches, all connected with one another.

" 5. The Principal Samaj shall possess various Vedic works in Sanskrit and Aryabhasha (Hindi) for the dissemination of true knowledge, and it shall issue a weekly paper under the name of *Arya Prakash*, also an exponent of the Vedic teaching. The paper and the books shall be patronized by all Samajes.

" 8. The members of the Samaj shall be men of truth, of upright policy and principles, of pure character, and of philanthropic impulses.

" 9. The members shall give their spare time to the earnest service of the Samaj. Those that have no family to care for should, in particular, be always striving to promote the well-being of the society.

" 10. Every eighth day the President, the Secretary, and other members of the Samaj shall come together in the Samaj Mandir. . . .

" 11. Having assembled together, they should be calm and composed in their minds, and in a spirit of love, and free from bias, they may ask questions and obtain answers from each other. This done, they shall sing the hymns of the Sama Veda in praise of God, and songs bearing on the true Dharma, to the accompaniment of musical instruments. The *mantras* shall be commented upon and explained, and the lectures delivered on similar (Vedic) themes. After this there shall be music again, to be followed by an exposition of *mantras* and speeches.

" 12. Every member shall cheerfully contribute a hundredth part of the money he has earned honestly and with the sweat of his brow, towards the funds of the Samaj, the Arya Vidyala and the *Arya Prakash* paper. If he contributes more, the greater shall be his reward. The money thus contributed shall be used for the purposes specified and in no other way.

" 13. The more an individual bestirs himself for the fund of the Samaj for the purposes specified, and for the diffusion of a knowledge of the teachings of the Arya Samaj, the more honour shall he receive for his energy and zeal.

" 14. The Samaj shall do *stuti*, *prarthana*, and *upasana* (*i.e.*, shall glorify, pray to and hold communion with the one only God), in the manner commended by the Vedas. They believe God to be formless, almighty, just, infinite, immutable, eternal, incomparable, merciful, the father of all, the mother of the entire universe, all-supporting, all truth, all intelligence, all happiness, and the supreme and the only lord of the universe ; as also all-pervading and the knower of all hearts, indestructible, deathless, everlasting, pure and conscious ; as endless, the bestower of happiness, the giver of righteousness, wealth, comfort and salvation ;—to speak of Him as endowed with such and similar other qualities and attributes, is to do his *stuti* (*i.e.*, to glorify and praise Him). Asking His help in all righteous undertakings, is identical with *prarthana* (*i.e.*, praying to Him), and to become absorbed in the contemplation of His Essence, which is absolute Happiness, is termed *upasana* (*i.e.*, holding communion with Him). He alone shall be adored, and naught besides.

" 15. The Samaj shall perform Vedic *sanskars* (ritual), such as *Anteshthi* (the death ceremony), etc.

" 16. The Vedas and the ancient Arsha Granthas shall be studied and taught in the Arya Vidyala, and true and right training, calculated to improve males and females, shall be imparted, on Vedic lines.

" 17. In the interests of the country, both kinds of reform shall receive thorough attention in the Samaj, spiritual as well as worldly. There shall be uplifting in both directions for the promotion of purity ; indeed, the welfare of entire mankind shall be the objective of the Samaj.

" 18. The Samaj shall believe only in what is right

and just, *i.e.*, in the true Vedic Dharma, free from prejudice, and tested by all tests laid down by the ancient authorities by which truth is distinguished from falsity.

" 19. The Samaj shall send learned men, of approved character, everywhere to preach truth.

" 20. In the interests of the education of both males and females, separate schools shall be established, if possible, in all places. In the seminaries for females the work of teaching and that of serving the students shall be carried on by *females only*, and in the schools for males the responsibility of doing the same shall lie with *males*. Never shall this rule be infringed. . . .

" 22. The President and the other members of the Samaj shall, for the maintenance of mutual goodwill, keep their minds wholly divested of all feelings of pride, hate, anger, etc., and, with such vices shut out, they shall, being free of enmity and pure of heart, love one another, even as each loves his own self.

" 23. When deliberating on a subject, that which has been, as the fruit of this deliberation, ascertained to be in thorough accord with the principles of justice and universal benevolence, and absolutely true, the same shall be made known to the members and believed in by them. Acting thus is termed rising above bias or prejudice.

" 24. He alone who conforms his conduct to the principles specified, and is righteous and endowed with true virtues, shall be admitted to the higher circle of the Samaj, while he who is otherwise shall be but an ordinary member of the Samaj. But the individual who openly appears to be utterly depraved and debased shall be expelled. Such a step, however, shall not be dictated by prejudice; on the contrary, everything shall be done after due deliberation by the exalted members of the Samaj, and not otherwise.

"27. Whenever an occasion for giving charity arises, as, for instance, in connection with a marriage, the birth of a son, or a death in the family, and so on, the Arya Samajist concerned shall be expected to make a donation to the Samaj.

"28. Whenever an addition is made to the principles or rules above laid down, or whenever any of these is altered or amended, such an addition, alteration or amendment shall invariably be the result of thorough deliberation on the subject by the exalted *Sabhasads* of the Samaj, after due and proper notice to all concerned."

Note.—We have omitted a few unimportant Articles.

Here again, as also at Poona, Dayananda came in close touch with the educated mind of the Hindu community, *i.e.*, with such as had received their education in the schools and colleges and at the universities established and maintained after the European model. But the next step in the evolution of the Arya Samaj was not taken till two years later, in Lahore, the capital of the province of the Punjab, in Northern India. Here the Samaj took its final shape, which it maintains at this day: the principles were finally revised, and the constitution re-framed and finally settled. All the Arya Samajes in India or elsewhere accept these principles and are governed by this constitution. There has been no change in the former, but the latter may have been changed in minor particulars to suit local conditions. We will speak of both in greater detail later.

2. *Death*

The remaining part of his life—from 1877 to October, 1883—was spent by the Swami in preaching and teaching and writing books, as well as in establishing and organizing Arya Samajes throughout India. The only part which the Swami could not reach was Madras.

In the Punjab, the United Provinces of Agra and Oude, and in Rajputana and Gujerat, he met with the greatest success. In these provinces a network of Arya Samajes had been established before his death, but the progress made since then may be inferred from the fact that the membership of 243,000 in 1911 was two and half times what it was in 1901, and six times that of 1891. Some of the noblest and highest in the land accepted his faith, and became his disciples and pupils: for example, the Maharana of Udaipur, the most ancient and the most respected of the Hindu chiefs, whose family has wielded the royal sceptre in an unbroken line of succession for over a thousand years. Never had this proud family bowed the knee to the Musulmans. Even the great Akbar was unable to win their allegiance, although his son (himself borne by a Hindu mother) eventually succeeded in making a temporary alliance with the head of this state.

Maharana Sajjan Singh studied Hindu law and Hindu jurisprudence with Dayananda, and the company of the latter had for a time a very chastening influence on the otherwise dissolute prince. It was at Jodhpur, the capital of the only other Hindu state in British India which claims as ancient a lineage as that of Udaipur, that he caught the fatal illness which carried him off. There he had gone in response to an invitation from the Maharaja, who was anxious to be his disciple and to study with him. To the misfortune of both, but to the greater misfortune of the country, the Swami took a very strong exception to the Maharaja's living with a concubine, a Musulman woman, who accordingly regarded him with violent dislike. It is said that she contrived to have a subtle poison mixed in his food, thereby causing mortal illness. The Maharaja, of course, had no hand in this alleged crime, and was genuinely stricken with grief when informed of the Swami's malady. He did everything in his power to obtain for the patient the best available medical aid and every comfort that money could procure. But there was no relief, and the Swami succumbed to his illness and died at Ajmere, in British territory, whither he had been removed by his friends a few days before.

This sad event took place on October 30th, 1883. Those who were present by the side of his deathbed are unanimous in testifying that he was perfectly calm at the time of his death, the exact time of which he had foretold several hours before.

It was at Jodhpur that Maharaja Pratab Singh,

the brother of the reigning chief (now General Sir Pratab Singh, G.C.S.I., G.C.V.O., K.C.B., etc.), became his disciple, a fact which he always recites with pride.

The amount of obloquy and persecution to which Swami Dayananda was exposed in his lifetime may be gathered from the fact that numerous attempts were made on his life by the orthodox Hindus; assassins were hired to kill him; missiles were thrown at him during his lectures and disputations; he was called a hired emissary of the Christians, an apostate, an atheist, and so on. The spirit in which he met this fierce opposition may be judged from the following anecdote which we cull from Madame Blavatsky's account of him in her book called *The Caves and Jungles of Hindusthan.*

"One is inclined to think," says Madame Blavatsky, "that this wonderful Hindu bears a charmed life, so careless is he of raising the worst human passions, which are so dangerous in India. At Benares, a worshipper of the Shiva, feeling sure that his cobra, trained purposely for the mysteries of a Shivaite pagoda, would at once make an end of the offender's life, triumphantly exclaimed: 'Let the god *Vasuki* (the snake god) himself show which of us is right!'

"Dayananda jerked off the cobra twisting round his leg, and with a single vigorous movement crushed the reptile's head. 'Let him do so,' he quietly assented, 'your god has been too slow. It is I who have decided the dispute. Now go,' added he, addressing the crowd, 'and tell every one how easily perish all false gods.' Truly, a marble statue could not be less moved by the raging wrath of the crowd. We saw him once at work. He sent away all his faithful followers, and forbade them either to watch over him or to defend him, and stood alone before the infuriated crowd, facing calmly the monster, ready to spring upon him and tear him to pieces."

In the same work, Madame Blavatsky pays the following compliment to his learning and scholarship:

"It is perfectly certain that India never saw a more learned Sanskrit scholar, a deeper metaphysician, a more wonderful orator, and a more fearless denunciator of any evil, than Dayananda, since the time of Shankaracharya." [1]

Another testimony to his erudition, and we have finished our account of the Swami's life. This is an unwilling admission of his great powers by his opponents among the orthodox Hindus; we give it in the words of Professor Max Müller:

"At a large convocation at Calcutta, about 300 Pandits from Gauda, Navadipa, and Kasi discussed the orthodoxy of his opinions. . . . But, although the decision was adverse, the writer of the report adds: the mass of young Hindus are not Sanskrit scholars, and it is no wonder that they should be won over by hundreds to Dayananda's views, enforced as they are by an oratorical power of the highest order, and a determined will force that breaks down all opposition."[2]

[1] The famous founder of the Vedantic school of Indian thought, of whom Max Müller and other German scholars have spoken in the highest terms of praise, and who flourished 800 A.D.

[2] *Biographical Essays,* by Max Müller, 1884, pp. 179-80.

His death elicited the highest tributes from all classes of people, Indian and non-Indian, Hindus, Musulmans, Christians, and Parsis. The greatest among his contemporaries wrote or spoke of him in the highest terms and deplored his early death: of these we may mention the late Sir Syed Ahmad Khan, the greatest nineteenth-century leader of the Moslems of India; Colonel Olcott, president of the Theosophical Society, and Madame Blavatsky, its founder. But the most characteristic tribute came from Professor Max Müller, who compared him with Dr. Pusey, of England, and wrote a remarkably eulogistic notice of the man and his work.[1]

"Deeply read in the theological literature of his country . . . he was opposed to many of the abuses that had crept in, as he well knew, during the later periods of the religious growth of India, and of which, as is now well known, no trace can be found in the ancient sacred texts of the Brahmans, the Vedas. . . . In his public disputations with the most learned Pandits at Benares and elsewhere, he was generally supposed to have been victorious, though often the aid of the police had to be called in to protect him from the blows of his conquered foes."

We give as a fitting conclusion of this chapter a few passages from a long tribute which appeared in the official organ of the Theosophical Society, *The Theosophist*:

"A master spirit has passed away from India. Pandit Dayananda Saraswati . . . is gone; the irrepressible, energetic reformer, whose mighty voice and passionate eloquence for the last few years

[1] *Biographical Essays*, p. 167.

raised thousands of people in India from lethargic indifference and stupor into active patriotism, is no more. . . .

" *De mortuis nil nisi bonum.* All our differences have been burnt with the body. . . . We remember only the grand virtues and noble qualities of our former colleague and teacher, and late antagonist. We bear in mind but his life-long devotion to the cause of Aryan regeneration ; his ardent love for the grand philosophy of his forefathers ; his relentless, untiring zeal in the work of the projected social and religious reforms ; and it is with unfeigned sorrow that we now hasten to join the ranks of his many mourners. In him India has lost one of her noblest sons. A patriot in the true sense of the word, Swami Dayananda laboured from his earliest years for the recovery of the lost treasures of Indian intellect. His zeal for the reformation of his mother-land was exceeded only by his unbounded learning. Whatever might be said as to his interpretation of the sacred writings, there can be but one opinion as to his knowledge of Sanskrit, and the impetus to the study of both received at his hands. There are few towns and but one province we believe—namely, Madras—that Pandit Dayananda did not visit in furtherance of his missionary work, and fewer still where he has not left the impress of his remarkable mind behind him. He threw, as it were, a bomb-shell in the midst of the stagnant masses of degenerated Hinduism, and fired with love for the teachings of the Rishis and Vedic learning the hearts of all who were drawn within the influence of his eloquent oratory. Certainly there was no better or grander orator in Hindi and Sanskrit than Dayananda throughout the length and breadth of this land.

"As soon as the sad rumour was confirmed, Colonel Olcott, who was then at Cawnpore, paid a public tribute to the Swami's memory. He said that whatever might have been our rights or wrongs in the controversy, and whatever other pandits or orientalists could say against the Swami, there was room for no two opinions as to his energetic patriotism or of the nationalising influence exerted upon his followers. In Pandit Dayananda Saraswati there was a total absence of anything like degrading sycophancy and toadyism towards foreigners from interested motives.

"Truly, however heretical and blasphemous might have appeared his religious radicalism in the sight of old orthodox Brahminism, still the teachings and Vedic doctrines promulgated by him were a thousand times more consonant with *Shruti* or even *Smriti* than the doctrines taught by all other native Samajes put together. If he merged the old idols into One Living Being, Ishwara, as being only the attributes and powers of the latter, he yet had never attempted the folly of forcing down the throats of his followers the hybrid *compound* of a *Durga-Moses, Christ-and-Koran,* and *Buddha-chaitanya* mixture of the modern reformers. The Arya Samaj rites certainly make the nearest approach to the real Vedic national religion."

CHAPTER IV

THE TEACHINGS OF DAYANANDA

अयमग्ने जरिता त्वे अभूदपि सहसः सूनो नह्यन्यदस्त्या-
प्यम् ॥ १ ॥ ऋ० १० । १४२ । १

"He hath paid sacrifice, toiled in worship and offered gifts to wealth-increasing Agni, Him the displeasure of the mighty moves not; outrage and scorn affect not such a mortal."

—R. VI., 3, 2.

1. *His attack on Mythological Hinduism and Caste*

In the preceding chapters we have given a summary of the main incidents of Swami Dayananda's life, in order to give the reader a clear idea of the conditions of the time in which he lived and of the environment in which he was born, bred, and educated. No one can appreciate the magnitude of the task that the Swami set himself to do, or of his achievements towards it, unless he is fully acquainted with what Hindu religion and Hindu society stood for when Dayananda began his career. When we use the past tense we do not necessarily imply that the Hinduism of the uneducated masses is very materially different to-day from what it was then. There is no doubt that a great change since then has come over orthodox Hinduism by its contact with Western thought, and still more by the constant searchings to which it has been subjected in the light of the aggressive propaganda of the Arya Samaj. Not only have the educated classes (though still orthodox) changed their point of view, but even the extremely ignorant and superstitious masses are not what they were in the infancy of Dayananda. Yet, speaking generally, what we are about to say of the Hinduism of Dayananda's time is perhaps as true of the Hinduism of to-day. The principal difference is that what was of universal application then has had its area contracted and narrowed by general education as well as by the propaganda of reforming bodies like the Arya Samaj.

In giving a general idea of popular Hinduism in contrast with the beliefs and teachings of Dayananda, we will begin with the personal authority of the priest, to which class Dayananda himself belonged by birth. Hindu priests are called Brahmins. When Dayananda reached the age of discretion he found that the Brahmin was everything in Hindu religion, and the ordinary individual nothing. Every Brahmin represented God Himself, and was the sole exponent of God's wishes and commands. His word was law, and could not be disregarded excepting on pain of eternal damnation. A Brahmin was neither selected, appointed, nor ordained. He was so by mere birth, and his authority as a priest had nothing to do with his education or other qualifications. He alone could say what was religion and what was not. He alone could lay down for every man what he was to believe and to do. The right of independent judgment did not exist. He alone knew, or was supposed to know, the Scriptures; although, as a matter of fact, not even one Brahmin in a thousand knew the Vedas. But then, everything in Sanskrit was as sacred as the Vedas. Anything said by a Brahmin was the essence of the Vedas, be it from the Puranas, or from the Epics, or even from an ordinary Sanskrit poem or drama. But it mattered not even if the Brahmin knew absolutely nothing of Sanskrit. By the mere fact of his birth he was supposed to be divine. Such was the influence of the Brahmins on the great mass of Hindus when Dayananda was born that the worship of the Brahmin was the primary test of Hinduism. Everything else was secondary. Even now Hinduism is so vast a sea of creeds, dogmas, beliefs, rituals and customs that the Census authorities have considered the worship of the Brahmin to be the principal test of this faith. In his report for the United Provinces of Agra and Oude for the year 1911, Mr. Blunt says:

"Though it is legitimate to assert that the *Brahmans'* influence on the growth of Hinduism has been overrated, at the expense of more natural causes, it is impossible to overrate their omnipotence in matters of religion and the completeness of their rule over the members of the Hindu system. The mediæval popes were spiritual despots: but, compared with the autocracy of the Brahmans, they were mere constitutional monarchs. . . . The *Brahman* may not be God, but he is at all events Godlike, a subject not only of veneration but of actual worship." He thus comes to the conclusion that "the first great criterion by which a Hindu is determined" is that "every Hindu must acknowledge the Brahman's superiority and his omnipotence in spiritual and social matters."

This is certainly a correct description of matters as they existed 100 years ago, or even in some parts as they existed 50 years ago; but it is not true of to-day. At the present moment there must be some hundreds of thousands of Hindus, both in and out of the Arya Samaj, to whom this criterion would not apply. The "divine right" by birth of the Brahmin is fast melting away. The monopoly of the Brahmin in administering religious sacraments and in performing religious ceremonies is being slowly but perceptibly undermined. Even in unlettered circles his authority is being questioned.

Yet no more than fifty years ago the description we have quoted was literally true. The authority of the mere Brahmin was the central point of Hindu religion. It was this central authority that ruled and controlled the whole system of Hindu life; its pantheon of gods and goddesses, its dogmas, its philosophy, its rituals, its social economy and all that is related thereto.

The organization of Roman Catholicism pales in comparison with the marvellously intricate and rigid organization of Hinduism effected by the Brahmins. It was the greatest organization the world had ever known. It encompassed the minutest details of individual and social life. The Brahmin's eye comprehended almost every moment of a Hindu's existence. There was nothing, however sinful, monstrous, or atrociously vicious, which a Hindu could not do, so long as it had the sanction of the priest, or so long as a Brahmin could be prevailed upon to make matters right by processes of expiation promulgated by him and known to him and to him alone. Various rites and ceremonies had been invented and used as accompaniments, or rather as accessories, to this redemption. Multitudinous and mysterious were the ways and practices whereby " forgiveness of sins and redemption, coupled with the guarantees of a pass to heaven after death, were brought about." The simple and spiritual religion of the Vedas, the philosophical teaching of the Upanishads, had been superseded by what was only an " affair of temples and material sacrifices, of shows and processions, of festivals spread over the whole year in honour of innumerable deities," accompanied by all the paraphernalia of " bells and candles and vestments and ceremonials and incantations and tunes, unintelligible to those who heard them," and in some cases even to those who uttered them.

With a keen eye, bent upon finding out the origin of things and tracing their development in their successive stages of rise and fall, with an intuitive faculty for going to the root of the matter in hand, Dayananda saw that the authority of the Brahmin was the pivot and the central curse of the whole system, and that no symbolic treatment of Hinduism was possible. Neither by habit nor by training was he given to diplomacy or duplicity: subtlety of speech or action was foreign to his nature. He felt the supreme importance of speaking the truth, the naked truth, and the whole truth. He therefore went straight to the point, attacked the central fortification of the citadel, and aimed to dash it from its foundations. He questioned the authority of the mere Brahmin by birth. The Brahmin relied on Manu for his rights and privileges, and the Swami showed, on the authority of Manu himself, that a Brahmin must be learned in the Vedas, above the very suspicion of avarice and greed and thoroughly calm and composed in his demeanour : and that a Brahmin who did not come up to that standard did not deserve to be treated and respected as such. He quoted chapter and verse in support of his contention, and showed, from those very books which the Brahmins relied upon, how in ancient times persons not born of Brahmin parents acquired the position of Brahmins by learning and piety, and how those born of Brahmin parents were degraded to lower positions according to their personal qualifications. He denied the right of any human being to control the free judgment of his fellow men or women, in matters relating to the soul, by the mere fact of his having been born in a certain caste or class. He held that the born Brahmin was nothing more than an ordinary man who, on account of his hereditary inclinations, had, perhaps, a better chance of becoming a real Brahmin than other persons not so born but who had an equal right to become Brahmins by the force of their personal character. He maintained that even a real Brahmin was not to be worshipped in the sense in which God is worshipped, and that he was no more than a leader, a teacher, a preceptor, a guide and a philosopher. He denounced the worship of gods and goddesses, and preached that only the Supreme Being, the Primal Cause of the Universe, the Universal and All-pervading Spirit, should be worshipped, and *none else;* that God and God's Word revealed in the beginning of the world were the only final and infallible authorities in religion ; that all truth and purity and goodness emanated from God ; that no one had any right to stand between man and God ; and that it was the right and duty of every man to seek inspiration and illumination from God Himself, and to live in the consciousness of a personal and direct relationship with Him.

For ages the Brahmins had prohibited the study of the Vedas to the other castes. For a Sudra to hear a Vedic verse was the highest sin. The other castes were allowed, in theory, to hear and study the Vedas, but in practice no Brahmin ever taught the Vedas to any but a born Brahmin. As a matter of fact, however, even among Brahmins the Vedas were known in parts only and to a few—say, to one in ten thousand in Upper India and to one in a thousand in the Deccan. All the four Vedas were known to a very few only, and their knowledge was only of the text. The majority of them understood no more than a few verses required for ritual purposes, or that formed part of the daily prayer-book. The great bulk of Brahmins were as ignorant of the Vedas as were the other Hindus. Even ceremonies were not necessarily performed with Vedic texts. Formulæ and texts had been culled from later literature and the necessary ceremonies were performed with their help. As for interpreting the Vedas, only one man had dared to do so within the 1,500 years immediately preceding the birth of Swami Dayananda, and he had done nothing more than compile a huge commentary based on current and traditional interpretation. To try to put an independent interpretation on the Vedas was an act of the highest audacity, amounting in fact to blasphemy, for which no human punishment could be adequate. It is true that, centuries before, the ancestors of the Hindus had been a most devout and God-loving people. Many inspired ones had risen among them—prophets and teachers of the highest rank, who had realized God and the highest knowledge in their own persons, and had left a spiritual and intellectual legacy of the noblest kind. But the time came when their descendants forgot God, began to indulge in intellectual quibbles, wedded themselves to dead forms, and neglected the noble heritage left to them by the pioneer souls of their race.

Pharisees arose who organized the most subtle and exacting ecclesiasticism ever invented by the legislative genius of man, reducing religion to dead dogma and dry form, and shutting and sealing the soul's windows of the nation. It is true that all this was done in the name and on the ostensible authority of the inspired ones of the past, but the spirit had vanished and there was no realization in actual life. The caste, the law, and the authority had become everything.

Into these surroundings came young Dayananda with a clear vision of the original truth and of its vast possibilities for his people in particular and for the human race in general. He began in right earnest, and, with a marvellous insight, attacked at once the root cause of the evil—the unquestioned authority of the mere Brahmin by birth. His educated countrymen had evidently told him of the Popes of Rome, and he gave that name to the Brahmins of India and denounced them with all the vehemence of his intensely vehement nature.

2. *The Right to Study the Scriptures.*

To ensure lasting success for his crusade, it was necessary that the restrictions imposed by the ecclesiastical system on the study of the Hindu Scriptures—the Vedas—should be removed, and the huge mass of literature, the growth of centuries, which had accumulated as a natural consequence of the system, should be divested of all authority excepting in so far as it followed the revealed literature. The Brahmins had clothed with divine authority everything written or composed by them: Dayananda exposed the trick and lifted the veil. He called upon all people, regardless of caste and creed, to study the Vedas, and he conceded to every human being the right of interpreting the Vedas for himself, provided he gave them their etymological and philosophical meanings and conformed to the ancient and approved canons of understanding and interpreting them. This was verily a revolution which, by a single stroke, broke the shackles which Hindus had worn for centuries. Dayananda loosed their chains and restored their pristine liberties. He led the way, and, discarding tradition and custom, began to interpret the Vedas for himself. His memory was well stocked with the sacred texts. His knowledge of Vedic literature was almost unsurpassed among his contemporaries. Thus he was able to justify everything he said, not merely by reason and logic alone, but also, above all, by profuse quotation from sacred literature—from the *Brahmanas*, the *Upanishads*, and the *Sutras*.

Any one seeing modern India in the twentieth century can scarcely conceive that within thirty years of the close of the nineteenth century the Vedas were a sealed book in India, and no one could even read them, much less quote them in open meetings composed of all classes of men, Hindus and non-Hindus alike. At the present moment the Vedas are being read, studied and commented upon by all classes and castes of Hindus, from the highest to the lowest. The Word of God has been spread before God's sons, irrespective of caste, creed and colour. This is the greatest service rendered by Dayananda to the cause of religious and intellectual as well as social freedom in India, and this alone entitles him to be called the saviour of Hindu India.

3. *The Key to the Vedas: Canons of Interpretation*

Swami Dayananda did not accept the existing commentaries on the Vedas as binding on any one. Those of *Sayana*[1] and *Mahidhar* he rejected altogether. The latter he thought was deliberately, mischievously and viciously perverse in his interpretation of the Vedas, and the former was misguided,

[1] European scholars speak of *Sayana* as "a mere drag on the progress of Vedic scholarship."—*Sacred Books of the East,* Vol. XXXII., Vedic Hymns, p. xxxii. Mahidhar is hardly relied upon by European scholars.

partial and prejudiced. His interpretation and commentary aimed at the justification of the prevailing theology and its concomitant institutions.

Sayana lived and wrote at a time when the sun of Hindu greatness had long set; when Hindu life and institutions had been perverted by an exacting priesthood, possibly with an eye to saving it from the inroads of a strong, proselytising creed like Islam in the fulness and splendour of its political and military glory. It was a logical consequence of Dayananda's teachings about the Vedas that he should supply a key to unlock their hidden treasures, so that his hearers might be assisted in their further studies. This he did by explaining the rules of Vedic interpretation and insisting on Vedic language being operated upon in the spirit of Vedic times.[1] The Sanskrit of the Vedas is mostly obsolete and quite different from modern Sanskrit as it has been written and read within the last 2,500 years. Even the grammar has undergone considerable changes. Modern grammar is of little assistance in understanding the sense of the Vedas. Swami Dayananda, therefore, insisted that the Vedas should be studied in the light of *Vedic* grammar, and with the help of literature that has no trace of modernism in it.

The first canon for the interpretation of Vedic terms laid down by admittedly the greatest authority

[1] Speaking of the difficulties of understanding the Vedas, Prof. Max Müller says: "Though we may understand almost every word, yet we find it so difficult to lay hold of a connected chain of thought and to discover expressions that will not throw a wrong shade on the original features of the ancient words of the Veda."—*Sacred Books of the East,* Vol. XXXII., p. xxxii.

on the subject, *Yaska*, the author of *Nirukta*, is that the Vedic terms are all "*yaugika*."[1]

Patanjali, the author of the most authoritative and universally accepted commentary on Vedic grammar, supports that view. Pandit Gurudatta Vidyarthi, in his learned brochure called *The Terminology of the Vedas*, to which Professor Max Müller refers approvingly in his monumental work on Vedic hymns (*Sacred Books of the East*, Vol. XXXII.), has said that all the *Rishis* and *Munis* of ancient India—*i.e.*, all the ancient authors and commentators—were unanimous on this point.[2] In his *History of Ancient Sanskrit Literature*, Professor Max Müller has admitted this, at least as regards certain portions of the Vedas. "But there is a charm," says he, "in these primitive strains discoverable in no other class of poetry. Every word retains something of its radical meaning, every epithet tells; every thought, in spite of the most intricate and abrupt expression, is, if we once disentangle it, true, correct and complete."[3]

Further in the same work, Müller says: "Names . . . are to be found in the Veda, as it were, in a still fluid state. They never appear as *appellations*, nor yet as *proper names*; they are organic, not yet broken or smoothed down."[4]

[1] A *yaugika* term is one that has a derivative meaning, that is, one that only signifies the meaning of the root together with the modifications effected by the affixes. In fact, the structural elements of which the word is compounded afford the whole and the only clue to the true signification of the word. The word is purely connotive.—(Pandit Gurudatta Vidyarthi, *Terminology of the Vedas*, Chicago edition, p. 7.)

[2] *Vedic Terminology*, p. 8.

[3] Max Müller's *History of Ancient Sanskrit Literature*, p. 553.

[4] *Ibid.*, p. 755.

Pandit Gurudatta points out how the neglect of this simple rule by *Sayana* and the European scholars has led to the idea that the Vedas inculcate the worship of innumerable gods and goddesses, called *devatas.* " This word, *devata,*" says the Pandit, " is a most fruitful source of error, and it is very necessary that its exact meaning and application should be determined. Not understanding the Vedic sense of this word, *devata*, and easily admitting the popular superstitious interpretation of a belief in mythological gods and goddesses, crumbling into wretched idolatry, European scholars have imagined the Vedas to be full of the worship of such materials and have degraded its religion even below polytheism and perhaps at par with atheism, calling it '*henotheistic.*' " He again quotes the ancient authorities on the true meaning of the word, *devata*, when used in connection with Vedic texts, and shows by several examples how European scholars have misunderstood and misinterpreted the Vedas by their ignorance and neglect of these authorities. The discussion is concluded by the following observations, which are well worth quoting in full :

" We have seen that Yaska regards the names of those substances whose properties are treated of, in the *mantra,* as the *devatas.* What substances, then, are the *devatas*? They are all that can form the subject of human knowledge. All human knowledge is limited by two conditions, *i.e.*, *time* and *space.* Our knowledge of causation is mainly that of succession of events. And succession is nothing but an order in time. Secondly, our knowledge must be a knowledge of something, and that something must be somewhere. It must have a locality of its existence and occurrence. Thus far, the *circumstances* of our knowledge, *time* and *locality*. Now to the essentials of knowledge. The most exhaustive division of human knowledge is between objective and subjective. Objective knowledge is the knowledge of all that passes without the human body. It is the knowledge of the phenomena of the external universe. . . . In speaking of the subjective knowledge, there is, firstly, the ego, the *human spirit*, the conscious entity ; secondly, the internal phenomena of which the human spirit is conscious." These latter are again divided into "*deliberate activities*" and "*vital activities*," and it is concluded that, since our prior analysis of the knowable leads to six things, *time, locality, force, human spirit, deliberate activities* and *vital activities*, these are fit to be called *devatas :* and, if the account of the *Nirukta* concerning Vedic *devatas* be accepted as true, the Vedas should be understood to inculcate these six things as *devatas* and no others. We have given this lengthy quotation as making clear the position of Swami Dayananda with regard to the true canons of Vedic interpretation.[1]

For over 2,500 years had these canons been neglected, resulting in a hopeless tangle of confusion as to the religion of the Vedas. The cry of "Back to the Vedas !" would have been meaningless but for

[1] As an instance of the perversity of the missionary mind in reading mythological gods and goddesses in the Vedas, reference may be made to a paper written by Mr. Griswold, M.A., of Lahore, wherein he presumes to differ from *Yaska*, the author of *Nirukta*, the greatest authority on Vedic interpretation.

the supplying of this key for the unlocking of the treasures hidden there. We are therefore disposed to think that this was the most important of the Swami's teachings, the keystone of the structure raised by him.

We know that both Hindu and European scholars take strong exception to his commentary on and interpretation of the Vedas. They consider it "more ingenious than ingenuous,"[1] but the Swami's claim to be a great scholar and a great reformer does not rest upon the accuracy of his voluminous Commentary on the Vedas. What matter for us are the principles he has laid down: (*a*) the right of every human being to read and interpret the Vedas for himself and for others; (*b*) the duty of every Arya to do so; and (*c*) the canons of its interpretation, as stated above. This alone would have entitled him to a niche in the Temple of Fame: but he did much more.

4. *The World-Apostle of Hinduism*

For the first time in the history of Hinduism since its fall, a Hindu scholar, born of Brahmin parents, opened the sealed gate of Hinduism to the rest of mankind. This followed as a logical consequence of his position in relation to the Vedas. The Vedas were the Word of God; they had been revealed in the beginning of creation, for the good of the race; they alone were the primeval revelation. It was therefore the right of every human being to know them and to join the Society which accepted them as the Word of God. He maintained that the Vedas

[1] *United Provinces Report* for 1911, by Mr. Blunt, p. 133.

themselves said so, and that it was the duty of all who knew the Vedas to disseminate their knowledge throughout the world for the benefit of all mankind. The Christians believed in the eternal damnation of those who would not accept Christ as their Saviour. They claimed the monopoly of salvation for a belief in Christ and the Holy Bible. The Hindus advanced neither of these claims for the Vedas. They held that salvation could be reached by different paths, that a good Muslim, a good Christian, or one who was neither, had as much chance of being saved as a good Hindu. Salvation, according to them, depended on true knowledge followed by true conduct. They did not hold that it was necessary to be a Hindu to fulfil either condition. The modern Hindus, however, implicitly believed, and the vast bulk of them still believe, that a Hindu could be such by birth only, and that none born outside the pale of Hindu society could ever become a Hindu. "Hinduism," says Sir Alfred Lyall in his *Asiatic Studies*, Part I, "is a matter of birthright and inheritance. . . . A man does not become a Hindu, but is born into Hinduism." Hindu society was thus a constantly diminishing entity. It was a self-contained community—a charmed circle, closed against all outsiders. Swami Dayananda broke that charm and unbarred the closed doors. The Arya Samaj was meant to be, and is, an essentially Hindu organization—Hindus and non-Hindus are all agreed on that point. Yet it is open to every one, regardless of caste, colour or nationality, who subscribes to its principles and desires to be enrolled as a member. Once a member, he has all the rights and privileges of a member, whether he be a Hindu or not. How this principle has worked in practice will be stated in another chapter.

5. *Dayananda's Beliefs*

As for the remainder of Dayananda's religious teachings, we shall give them in his own words. At the end of his great work, called *Sattyarath Prakash* (*lit.*, "The True Exposition"), he summarizes his beliefs in categorical order, with a short explanatory preface from which we extract the following passages:

" I believe in a religion based on universal and all-embracing principles which have always been accepted as true by mankind, and will continue to command the allegiance of mankind in the ages to come. Hence it is that the religion in question is called the *Primeval Eternal Religion*, which means that it is above the hostility of all human creeds whatsoever.

" My conception of God and all other objects in the Universe is founded on the teachings of the Veda and other true *Shastras*, and is in conformity with the beliefs of all the sages, from *Brahma* down to *Jaimini*. I offer a statement of these beliefs for the acceptance of all good men. That alone I hold to be acceptable which is worthy of being believed in by all men in all ages. *I do not entertain the least idea of founding a new religion or sect.* My sole aim is to believe in truth and help others to believe in it, to reject falsehood and to help others in doing the same. . . . He alone is entitled to be called a man who possesses a thoughtful nature and feels for others in the same way as he does for his own self, does not fear the unjust, however powerful, but fears the truly virtuous, however weak. Moreover, he should always exert himself to his utmost to protect the righteous, and advance their good, and conduct himself worthily towards them, even though they be extremely poor and weak and destitute of material resources. On the other hand, he should constantly strive to destroy, humble and oppose the wicked, sovereign rulers of the whole earth and men of great influence and power though they be. In other words, a man should, as far as lies in his power, constantly endeavour to undermine the power of the unjust and to strengthen that of the just. He may have to bear any amount of terrible suffering, he may have even to quaff the bitter cup of death in the performance of this duty, which devolves on him on account of being a man, but he should not shirk it."

We proceed to give his beliefs in the order in which he has recorded them :

" 1. He, who is called *Brahm* or the Most High ; who is *Parmatma*, or the Spirit who permeates the whole universe ; who is Truth, Intelligence, and Happiness ; whose nature, attributes and characteristics are holy ; who is omniscient, formless, all-pervading, unborn, infinite, almighty, just, and merciful ; who is the author of the universe, sustains and dissolves it ; who awards all souls the fruits of their deeds in strict accordance with the requirements of absolute justice ; and who is possessed of other like attributes—even *Him* I believe to be the Lord of creation.

"2. The four Vedas, the repository of Knowledge and Religious Truth, are the Word of God. They comprise what is known as the *Samhita—Mantra Bhag* only. They are absolutely free from error, and the supreme and independent authority in all things. They require no other book to bear witness to their Divine origin. Even as the sun or a lamp is, by its own light, an absolute and independent manifester of its own existence—yea, it reveals the existence of things other than itself—even so are the Vedas.

"The commentaries on the four Vedas, viz., the *Brahmanas*, the six *Angas*, the six *Upangas*, the four *Up-Vedas*, and the eleven hundred and twenty-seven *Shâkhâs*, which are expositions of the Vedic texts by Brahma and other great Rishis—I look upon as works of a *dependent* character. In other words, their authority is to be followed only so far as they conform to the *teachings of the Vedas*. Whatever passages in these works are opposed to the Vedic teaching, I reject them entirely.

"3. That which inculcates justice and equity, which teaches truthfulness of thought, speech and deed—in a word, that which is in conformity with the Will of God, as embodied in the Vedas, even *that* I call Dharma. But that which is intermixed with what is partial, which sanctions injustice, which teaches untruthfulness of thought, speech or deed—in a word, that which is in antagonism to the Will of God, as embodied in the Vedas, *that* I term Adharma.

"4. The immortal, eternal Principle which is endowed with thought and judgment, with desire and hate, which is susceptible of pleasure and pain, whose capacity for knowledge is *limited*—even that is 'Soul.'

"5. God and Soul are two distinct entities. Each has certain attributes which are not and *cannot* be predicable of the other, and each performs certain functions which the other does not and *cannot* perform. They are, however, inseparable one from the other, being related to each other as the *pervader* and the *pervaded*, and have certain attributes in common. Even as a material object is, was, and shall always be, distinct from the space in which it exists and as the two cannot, were not, and shall never be, *one and the same*, even so God and the Soul are to each other. Their mutual relation is that of the *pervader* and the *pervaded*, of *father* and *son*. *This* worships and *that* is worshipped.

"6. Three things are eternal, namely *God*, *Soul*, and *Prakriti*—the material cause of the universe. These are also known as the *eternal substances*. Being eternal, their essential qualities, their functions, and their natures are eternally the same.

"7. Substances, properties, and functions, which result from combination, cease to exist on dissolution. But the power or force, by virtue of which a substance unites with another or separates from it, is eternally inherent in the substance, and this power will compel it to seek similar unions and disunions in future. The *unions* and *disunions*, as well as the *power* by virtue of which they take place, are also *eternal*, in consequence of the regularity of their succession.

"8. That which results from a combination of primary elements, compounded together consistently with a thorough and complete knowledge of the distinctive properties of every separate element and with all the perfection of design—even *that*, in all its infinite variety, is called *creation*.

" 9. The purpose of creation is the essential and natural exercise of the creative energy of the Deity. A person once asked some one: 'What is the purpose of the *eyes* ?' 'Why, *to see with*, to be sure,' was the reply. The same is the case here. God's creative energy must have play, and the Souls must reap the fruits of their *karma*.

" 10. The creation has a Creator. The existence of a design in the universe as well as the fact that dead unconscious matter is incapable of forming itself into seed or any other thing endowed with life and vitality, shows that it *must have* a Creator.

" 11. The earthly bondage of the Soul has a cause. This cause is *ignorance*, which is the source of sin as, among other things, it leads man to worship things other than the Creator and obscures his intellectual faculties, whereof pain and suffering is the result. Ignorance is termed *bondage*, as it involves the Soul in pain which everybody wants to escape but which he *must suffer* if he is ignorant.

" 12. The emancipation of the Soul from pain and suffering of every description, and a subsequent career of freedom in the all-pervading God and His immense creation, is termed *Salvation*. Salvation lasts for a period only, on the expiration of which the saved Soul again assumes a body.

" 13. The means of salvation are the worship of God or the contemplation of His nature and attributes with concentrated attention, the practice of virtue, the acquisition of true knowledge by the practice of

Brahmcharya, the company of the wise and learned, the love of true knowledge, purity of thought, active benevolence, and so on.

"14. *Artha* is wealth acquired righteously, but that which is acquired by foul means is *anartha*.

"15. Righteous enjoyment of legitimate desire is *kama*.

"16. The 'caste' of an individual is determined by merit and sterling worth only. . . .

"19. He who always thinks and judges for himself, who is ever ready to accept truth and reject falsehood, who puts down the unjust but helps the just, who has as much regard for the happiness of others as for his own—even *him* I call *just*.

"20. *Devas* (gods) are those who are wise and learned ; *asuras*, those who are foolish and ignorant ; *rakshas*, those who are wicked and sin-loving ; and *pishachas*, those whose mode of life is filthy and debasing.

"21. *Devapûja* (or the worship of the gods) consists in showing honour and respect to the wise and learned, to one's father, mother and preceptor, to the preachers of the true doctrine, to a just and impartial sovereign, to lovers of righteousness, to chaste men and women. The opposite of this is called *adevapûja*, or the worship of demons. To respect and serve the good (as explained and detailed in this paragraph) is real worship, but the worship of the dead (in the belief that it benefits them) I hold to be wrong.

"22. That, of which the fruit is the acquisition of knowledge, courteousness and good behaviour, uprightness of principle, and purity of thought, which conduces to self-control and other similar virtues, which dispels ignorance—even that is *education.*

" 23. The *Puranas* (ancient commentaries on the Vedas and other works on theology) are the *Aitreya Brahmanas* and similar compositions by the great Rishis like *Brahma* and others. In *Itihas* or history I include *Kalpa, Gâthâ,* and *Nârâshansi.* The *Bhâgwat* and other books of that sort are *not* the *Puranas.*

" 24. *Tirtha* is that by means of which the ' sea of pain ' is crossed. It consists in truthfulness of speech, in the acquisition of true knowledge, in cultivating the society of the wise and good, in the practice of morality, in contemplating the nature and attributes of the Deity with concentrated attention, in active benevolence, in the diffusion of education, and so on. Rivers and other so-called holy places are not *Tirthas.*

" 25. An energetic and active life is preferable to passive acquiescence in the decrees of fate, inasmuch as *destiny* is the consequence of *acts.* A life of virtuous activity will secure the Soul a good *destiny,* as a life of wickedness will produce the opposite result. Hence *acts,* being the *makers* of destiny, virtuous activity is superior to passive resignation.

" 26. The most approved behaviour of one man towards his fellow-creatures lies in his treating everyone according to his worth, in his treating him as he would wish himself to be treated by others, in sympathizing with him, from the core of his heart, in his joys and sorrows, in his losses and gains. The contrary conduct is reprehensible.

"27. *Sanskar*, or sacrament, is that which contributes to man's physical, mental, and spiritual improvement. The *sanskars* are sixteen in number. Their due and proper observance is obligatory on all. Nothing should be done for the departed after the remains have been cremated.

"28. The performance of *yajna* is most commendable. It consists in showing honour and respect to the wise and learned, in the proper application of the principles of chemistry and other physical sciences to the affairs of life, in the dissemination of knowledge, in the performance of *Agnihotra*, which, by contributing to the purification of the air and water, and the healthy growth of vegetables, directly tends to promote the well-being of all sentient creatures.

"29. *Aryas* are men of exalted principle, and *Dasyus* those who lead a life of wickedness and sin.

"30. This country is called Aryavarta, because it has been the residence of the Aryas from the very dawn of creation. . . .

"31. He alone is an *Acharya* (or true teacher) who can teach the sciences of the Vedas and their commentaries, who inculcates, both by example and precept, the practice of virtue and the avoidance of what is impure and immoral.

"32. He alone is a *Shishya* (true pupil) who has the capacity for assimilating knowledge and grasping the truth, whose moral character is unimpeachable, who is eager to learn, and devoted to his teacher.

"33. The term *Guru* includes father, mother, and preceptor. It also applies to all those through whose instrumentality the mind is grounded in truth and weaned from falsehood. . . .

"39. All truth must satisfy *five* tests: (1) It must not militate against the nature and attributes of God; (2) it must not be opposed to the teaching of the Vedas; (3) it must stand the test of the well-known eight kinds of proofs based on natural laws; (4) it must have the sanction of '*ápt purshas*' (*i.e.*, men learned, true and holy); and lastly (5) it must be in consonance with the dictates of one's own conscience. Every doctrine must be subjected to these five tests, and accepted if it fulfils them. . . .

"41. The Soul is a free agent—at liberty to act as it pleases, but it is dependent on God's grace for the enjoyment of the fruit of its actions. God is free as well as just.

"42. *Swarga* (heaven) represents the state of happiness.

"43. *Narka* (hell) represents pain and suffering.

"44. *Janma*, or birth, is the Soul's assumption of the gross, visible body. Viewed in relation to time its existence is three-fold, *viz.*, *past*, *present*, and *future*.

"45. *Birth* means the *union* of the Soul with the body, as *death* means their *separation*.

"46. When, according to the rules prescribed by the Shastras, a person bestows, as the result of reciprocal affection, his or her hand upon one of the opposite sex and in a public manner, he or she is said to contract *marriage*.

"47. *Niyoga* is a temporary union of a person with another of the opposite sex belonging to his or her plane, for the raising of issue, when marriage has failed to fulfil its legitimate purpose. It is resorted to in *extreme* cases, either on the death of one's consort, or when protracted disease has destroyed productive energy in the husband or in the wife.

"48. *Stuti* (or praise) is the enumeration of Divine attributes and qualities, with a view to fix them in the mind and realize their meaning. Among other things it inspires us with love towards God.

"49. *Prarthana* is praying to God for the gift of knowledge and similar other blessings which result from a communion with Him. Its principal fruit is humility and serenity of mind. Prayer does not dispense with effort.

"50. *Upâsna* is conforming, as far as possible, in purity and holiness to the Divine Spirit. It is feeling the presence of the Deity in the Soul by the realization of His all-pervading nature. *Upâsna* extends the bounds of our knowledge.

"51. *Sagun Stuti* is praising God by the enumeration of the qualities and attributes which He possesses, but *Nirgun Stuti* is praising God by those qualities and attributes which are foreign to His nature.

"*Sagun Prarthana* is praying to God for virtuous qualities; but *Nirgun Prarthana* is imploring the Deity to cast out from us that which is evil.

"*Sagun upâsna* is the realization, in the Soul, of the presence of God as possessing the attributes which are inherent in Him, while *Nirgun upâsna* is the realization, in the Soul, of the presence of God as distinct from what is foreign to His nature."

We have omitted some articles as unimportant, or because they were included in others but had been treated of separately for the sake of elucidation only.

But Swami Dayananda was more than a religious propagandist. He was a social reformer also, and a true patriot. His opinions on social and political questions will come under review in succeeding chapters, when we proceed to discuss the social work of the Arya Samaj and its politics.

CHAPTER V

DAYANANDA'S TRANSLATION OF THE VEDAS

नावेदविन्मनुते तं बृहन्तम् । तै॰ ब्रा॰ ३ । १२ । ९ ॥

"He who does not know the Vedas, does not know Him who is great."

As for Dayananda's translation of the Vedas being "ingenious," it should be borne in mind that it is no easy task to understand the real sense of the Vedas, much less to interpret it. In 1869, when Professor Max Müller published the first edition of his *Vedic Hymns*, Part I, he characterized his work as one of "deciphering," and more than twenty years afterwards, when bringing out the second and revised edition of the same work, he again said: "I hold that they (*i.e.*, the first translators) ought to be decipherers."[1] Referring to his adversaries in the task of translating the Vedas (a whole host of German professors), he says: "There is another point also on which I am quite willing to admit that my adversaries are right. 'No one who knows anything about the *Veda*,' they say, 'would think of attempting a translation of it at present. A translation of the

[1] *Sacred Books of the East*, Vol. XXXII., Vedic Hymns, Part I., Introduction, p. ix.

Rig-Veda is a task for the next century.' "[1] In another place he says[2]: "If by translation we mean a complete, satisfactory and final translation of the whole of *Rig-Veda*, I should feel inclined to go even further than Professor von Roth. Not only shall we have to wait till the next century for such a work, but I doubt whether we shall ever obtain it."[3] Then he compares his own translation of the 165th Hymn of the first Mandala of the *Rig-Veda* with that of Professor von Roth, and concludes that a comparison like this "will disclose the unsettled state of Vedic scholarship, but the more fully this fact is acknowledged the better, I believe, it will be for the progress of our studies. They (*i.e.*, the translations of the *Vedas* by European scholars) have suffered more than anything else from the baneful positivism which has done so much harm in hieroglyphic and cuneiform researches. That the same words and names should be interpreted differently from year to year is perfectly intelligible to everyone who is familiar with the nature of the decipherments. What has seriously injured the credit of the studies is that the latest decipherments have always been represented as final and unchangeable. . . . When we come to really difficult passages, the Vedic hymns often require a far greater effort of divination than the hymns addressed to Egyptian or Babylonian deities."

[1] *Ibid.*, p. xi.

[2] *Ibid.*, p. xxi.

[3] "The *Veda*, I feel convinced, will occupy scholars for centuries to come, and maintain its position as the most ancient of books in the library of mankind."—Max Müller, in *The Sacred Books of the East*, Vol. XXXII., Vedic Hymns, p. xxxi.

Max Müller certainly voices a crying grievance when he complains of the "baneful positivism" of European scholars as to interpretations which are little better than guess-work; yet his own conclusions on the Vedas and other Sanskrit writings, and on the religion of which they are the vehicle, are open to similar criticism. The conclusions of European scholars on ancient civilizations are vitiated also, in many cases, by their judging these older civilizations by Christian or other modern standards, which they assume to be true and permanent. They forget that all standards are mutable—that the one whose permanence they tacitly assume is dissolving here and reforming there before their very eyes. While we are deeply grateful to the Western scholars for the time and labour they have bestowed on Vedic research, which is likely to be of the greatest possible value to the rising generation of Indians who are devoting themselves to the study and interpretation of the Vedas, we cannot help remarking that their hasty conclusions as to the religion of the Vedas did great and unnecessary harm by creating a mass of prejudice against Vedic religion on the part of the earlier generations of educated Hindus. The Missionary propagandists in their zeal for conversion, in their anxiety to show the superiority of the Christian Bible, condemned the Vedas in the most positive language at their command. For this purpose they even transgressed the rules of fair and honest controversy by quoting the conclusions of European scholars on Vedic religion and Vedic culture without giving the accompanying qualifications, and without giving the reader any idea of

PANDIT GURUDATTA VIDYARTHI, M.A.
Who died at the age of 25.

the unsatisfactory character of the translations on which those conclusions were based, though well known to and acknowledged by themselves. It is not wonderful, therefore, that, misled by these garbled quotations, many an educated Indian rejected the Vedas, and accepted Christian thought, though not Christian religion, especially in Bengal and Bombay.

Swami Dayananda made it his mission to stem the flow of this anti-Vedic and anti-Hindu current by showing that the conclusions of European scholars were faulty, and often affected by their conscious or unconscious Christian bias. In any case, in the language of the European scholars themselves, their translations are only provisional. Swami Dayananda did not know any of the European languages, not even English. His criticism of Max Müller, etc., in his commentaries on the *Rig-Veda*, is therefore based on information supplied to him by friends who were acquainted with English.

After him, Pandit Gurudatta Vidyarthi, an erudite scholar of modern science and modern thought, as well as of Sanskrit, examined some of the conclusions of the European translators in the light of Sanskrit grammar and philosophy and literature, and showed how misleading and erroneous they were.[1]

Those who may be disposed to sit in judgment on Swami Dayananda and to pronounce on the merits of his translation of or Commentaries on the Vedas would do well to bear in mind :

(*a*) That this was his first attempt.

[1] See his lectures on Prof. Sir Monier Williams's *Indian Wisdom*, and his articles on *European Scholars and the Vedas.*

(*b*) That all this great work was accomplished within a short period of less than seven years. The first instalment, or the first part of his Commentaries, containing an exposition of a few *Mantras* only, came out at the end of 1876, and he died on October 30th, 1883.

(*c*) That this period was the busiest of his life, when most of his time was taken up by propaganda work. It was during this period that he established the Arya Samajes, conducted public and private discussions, replied to criticism of his views and writings, and, besides the Commentaries on the Vedas, wrote and published a number of other books in Sanskrit and vernacular, which so far have been the chief support of the Arya Samaj. Moreover, he gave a part of his time to teaching. We have already stated that several princes studied with him, but among his pupils were also priests, *Sadhus* and laymen.

(*d*) That he had to do most of his work single-handed. He employed Pandits to write from his dictation (*i.e.*, as amanuenses), to translate his Sanskrit into vernacular and then to make fair copies for the Press. But beyond that he had no help from anyone in his translation of the Vedas, for the simple reason that no one knew the Vedas so well as to be of any help. Those who knew a little considered it to be sacrilegious to attempt to translate them.

(*e*) That he had no time to revise and to reconsider.

Under the circumstances, what he did was more than creditable, and deserves indeed our unstinted admiration. The Arya Samaj does not claim infallibility for his translation, nor did he. But his honesty of purpose is clearly written on every page of his work, in that, unlike most of the European translators of the Vedas (Max Müller excepted), he has not contented himself with giving his own empirical view of the text, but in almost every case has supported it with reasons and explanations and often by quotations from ancient authors credited with a better and deeper knowledge of the Vedas on account of the nearness of their time to the Vedic period of Indian civilization.

His translation of the text is always preceded by a full analysis of the grammatical and etymological construction of the words composing a *Mantra* (verse). Then follows the meaning of every word; then the translation of the whole, and finally the commentary and its general sense as he understood it.

All this appears in his own language in Sanskrit, which has been translated into vernacular in full for him by the Pandits whom he employed for that purpose. It was the boldest act of his life to have issued a translation of the Vedas in Hindi, the vernacular of North India, since this translation had never even been attempted before. This fact should be the best proof of the transparency and the honesty of his motives.

Speaking of his own efforts to understand and then translate the Vedas for the public, Prof. Max Müller says that it is a mere beginning, "a mere contribution towards the better understanding of the Vedic hymns," and he felt convinced that on many points his translation was liable to correction and to be replaced sooner or later by a more satisfactory one. "There are," continues he, "as all Vedic scholars know, whole verses which as yet yield no sense whatever. There are words the meaning of which we can but guess."[1]

All that we claim for Dayananda's translation of the Vedas is that, from the Hindu point of view, it is the best and the most scholarly translation of that ancient book so far given to the public; yet, that Dayananda has only shown the way to the coming generation how to approach the Vedas—how to interpret them. It would take centuries of hard labour and incessant care before anything like a complete and thoroughly intelligent translation of the Vedas could be made. Generations of learned Hindus will have to devote their lives to the study of the Vedas in a spirit of reverent humility and with a determination to master all their difficulties, before these ancient scriptures yield up even a fraction of their treasures of beauty and of truth.

[1] *Sacred Books of the East*, Vol. XXXII., Vedic Hymns, Part I., p. xxxii.

PART II

THE ARYA SAMAJ

CHAPTER I

RELIGIOUS TEACHINGS

वेदाहमेतं पुरुषं महान्तमादित्यवर्णं तमसःपरस्तात् ।
तमेव विदित्वाति मृत्युमेति नान्यः पन्था विद्यतेऽयनाय ॥
य० । अ० ३१ । मं० १८ ॥

"I know the all-pervading Supreme Being who is exalted above all, glorious like unto the suns and aloof from darkness. By knowing Him alone is death conquered. Except this, there is no other road leading to Salvation."

1. *The Ten Principles*

In previous chapters we have described the genesis of the Arya Samaj. It was originally founded at Bombay in 1875, but was revised at Lahore in 1877, when its principles received their final shape and its constitution was finally settled. The Ten Principles to which every Arya is required to subscribe when he applies for membership constitute the only authoritative exposition of its beliefs and its doctrines :

1. God is the primary cause of all true knowledge and of everything known by its means.

2. God is All-truth, All-knowledge, All-beatitude,

Incorporeal, Almighty, Just, Merciful, Unbegotten, Infinite, Unchangeable, Without a beginning, Incomparable, the Support and the Lord of All, All-pervading, Omniscient, Imperishable, Immortal, Exempt from fear, Eternal, Holy and the Cause of the Universe. *To Him alone* worship is due.

3. The Vedas are the Books of true knowledge, and it is the paramount duty of every Arya to read or hear them read, to teach and read them to others.

4. An Arya should always be ready to accept truth and to renounce untruth.

5. All actions must conform to virtue, *i.e.*, should be performed after a thorough consideration of right and wrong.

6. The primary object of the Samaj is to benefit the whole world, viz., by improving the physical, spiritual, and social condition of mankind.

7. All ought to be treated with love, justice and with due regard to their merits.

8. Ignorance must be dispelled and knowledge diffused.

9. No one should be contented with his own good alone, but every one should regard his or her prosperity as included in that of others.

10. In matters which affect the general social well-being of our race, no one should allow his or her individuality to interfere with the general good, but in strictly personal affairs everyone may act with freedom.[1]

[1] The translation of these Principles must be regarded as approximate only. Some of the original words, such as *Dharma* and *Adharma*, have no exact equivalents in English. The tenth Principle is intended to make personal freedom subordinate to the general welfare.

Nothing beyond these Ten Principles has any binding force. The only doctrinal teaching included therein is what is contained in the first three Principles, which sum up the belief of the Arya Samaj in God, its conception of the Godhead, and its teaching about the Vedas. This, surely, is the simplest of creeds, to which no Hindu, at any rate, should have any difficulty in subscribing. A comparison of these Principles with those laid down originally at Bombay, in 1875, lends weight to the suggestion that their revision was intended to keep all dogma in the background and to free the Principles from all controversial matter. It is said, in fact, that the object was to make the Arya Samaj as Catholic as it possibly could be without sacrificing its Hindu character.

We have already stated that on the occasion of the Swami's visit to Calcutta in 1869 the leaders of the Brahmo Samaj conferred with him with a view to win him over to their society and secure his powerful support for their propaganda. It took but little time, however, to make it clear that such an agreement was well-nigh impossible. The Brahmo Samaj would not accept the infallibility of the Vedas or the doctrine of the transmigration of souls: it was pledged to the negation of both. Swami Dayananda, on the other hand, could not be a party to any propaganda which would militate against or ignore either. In the words of Max Müller, "he considered the Vedas not only as divinely inspired, but as prehistoric or prehuman." To him everything contained in the Vedas was perfect truth. In this he was in full agreement with the ancient theologians of India, who all, without any exception, looked upon the

Vedas as divine, or superhuman. To him a Church that ignored that basic principle of faith was unthinkable—much more a Church that should be Aryan or Hindu in its origin and conception. His object was to revive the Vedic faith and the Vedic worship, not to destroy them. He took his stand on the Vedas. These holy writings were his great weapon against the stronghold of latter-day and corrupt Hinduism. Whatever was found in them was to him beyond the reach of controversy, and in this position he had the unanimous support of all that was sacred to the Hindu. Every branch of the sacred literature of the Hindus, from the very earliest times, down to the most modern compositions of the different forms of Hindu faith, was agreed on that point, and unhesitatingly accepted the authority of the Vedas as final and conclusive. From the Upanishads, to which Schopenhauer has paid the highest compliment possible for any human composition,[1] downward to the latest manual of Puranic Hinduism, all branches of Hindu literature are agreed on that point. Even the philosophers and freethinkers would not reject the Vedas: the great founders of the six schools of Hindu philosophy, each in his own way, accept the authority of the Vedas as conclusive. So does *Shankaracharya*; and so do the great law-givers, viz., *Manu*, *Yajnyavalka*, *Parasara*, *Apasthamba*, and others. Even the *Tantrikas* profess to base their

[1] "Oh! how thoroughly is the mind here washed clean of all early engrafted Jewish superstition and of all philosophy that cringes before that superstition! In the whole world there is no study except that of the originals so elevating as that of the Upanishads. It has been the solace of my life, and it shall be the solace of my death."

propaganda on their reading of the Vedas. The Puranas, of course, with one voice, accept them as divine and infallible. In fact, in the whole range of Indian thought and Indian culture, the only dissentient voices on the point are those of the *Buddhists*, the *Jains*, and the *Charvakas* (atheists), who were originally considered to be outside the pale of Hinduism. Even the Brahmo Samaj[1] had begun with faith in the revealed character and divine origin of the Vedas. The Vedas were the sheet-anchor of Dayananda's propaganda and his scheme of reform. In the words of Max Müller, the idea had taken " such complete possession of his mind that no argument could ever touch it." It was impossible to shake him from that position, and this the leaders of the Brahmo Samaj soon found out. So the attempt to win him over to the Brahmo Samaj had failed so early as 1869.

In 1877 again, when most of India's great men were gathered at Delhi on the occasion of the great Durbar which Lord Lytton, the Viceroy and Governor General of India, had convened to announce the assumption of the title of " Empress of India " by Her Majesty Queen Victoria, an attempt was made to formulate doctrines which should be acceptable to all Indians—Hindus, Musulmans, Christians, and Parsis—alike. Dayananda, Syed Ahmad,

[1] Max Müller, in his *Biographical Essays,* says : " Ram Mohan Roy also and his followers held for a time to the revealed character of the Vedas, and in all their early controversies with Christian missionaries they maintained that there was no argument in favour of the divine inspiration of the Bible which did not apply with the same or even greater force to the Vedas." (Page 168.) Speaking of Ram Mohan Roy, Prof. Max Müller says : " He never became a Mahomedan, he never became a Christian, but he remained to the end a Brahman, a believer in the Veda and in the one God, Who, as he maintained, had been revealed in the Veda." (Page 33.)

and Keshub Chunder Sen were among those who took part in this conference, but they soon found out that the attempted reconciliation was impossible. In our opinion it was even preposterous, however patriotic the attempt might have been from a social and political point of view. Even on that occasion, Swami Dayananda would not consider any religion that ignored the Vedas.

We have reason to think that soon afterwards, when he visited Lahore, some persons tried to induce him to omit from the Principles of the Arya Samaj the article relating to the Vedas; but this was a proposition to which he would not listen, and with good reason. His aim was the revival of the Vedic religion and the reform of the abuses that had crept into Hindu society, not the establishment of a new creed which would mean the uprooting of the venerable faith that had grown with the growth of the Hindu nation. All that he would assent to, was a change in the wording of the Principle in question so as to make it include all the different opinions expressed about the Vedas by the eminent thinkers and writers of the various schools of Hindu thought prior to the birth of the Buddha.[1] It was not his desire to impose his own faith on all who would join

[1] "One more common element presupposed by Indian philosophy might be pointed out in the recognition of the supreme authority and the revealed character ascribed to the Veda. . . . The Sankhya philosophy (Agnostic school) is supposed to have been originally without a belief in the revealed character of the Vedas, but it certainly speaks of Sruti (Sutras, I. 5). As long as we know the *Sankhya,* it recognizes the authority of the Veda, calling it *Sabd* (Word), and appeals to it even in matters of minor importance." —*The Six Systems of Indian Philosophy,* Max Müller, 1903, p. 111. For a fuller discussion of the subject see page 206 of the same work.

the Arya Samaj. He wanted them to follow the unanimous opinion of the great Arya sages, divines and scholars who had made all that was glorious and sublime in Hindu thought and Hindu culture, since he himself was no more than an humble follower of his illustrious predecessors. When, therefore, it was suggested to him that in wording the Principles of the Arya Samaj he should adopt the language of the *Rishis*, he received the suggestion gladly and put it into effect.

Thus is explained the obvious difference between the language of the Principles as enunciated at Bombay in 1875, and as finally settled at Lahore in 1877.

2. *The Split in the Arya Samaj*

A great controversy has raged in the Arya Samaj for the last twenty-five years as to how far the opinions expressed by Swami Dayananda are binding on the Arya Samaj as a body. In 1892 the Arya Samaj split into two sections, ostensibly on a difference of opinion (1) as to the righteousness of meat diet, and (2) as to the lines on which the Dayananda Anglo-Vedic College, founded in memory of Swami Dayananda in 1886, was to be conducted. The principle that underlay this difference concerned the authority of Dayananda. The party that was opposed to a meat diet and considered it unrighteous maintained that, Swami Dayananda having expressed that opinion, it was binding on the Arya Samaj, and no one who held a different opinion could be or remain a member of that body. Some members of this party—and their number was not inconsiderable then—went to the length of maintaining that the Swami was infallible; others held that, so long as a greater authority on the Vedas was not born, the Arya Samaj was bound by the teachings of Dayananda and by his interpretation of the Vedas. The opposite party would not accept that position. They maintained that the teachings of Swami Dayananda were not binding on the Arya Samaj, and that a member need believe in the Ten Principles only, and in nothing further; that, although it was true that Swami Dayananda had expressed an opinion unfavourable to meat diet and the Samaj had tacitly accepted that position, yet the Samaj had no right to question the individual's right of private judgment in matters not covered strictly by the Principles. They conceded the right of the majority to determine what should be preached from the pulpit of the Samaj, but they would not agree to the majority sitting in judgment on individuals and dictating what they must believe, beyond what was contained in the Principles of the Samaj.

When the split actually took place, it presented the strange spectacle of a large number of vegetarians, who were so both by conviction and by caste rules, joining the ranks of those who stood for liberty of thought and conscience for the individual, and of some who actually indulged in meat diet remaining with the other party. The position of the former party may be summed up in the language of one of its best exponents (namely, Mulraj, M.A., the first President of the Arya Samaj when it was established at Lahore in 1877) in the following extracts from a lecture delivered at Lahore in 1892:

"It is known to all that he founded the Arya Samaj on the Ten *Niyams* (Principles, or Articles of Faith). He required that to become a member of the Arya Samaj one should believe in the Ten *Niyams*. If a man believed in the Ten *Niyams*, the Swami thought that he could become a member of the Arya Samaj whatever his opinion on other subjects might be. He did not make it an essential condition for membership of the Samaj that a man should believe his translation of the Vedas to be correct, or the opinions expressed by him in his works to be sound. . . . He was not questioned as to his belief or disbelief in the many excellent theories and philosophical opinions with which the works of Swami Dayananda abound. He was never asked what he thought of the works of Swami Dayananda and of the translation he was making of the Vedas. He was never required to believe Swami Dayananda's translation of the Vedas to be infallible, or to state that he regarded the works of Swami Dayananda to be free from mistakes. He was never required to sacrifice his freedom of thought and speech."

Again:

"I believe the religion which the Arya Samaj preaches is the only religion which can become the common or national religion of the Hindus. It suits the masses and also the *advanced* section of the people. It can satisfy the orthodox Hindus as well as those who have received an English education. It can be accepted by people who are in different stages of intellectual development. It is simple and so can extend over a large tract, if it cannot become universal. It requires belief in one true God and in the Vedas only. There are no theoretical questions or doctrines included in the Principles of the Arya Samaj. If Swami Dayananda had made it an essential condition for entering the Arya Samaj that a man should believe in particular doctrines, I do not think he could have succeeded so well in the achievement of his great object—the revival of the study of Vedas and the worship of one true God. Belief in particular doctrines presupposes a certain amount and line of education and a particular bent of mind. Only those who have a certain kind of education and the required mood of mind and training can accept a particular doctrine or philosophical theory. Those whose minds are not prepared for the understanding or reception of a theory can neither understand it nor believe it to be correct. The greater the number of the theories which a religion requires its followers to believe in, the smaller will be the number of men who can embrace that religion. If, then, Swami Dayananda had introduced philosophical questions, doctrines and theories into the Articles of Faith of the Arya Samaj, he would have limited the number of men who could have entered it. He would have thus curtailed the usefulness of the Arya Samaj by limiting the sphere of its action, and defeated his own object. For, the greater the number of men who can join together to revive the study of the Vedas and the worship of the unincarnate God, the greater will be the good they can do to themselves and to humanity. The greater the number of men who can enter the Arya Samaj, the greater will be the good they can do by spreading pure religion, truth, and godliness.

"We must be thankful that the Arya Samaj has been placed upon a very broad and catholic basis: the basis of belief in one eternal God and in the Vedas. We must be thankful that doctrines, philosophical matters and theoretical questions have not been included in the Articles of Faith of the Arya Samaj. The Hindus must be thankful that Swami Dayananda has turned their attention to one religion which is pure and grand. He has not given them any new religion. He has drawn their attention to what was old and latent in the Hindu mind. He told them that the Aryas who were the ancestors of the modern Hindus, believed in one true God and in the Vedas, and he asked them to believe in the Vedas and to worship the Almighty God sung in them. The religion which the Arya Samaj preaches can be truly called a national religion. On the broad and common platform of this religion, which is simple and free from philosophical theories, men whose minds are in different stages of development and who have different modes of thinking can come together to revive the study of the Vedas and to worship and glorify the Omnipresent Being Who was adored by our ancestors.

"I cannot help admiring the greatness and moderation of Swami Dayananda Saraswati. He was a great Sanskrit scholar. . . . He placed before the public his translation of the Vedas and the views he had on philosophical questions, and left the public to believe what was good in his interpretation and exposition. . . . He admitted that the *Rishis* who had gone before him, the *Rishis* who had composed the *Brahmanas*, the *Sutras*, the *Angas*, *Upangas*, and the *Upvedas* were greater men than himself, and much better and abler scholars, and that his translations and expositions must be read with the light of the old commentators. He did not claim to be infallible. . . .

"Swami Dayananda purposely abstained from entering in the *Niyams* any doctrinal points and philosophical questions. He believed in all he wrote, but he had toleration for the views of others. He knew that it is almost impossible to make all men have the same and identical views on doctrinal points and philosophical questions. He therefore wisely excluded from the *Niyams* all doctrinal points and philosophical questions, though he was not afraid of expressing his opinions on those matters frankly and boldly in his works. It would be indeed absurd to make a belief one way or the other in philosophical questions to be an essential condition for entering a religious society. . . . Is it not absurd that a man should be told that he cannot become a member of the Arya Samaj unless he believes in the doctrine of *Niyog* or the theory that vegetables have souls? Swami Dayananda was a wise man and saw this, and so purposely excluded doctrinal points and philosophical matters from the Principles of the Arya Samaj."

We have given this quotation from the lecture of Mulraj, M.A., because the lecturer had a certain right to say what were the intentions of those who co-operated with Swami Dayananda in reforming the Samaj in 1877, and in giving final shape to its Principles. He was the first President of the reconstituted Samaj, and was in the confidence of the founder up to the latter's death, as evidenced by the fact that in 1882, when he executed his will, he assigned Mulraj a high position (that of Vice-President) in the body which he nominated therein to act as his executors, with the Maharana Sajjan Singh, the ruling chief of Udaipur, as its President. It is clear from this quotation that the founder and those associated with him in reorganizing the Samaj in 1877 had no intention of imposing a creed on the members thereof beyond what was contained in the first three Principles, but it was soon manifest that it was impossible to carry on propaganda on those lines. The beliefs of Swami Dayananda were tacitly accepted as the doctrines of the Arya Samaj and formed its propaganda. No one raised any question for fully fifteen years, when the question of meat diet was unfortunately pushed to the front on grounds more or less personal in their origin. Those who stood by this practice argued that the Samaj had by its conduct given it the character of an unwritten law, and that without a definite creed it was impossible to carry on any religious propaganda. They saw the dangers of eclecticism, which had retarded the progress of the Brahmo Samaj, and did not wish the same fate to overtake the Arya Samaj. The chief weakness of Hinduism lay in it being a vast sea of contradictory doctrines and beliefs, which made it an impossible religion for active propaganda work and which laid it open to the attacks of those who aimed in India to convert Hindus to alien faiths. The vagueness and the vastness of Hinduism were its most vulnerable points.

In discussing the position of Christianity in "its

relation to Hinduism," Mr. Blunt, I.C.S., makes the following observations in his *Census Report* for 1911:[1]

"The position of Christianity in India is very similar to the position it occupied in the early centuries of its era, in a Pagan Europe. . . . It is that of a definite, clear-cut religion in opposition to an enormous and unwieldy congeries of divergent beliefs, both high and low. Its strength lies in its definiteness; the weakness of its opponent in its lack of cohesion." The "Christian always possesses the same creed, whilst a Hindu possesses no creed." Whilst we question the correctness of the view that the Christian "always possesses the same creed," we accept the general accuracy of the statement about Hinduism. The founder of the Arya Samaj saw through the difficulty and aimed at defining Hinduism. His definition has the merit of comprehensiveness and was made as little credal as was possible under the circumstances; but its vagueness and indefiniteness exposed it to the same danger from which it aimed to extricate Hinduism. The early leaders of the Arya Samaj, quite unconsciously, felt this indefiniteness, and, without devoting any further thought to the matter, made good what was lacking by adopting the beliefs of Swami Dayananda as the creed of the Arya Samaj, and on the strength of that creed gave battle to all who opposed them. When, therefore, in the early nineties, the question was raised by the so-called "meat-eaters" how far the Arya Samaj was bound by the doctrines of Dayananda, some of the vegetarians began to say that Dayananda was infallible, but the bulk of them wished to

[1] Page 144.

keep the authority of Dayananda unimpaired on the grounds stated above. They thought that there could be no propaganda without a definite creed; that the Arya Samaj had virtually and unambiguously accepted the creed of Dayananda; and that this creed was binding upon them unless the majority ruled otherwise. The "meat-eaters" acquiesced in that position so far as propaganda was concerned, but they would not interfere with the liberty of the individual in the matter of beliefs outside the Principles.

There are difficulties in either view, and both parties recognize them. They are prepared to give a certain latitude to individual opinions in matters religious, but they are not prepared to go without a creed. They feel that the moment they decided to do so, they would lose what so far has proved to be an invaluable element of force and weight in the general progress of their movement, and in this view they are supported by the opinions of competent observers of other nationalities and creeds, as well as by the experience of the Brahmo Samaj.

In his *Expansion of England*, Sir John Seeley passes a rather adverse judgment on the "facile comprehensiveness of Hinduism," which, in his opinion, "has enfeebled it as a uniting principle and rendered it incapable of generating true national feeling."

In the opinion of Sir Herbert Risley, "it may be admitted that the flame of patriotic enthusiasm will not readily arise from the cold grey ashes of philosophic compromise, and that before Hinduism can inspire an active sentiment of nationality, it will have to undergo a good deal of stiffening and consolidation.[1]

" The Arya Samaj," he adds, " seems to be striking out a path which may lead in this direction, but the tangled jungle of Hinduism bristles with obstacles and the way is long." In another place he gives the Aryas the credit of " a definite creed resting upon scriptures of great antiquity and high reputation," and characterises their teaching as " bold and masculine " and " free from the limp eclecticism which has proved fatal to the Brahmo Samaj."[2]

A similar opinion has also been expressed by Mr. Blunt, I.C.S., in his *Census Report for United Provinces*, 1911.[3] In his opinion, an element of strength in the Arya Samaj is its freedom from " the formlessness and indefiniteness of Hindu polytheism on one side and the weak eclecticism of such reformed sects as the Brahmo Samaj on the other."[4]

To sum up, we are quite safe in saying that the teachings of Dayananda, though not embodied in the Principles of the Arya Samaj, constitute its creed for all practical purposes. The teachings of Dayananda are, in their turn, the teachings of the ancient sages of India, based on the Vedas.

3. *Creed of the Arya Samaj*

A detailed statement of the teachings to which we have referred has been made in a previous chapter.

[1] *The Peoples of India*, by Sir Herbert Risley, 1904, p. 280.

[2] *Ibid.*, p. 244.

[3] Page 133.

[4] " The Arya Samaj alone has provided a manly and straightforward creed which is in all essentials thoroughly Hindu."—*Census Report for U.P. for* 1911, p. 143.

Here we propose to discuss the meaning of the most important of them as accepted by the Arya Samaj.

The first and by far the most important is the Aryan conception of the Godhead. It is contained in the second of the Ten Principles of its official creed. In brief, the Arya Samaj believes in God and enjoins that He alone is worthy of our adoration. There is no longer any doubt in the minds of all competent and impartial students of Hindu scriptures and Hindu literature that the monotheism of Hinduism is of the highest, most exclusive and most exalted kind.[1] In support of this we give some citations from the Vedas with their translation in English :

[1] Schlegel says : "It cannot be denied that the early Indians possessed a knowledge of the true God. All their writings are replete with sentiments and expressions, noble, clear, lovely, grand, as deeply conceived as in any human language in which men have spoken of their God."

The Rev. J. Bryce admits that "there is every reason to believe that there existed a period in the Hindu history when the Brahma was the sole object of religious adoration."

The Rev. Mr. Ward says : "It is true, indeed, that the Hindus believe in the Unity of God. 'One Brahma without a Second' is a phrase very commonly used by them when conversing on subjects which relate to the nature of God. They believe also that God is Almighty, All-wise, Omnipotent, Omniscient."

Mr. Charles Coleman says : "The Almighty, Infinite, Eternal, Incomprehensible, Self-existent Being, He who sees everything though never seen, He who is not to be compassed by description and who is beyond the limits of human conception, is Brahma, the one unknown true Being, the Creator, the Preserver and Destroyer of the Universe. Under such and innumerable other definitions is the Deity acknowledged in the Vedas or the sacred writings of the Hindus."

Colonel Kennedy says : "Every Hindu who is in the least acquainted with the principles of his religion must in reality acknowledge and worship God in Unity."

Count Björnstjerna, after giving a quotation from the Vedas, says : "These truly sublime ideas cannot fail to convince us that the Vedas recognize only one God, who is Almighty, Infinite, Eternal, Self-existent, the Light and the Lord of the Universe."

Maurice is assured "that the Brahman is seeking after one

From the "Rig-Veda"

इन्द्रं मित्रं वरुणमग्निमाहुरथो दिव्यः स सुपर्णो गरुत्मान् ।
एकं सद्विप्रा बहुधा वदन्त्यग्निं यमं मातरिश्वानमाहुः ॥ १ ॥
ऋ० १ । १६४ । ४६ ।

1. They call Him Indra, Mitra, Varuna, Agni, and he is heavenly nobly-winged Garutman.[1] *He is one, sages call Him by many names*, viz., Agni, Yama, Matarisvan.

—R. I., 164, 46.

अग्ने भूरीणि तव जातवेदो देव स्वधावोऽमृतस्य नाम ।
याश्च माया मायिनां विश्वमिन्व त्वे पूर्वीः सन्दधुः
पृष्टबन्धो ॥ २ ॥ ऋ० ३ । २० । ३ ।

2. Many are Thy names, O Agni, Immortal, God, Divine, Jatavedas, and many Charms of Charmers,[2] All-inspirer! have they laid in Thee,[3] Lord of true attendants!

—R. III., 20, 3.

Divine Unseen Object, nay, that his aim in his whole life and discipline is to purify himself from outward, sensible things, that he may approach nearer to this one Source of Illumination."

Mr. Colebrook says: "The ancient Hindu religion, as founded on the Hindu scriptures, recognized but one God."

[1] *Garutman*—Sun.

[2] *Charms of Charmers*—attractive features and winning virtues.

[3] *They have laid in Thee*—the wise and pious sages have seen in Thee and realized them.

त्वामग्ने पितरमिष्टिभिर्नरस्त्वां भ्रात्राय शम्या तनूरुचम् ।
त्वं पुत्रो भवसि यस्तेऽविधत्त्वं सखा सुशेवः पास्याधृषः ॥ ९ ॥

ऋ० २ । १ । ९ ।

3. Agni! men seek Thee as a Father with their prayers. They win Thee, O source of light, to brotherhood by holy actions. Thou art a son to him who duly worships Thee. Thou guardest him from injury as a trusty Friend.

—R. II., I, 9.

यः प्राणतो निमिषतो महित्वैक इद्राजा जगतो बभूव ।
य ईशे अस्य द्विपदश्चतुष्पदः कस्मै देवाय हविषा विधेम
ऋ० १० । १२१ । ३ ॥

4. What God shall we adore with our oblation? The great One who is the Sole Ruler of all the moving world that breathes and slumbers, and is the Lord of bipeds and quadrupeds.

—R. X., 121, 3.

त्वद्विश्वा सुभग सौभगान्यग्ने वि यन्ति वनिनो न वयाः ।
श्रुष्टी रयिर्वाजो वृत्रतूर्ये दिवो वृष्टिरीड्यो रीतिरपाम् ॥ १ ॥

ऋ० ६ । १३ । १ ।

5. From Thee as branches from a tree, O Agni, from Thee, Auspicious God! spring all our blessings. Wealth (bestowed by Thee) swiftly, strength in battle with our foemen, the rain besought of heaven, the flow of waters.

—R. VI., 31, 1

इन्द्रो मह्ना रोदसी पप्रथच्छव इन्द्रः सूर्यमरोचयत ।
इन्द्रे ह विश्वा भुवनानि येमिर इन्द्रे सुवानास इन्दवः

॥ १४ ॥ ऋ० ८ । ३ । ६ ।

6. With might hath Indra spread out heaven and earth. By His power hath the sun been lighted up. In Him are contained all the creatures and in Him the purified Somas.

—R. VIII., 3, 6.

पुरुष एवेदं सर्वं यद्भूतं यच्च भव्यम् ।
उतामृतत्वस्येशानो यदन्नेनातिरोहति ॥ २१ ॥

ऋ० १० । ९० । २ ।

7. This Purusha (Being) is (in) all that hath been and all that is to be; the Lord of immortality, transcending all that grows by food.

—R. X., 90 2.

ईशे ह्यग्निरमृतस्य भूरेरीशे रायः सुवीर्यस्य दातोः ।
मा त्वा वयं सहसावन्नवीरा मा प्सवः परि षदाम मा दुवः ॥
ऋ० ७ । ४ । ६ ।

8. Agni is Lord of Amrita in abundance, Lord of the gift of wealth and heroic valour. O victorious God, let us not sit about Thee like men devoid of strength, beauty and worship.

—R. VII., 4. 6.

यस्येमे हिमवन्तो महित्वा यस्य समुद्रं रसया सहाहुः ।
यस्येमाः प्रदिशो यस्य बाहू कस्मै देवाय हविषा विधेम
॥ ३२ ॥ ४ ॥

9. What God shall we adore with our oblation? The great One whose are these snow-clad mountains as well as the terrestrial and celestial seas, and whose arms are these heavenly regions.

—R. X., 121, 4.

From the "Yajur Veda"

न तस्य प्रतिमा अस्ति यस्य नाम महद्यशः ।
हिरण्यगर्भ इत्येष मा मा हिंꣳसीदित्येषा यस्मान्न जात
इत्येषः ॥ ८७ ॥ यजु० ३२ । ३ ।

1. There is no measure of Him whose glory, verily, is great, etc., etc.

—Y. XXXII., 3.

अग्ने त्वन्नोअन्तमउत त्राता शिवो भवा वरूथ्यः ।
वसुरग्निर्वसुश्रवाअच्छा नक्षि द्युमत्तमꣳ रयिन्दाः ॥१.३॥
यजु० ३ । २५ ।

2. O Agni, be our nearest Friend: be Thou a kind Deliverer and gracious Friend. Excellent Agni, come Thou nigh to us and give us wealth most splendidly renowned.

—Y. III., 25.

देवकृतस्यैनसोऽवयजनमसि मनुष्यकृतस्यैनसोऽवय-
जनमसि पितृकृतस्यैनसो ऽवयजनमस्यात्मकृतस्यै-
नसोऽवयजनमस्येनस एनसोऽवयजनमसि। यच्चाहमेनो
विद्वाँश्चकार यच्चाविद्वाँस्तस्य सर्वस्यैनसोऽवयजन-
मसि ॥ ३ ॥ यजु० ८ । १३

3. Of sin against the gods Thou art atonement. Of sin against mankind Thou art atonement. For sin against the fathers Thou atonest. Of sin against oneself Thou art atonement. Of every sort of sin Thou art atonement. The sin that I have committed unconsciously, of all that wickedness Thou art atonement.

—Y. VIII., 13.

तमीशानं जगतस्तस्थुषस्पतिं धियंजिन्वमवसे हूमहे वयम्।
पूषा नो यथा वेदसामसद्वृधे रक्षिता पायुरदब्धः स्वस्तये
॥ १२ ॥ यजु० २५ । १८ ।

4. Him we invoke for aid who reigns supreme, the Lord of all that stands or moves, Inspirer of the Soul, that He may promote the increase of our wealth. He, our infallible Keeper and Guard and Well-wisher.

—Y. XXV., 18.

एषो ह देवः प्रदिशोऽनु सर्वाः पूर्वो ह जातः स उ गर्भे
अन्तः। स एव जातः स जनिष्यमाणः प्रत्यङ् जनास्तिष्ठति
सर्वतोमुखः ॥ ५ ॥ यजु० ३२ । ४ ।

5. This very God pervadeth all the regions. Yea, existent from the beginning, He abides in the centre of all. He has been and ever will be. Facing all directions He stands before you, O men.

—Y. XXXII., 4.

त्रातारमिन्द्रमवितारमिन्द्रꣳ हवे हवे सुहवꣳ शूरमिन्द्रम् ।
ह्वयामि शक्रं पुरुहूतमिन्द्रꣳस्वस्ति नो मघवा धात्विन्द्रः॥१०
य० २० । ५० ।

6. Indra the Rescuer, Indra the Helper, Hero who listens at each invocation. I call upon the mighty Indra invoked of many. May Indra, Bounteous Lord, prosper and bless us.

—Y. XX., 50.

तदेवाग्निस्तदादित्यस्तद्वायुस्तदु चन्द्रमाः ।
तदेव शुक्रं तद्ब्रह्म ता आपः स प्रजापतिः ॥ ७ ॥
यजु० ३२ । १ ।

7. Even He is Agni, He is Aditya, He is Vayu, He is Chandramas, He is Sukra, He is Brahma, He is Apa, He is Prajapati.

—Y. XXXII., 1.

विश्वो देवस्य नेतुर्मर्त्तो वुरीत सख्यम् ।
विश्वो राय इषुध्यति द्युम्नं वृणीत पुष्यसे स्वाहा ॥ ९ ॥
यजु० ४ । ८ ।

8. May every mortal elect the friendship of the guiding God. Each one solicits Him for wealth. Let him seek fame to prosper him.
—Y. IV., 8.

त्वमग्ने व्रतपा असि देव आमर्त्येष्वा । त्वं यज्ञेष्वीड्यो
रास्वेयत्सोमाभूयो भर देवो नः सविता वसोर्दाता वस्वदात्
॥ १० ॥ यजु० ४ । १६ ।

9. Thou Agni art the guardian God of sacred vows among mankind. Thou meet for praise at holy rites. Grant this much, Soma! bring yet more. Savitar who giveth wealth, hath given treasure unto us.
—Y. IV., 16.

अभि त्यं देवꣳसवितारमोण्योः कविक्रतु मर्चामि सत्यसवꣳ
रत्न धामाभि प्रियं मतिं कविम् । ऊर्ध्वा यस्यामतिर्भा अदि
द्युतत्सवीमनि हिरण्यपाणि रमिमीत ॥ ११ ॥
यजु० ४ । २५ ।

10. I sing my song of praise to Him, Savitar, pervading earth and heaven, strong with the wisdom of the wise, and the giver of virtuous impulses, bestower of wealth, the well-beloved thoughtful Sage. To Him I sing, at whose impulse the splendid light shone in heaven. Most wise, the

golden-handed, hath measured the sky with skilled design. —Y. IV., 25.

स नो बन्धुर्जनिता स विधाता धामानि वेद भुवनानि विश्वा।
यत्र देवा अमृतमानशानास्तृतीये धामन्नध्यैरयन्त ॥ २१ ॥
यजुः ३२ । १० ।

11. He is our kin, our Father and begetter, He knows all beings and all ordinances. Obtaining eternal life in Him, the gods have risen upward to the third high stage. —Y. XXXII., 10.

यो नः पिता जनिता यो विधाता धामानि वेद
भुवनानि विश्वा । यो देवानां नामधा एकऽएव तं
सम्प्रश्नं भुवना यन्त्यन्या ॥ य० अ० १७ मं० २७

12. He who is our father and the progenitor of all things, who rewards every one according to his deserts, who knows all the heavenly bodies and habitable globes, who gives names to the wise as well as to the worlds He creates, who is One without a second, in whom all things are comprehended :— Him let all strive to understand by means of friendly discussions.

तमिद्गर्भं प्रथमं दध्र ऽ आपो यत्र देवाः समगच्छन्त
विश्वे। अजस्य नाभावध्येकमर्पितं यस्मिन्विश्वानि भुवनानि
तस्थुः ॥ य० अ० १७ । मं० ३१ ॥

13. He in whom the souls (or the vital air) are clad in the eternal, expansive, subtle material cause of the universe, whom the *yogis*, with purified souls and enlightened minds, attain to, who is present in the

inmost recesses of the eternal souls and the primordial atom, who is sustained by His own power, in whom all the worlds are established :—*Him* do ye realize.

परो दिवा पर एना पृथिव्या परोदेवेभिरसुरैर्य्यदस्ति।
के स्विद्गर्भम्प्रथमन्दध्र ऽआपो यत्र देवाः समपश्ययन्त
पूर्व्वे ॥ य० अ० १७। मं० २९ ॥

14. He who extends beyond (or is exalted above) the luminous bodies, who extends beyond the earth, who extends beyond (*i.e.*, is above the reach of) even the wise, who extends beyond the ignorant, in whom the vital airs sustain desirable objects, whom the sages, rich in knowledge and wisdom, can alone *realize* :—Him do ye try to know.

यो भूतं च भव्यं च सर्वं यश्चाधितिष्ठति। स्वर्यस्य
च केवलं तस्मैज्येष्ठाय ब्रह्मणेनमः ॥ १ ॥ यस्य भूमिः प्रमान्त-
रिक्ष मुतोदरम्। दिवं यश्चक्रे मूर्द्धानं तस्मै ज्येष्ठाय ब्रह्मणे
नमः ॥ २ ॥ यस्य सूर्य्यश्चक्षुश्चन्द्रमाश्च पुनर्णवः । अग्निं
यश्चक्रे आस्यं तस्मै ज्येष्ठाय ब्रह्मणे नमः ॥ ३ ॥ यस्य
वातः प्राणापानौ चक्षुरंगिरसो भवन्। दिशो यश्चक्रे प्रज्ञा-
नीस्तस्मै ज्येष्ठाय ब्रह्मणेनमः ॥ ४ ॥ अथर्व ॥

न द्वितीयो न तृतीयश्चतुर्थो नाप्युच्यते ॥ १ ॥ न पञ्चमो
न षष्ठः सप्तमो नाप्युच्यते ॥ २ ॥ नाष्टमो न नवमो दशमो
नाप्युच्यते ॥ ३ ॥ स सर्वस्मै विपश्यति यच्च प्राणति यच्च
न ॥ ४ ॥ तमिदं निगतं सहः सएष एक एक वृदेक एव ॥
५ ॥ सर्वे अस्मिन् देवा एक वृतोभवन्ति ॥ ६ ॥ अथर्व० ॥

15. (1) To Him who rules the Past, the Present and the Future, who presides over the entire universe, who is the sovereign lord of all, above the reach of Time and Death (self-effulgent), immutable and absolute bliss—even to Him, the most exalted Brahm, be our homage !

(2) To Him, who makes the Sun and Moon, the eyes of the universe, at the commencement of every creation, who has made Fire like unto a mouth—even to Him, the most exalted Brahm, be our homage !

(3) To Him who has, in the universe, made the Earth and other habitable globes in place of the feet, who has made Space in place of the womb, who has made the Luminous Bodies in place of the head —even to Him, the most exalted Brahm, be our homage !

(4) To Him who has made the Atmosphere as the life of the creation, who has made the Rays of Light as its eyes, who has made the Directions of Space as the organs of hearing—even to Him, the most exalted Brahm, be our homage !

From the "Atharva Veda"

यथेमां वाचं कल्याणीमावदानि जनेभ्यः। ब्रह्म
राजन्याभ्याᳬं शूद्राय चार्याय च स्वाय चारणाय॥
यजु॰ अ॰ २६।२।

1. Renown and glory, force and happiness, the Brahman's splendour and food and nourishment to

him who knoweth this God *as one without a second.* Neither second nor third, nor yet fourth is He called. He is called neither fifth, nor sixth, nor yet seventh. He is called neither eighth, nor ninth, nor yet tenth.

He watcheth over creatures, all that breatheth and breatheth not. This conquering might is possessed by Him. *He is the sole, the simple one, the One alone.* In Him all gods become simple and One.

—A. XIII., 4, 14-21.

यावती द्यावापृथिवी वरिम्णा यावदापः सिष्यदुर्या-
वदग्निः । ततस्त्वम्० ॥ ४७, ॥
यावतीर्दिशः प्रदिशो विषूचीर्यावतीराशा अभिचक्ष-
णा दिवः । ततस्त्वम्० ॥ ४८ ॥
ज्यायान् निमिषतोसि तिष्ठतो ज्यायान्त्समुद्रादसि काम
मन्यो । ततस्त्वम्० ॥ ४९ ॥ अथ० ९।२।२०,२१,२३॥

2. Wide as the space which heaven and earth encompass, far as the flow of waters, far as Agni, vast as the quarters of the sky and regions that lie between them spread in all directions, vast as celestial tracts and views of heaven, stronger than these art Thou and great for ever, yea, stronger than aught that stands or twinkles, stronger art thou than Ocean, O Kama, O Manyu. To Thee, to Thee I offer worship.

—A. IX., 2, 20, 21, 23.

सर्वं तद्राजा वरुणो वि चष्टे यदन्तरा रोदसी यत् परस्तात्।
संख्याता अस्यनिमिषो जनाना मक्षानिव श्वघ्नी निमिनो-
ति तानि ॥ १५ ॥ अ० ४।१६।५।

3. All this the royal Varuna beholdeth, all between heaven and earth and all beyond them. He has counted even the twinklings of men's eyes. As one who plays, throws dice, He settles all things.

—A. IV., 16, 5.

त्वमिन्द्रस्त्वं महेन्द्रस्त्वं लोकस्त्वं प्रजापतिः। तुभ्यं
यज्ञो वि तायते तुभ्यं जुह्वति जुह्वतः॥ १८ ॥

अथर्व० १७।१।१८।

4. Indra art Thou, Mahendra art Thou, Thou art the world, the Lord of Life. To Thee is sacrifice performed: worshippers offer gifts to Thee.

—A. XVII., 1, 18.

सोर्यमा स वरुणः स रुद्रः स महादेवः ॥ ८ ॥
सो अग्निः स उ सूर्यः स उ एव महायमः॥ ९ ॥

अथ० १३।४।४,५।

5. (1) He is Aryaman, He is Varuna, He is Rudra, He is Mahadeva.

(2) He is Agni, He is Surya, he verily is Mahayama.

—A. XIII., 4, 4, 5.

(2) The Arya Samaj believes that some persons (of either sex) may have more of the divine in them, in proportion to the degree of exaltation to which their spirits have risen, but that they never can be the same as God, and therefore must remain imperfect. Such persons deserve all honour from ordinary men as prophets, teachers, leaders, or great men; but they never can be *mediators,* in the sense in which that term is used in orthodox Christianity. The Arya Samaj, in common with the rest of mankind, believes that these exalted persons are the great benefactors and uplifters of the human race; that they deserve the respect of every man, regardless of nationality, colour or creed; that human souls receive the greatest possible support and enlightenment by coming in contact with them and their thought, but that the salvation of each human soul must eventually depend upon his or her own exertions, and that faith in no other human soul can, *ipso facto,* save him or her. This teaching of the Arya Samaj is in direct conflict with popular Hinduism, as well as with popular Christianity.

(3) The Arya Samaj does not believe in the infallibility, or immunity from mistake or sin, of any human being, however exalted he may be in the spiritual sense. "To err is human" is thus accepted in its literal and widest sense.

(4) The only approved forms of worship are: Contemplation, Communion, and Prayer (*Stuti, Prasathna* and *Upasana*) coupled with purity of thought, word and deed. The only approved form of expiation is repentance as shown by determination not to sin again, in addition to such sacrifices as may

help in the purification and uplifting of the soul from the effects of the sin committed.

(5) The Arya Samaj believes in the doctrine of *Karma*,[1] that "acts must be followed by their consequences, that the results of actions cannot be warded off or atoned for by any means." Says an authority: "An act cannot wear away without bearing fruit, even in millions of years; a man must necessarily eat the fruit of his good and evil deeds." This leads to the doctrine of the transmigration of souls which forms a part of the propaganda of the Samaj.

(6) The Samaj does not believe in Fate, unless it be confounded with the doctrine of *Karma* stated in (5). Every one can make and unmake his or her own destiny, subject to the eternal laws of God, including the law of *Karma*. Action, right earnest action, with confidence and faith, is the only way to undo *Karma*, in the sense that the fruits of fresh energetic action may over-ride and supersede previous *Karma*. Surrender to inaction or Fate means death.

(7) Swami Dayananda did not recommend ancestor-worship, in the sense in which it is carried out by the Hindus in popular belief. In his opinion, such only of the dead ancestors deserve our loving remembrance, respect and homage as have been virtuous in their lives, or good and great and learned benefactors and leaders of the community, the nation, or the race. He enjoins, however, respect to and service of living parents and grandparents.

(8) The Samaj accepts the Vedas as infallible

[1] For Vedic authorities see *Sattyarath Prakash*, by Dayananda, and *Punjab Census Report for* 1911, footnote on p. 108.

and expects every man and woman to know them and to expound them for the benefit of others. As explained before, it leaves every individual free to interpret them for him- or her- self, subject to certain well-known laws of interpretation. The idea of progressive interpretation finds favour with some leaders of the Arya Samaj.

These constitute the principal religious teachings of the Samaj.

4. *Religious Observances and Practices*

Of these the Arya Samaj retains and enjoins the following :

1. The five daily *Mahayajnas, i.e.,* the five principal religious practices to be observed every day :

(*a*) *Brahma yajna,* which is two-fold—*Sandhya* and *Swadhyae.* The former is worship of God, morning and evening, by contemplation, communion and prayer ; and the latter is the regular reading of some portion of the Scriptures once a day.

(*b*) *Deva yajna.* This is the well-known *Homa, i.e.,* burning of *Ghi* (clarified butter) and other articles in the fire, and is one of the most ancient practices of the Hindus. No Hindu ceremony is complete without *Homa* in some form or other. The Vedic texts which are repeated in this ceremony are among the most elevating and uplifting pages in the Vedas. The Hindu's day must begin with *Homa,* which purifies the household both physically and spiritually. No period of Hindu history is known in which it was discarded. With the degeneration of Hinduism its daily performance by every householder has fallen into disuse, as have also the other daily *yajnas*.[1]

(*c*) *Pitri yajna* (*lit.*, the worship of parents). Some daily act of service towards one's parents, lest in the care of self and family, duty towards parents be forgotten. In the absence of a system of State Pensions for old age, this system ensures the care of the aged.

(*d*) *Athithi yajna.* The feeding of some learned man or ascetic who has not been invited beforehand, but who must be sought out every day. Hindu law recognizes no regular organization for the help of the student and the learned. The householders are supposed to look after and support them. To guard against personal idiosyncrasies or negligence, it has been provided that every householder must feed one or more students or scholars, or others who may be engaged in the work of religion. It was considered an act of religious duty that such persons should be fed and looked after before the householder's family is fed, in recognition of their services to the cause of learning and religion. The ancient Hindu system did not recognize regularly organized and well-endowed religious institutions; yet it enjoined on every one to devote the first part of life, up to 25 years, to study and the last years of life to religion and the service of mankind. The question of these persons' maintenance and living was solved by making it incumbent on every householder to entertain one

[1] For an explanation of *yajna*, see Müller's *Physical Religion*. (Collected Works), 1898, pp. 107-10.

or more of them every day. This voluntary provision was in lieu of some such compulsory provision as the rates levied on modern British householders to pay for the education and feeding of school children of the poorer classes, as well as for the maintenance of highways, street lamps, parks and other local public advantages. It was further enjoined that the householder should seek them out, bring them to his house and feed them, so that they might not feel humiliated as being the objects of charity.

(*e*) The fifth and the last daily duty was in recognition of human dependence on domestic animals, and also in recognition of one's *duty* towards the poor, the helpless, the crippled, and the orphaned of one's race. It is called *Bali vaishwa deva yajna*. It consists in giving food to as many of them as one can afford, according to one's means.

2. The sixteen *Sanskars*, *i.e.*, *sacraments* or sacred ceremonies, beginning with conception and ending with cremation after death. The ritual is generally very simple and inspiring. There is nothing new in it. It is as old as the Aryas and follows the lines laid down by ancient law-givers. All the later additions, accretions, and modifications have been dispensed with. Only as much is retained as is common to all schools of Hindu thought and is free from any kind of image-worship. All superstitious rites have been disallowed. These sixteen ceremonies are, so to say, sixteen mile-stones in each individual human life, and are therefore of some importance to be celebrated with a certain amount of

formality and display, according to the means of the householder who performs them.

Such is the only ritual recognized by the Arya Samaj, and is contained in a book compiled by Swami Dayananda from ancient authorities on the subject. This book is named *Sanskar Vidhi.*[1]

[1] " Orthodox Hinduism is too apt to lead to irreligion ; a religion which gives ritual in place of a creed and unintelligible *mantras* in place of religious instruction, is bound to have such a result. And a thoughtful man will often be driven to turn to other creeds. Amid all the religions such a man has the choice of four. Brahmoism is nothing but a limp eclecticism ; it has discarded the Vedas and put nothing in their place ; it has adopted a belief here and a doctrine there, and when doubt arises leaves the individual to decide the doubt for himself. Such a religion has little vitality. . . . Christianity and Islam are utterly irreconcilable with Hinduism in any shape or form. . . . But Aryaism is different. . . . It offers . . . a bold, straightforward monotheism ; it bids him discard all those superstitions which he most specially dislikes ; it bases the order and its whole teaching on the Vedas, which he reverences deeply, though he probably reverences nothing else ; it gives him a creed that he can believe, ceremonies that he can himself carry out, and a hope of salvation, if his deeds are good. At the same time, he need not break completely with the Hindù social system. . . ."—*United Provinces Census Report for* 1911, p. 138.

CHAPTER II

SOCIAL IDEALS AND AIMS

आयुर्यज्ञेन कल्पतां प्राणो यज्ञेन कल्पतां चक्षुर्यज्ञेन कल्पताᳬश्रोत्रं यज्ञेन कल्पतां पृष्ठं यज्ञेन कल्पतां यज्ञो यज्ञेन कल्पताम् । प्रजापतेः प्रजा अभूम स्वर्देवा अगन्माऽमृता अभूम ॥ ४ ॥ यजु० ९ । २१

"May life succeed through sacrifice, may life-breath thrive by sacrifice. May the eye thrive by sacrifice. May the ear thrive by sacrifice. May the back thrive by sacrifice. May sacrifice thrive by sacrifice. We have become the children of Prajapati. Gods, we have gone to heaven! We have become immortal."

"Thou (sacrifice) art the ladder by which the gods ascended."

1. *Its Social Basis*

THE social ideals of the Arya Samaj are the ideals of the ancient *Rishis* of India. They are based on:

(1) The Fatherhood of God and the Brotherhood of Man.

(2) The equality of the sexes.

(3) Absolute justice and fair play between men and men and nations and nations. Equal opportuni-

ties to all according to their nature, *karma*, and merit.

(4) Love and charity towards all.

The Caste System

The caste system of the Hindus has been their curse as well as their salvation. While it has been the principal cause of their social and political downfall, it has saved them from complete disruption and from total annihilation as a social and national organism. It has saved them from absorption into other religio-social systems that attained more or less ascendancy in India, in the different periods of the history of that country.

For the last two thousand years it has been more or less a defensive bastion in the fortress of Hinduism. The Arya Samaj repudiates caste by birth ; it condemns the numerous subdivisions into which Hindu society has been split up by reason of castes and subcastes ; it considers the artificial barriers which caste in India has created to divide men from their fellowmen as pernicious and harmful ; in its opinion, it is unnatural to divide society into, as it were, watertight compartments, or to exclude the possibility of people belonging to one having social relations with the other. Yet it cannot shut its eyes to the facts of life and has to recognize that by birth men are not equal ; that they differ from one another in physical powers, in intellectual and mental faculties, in moral dispositions, and also in spiritual development ; that they are born in different environments and that their position and status in life must from the very nature of things be affected by their environment ; that heredity also plays its part in making them what they are at birth or in life. Nevertheless, the Arya Samaj would give equal opportunities to all persons, men and women, to acquire knowledge and to qualify themselves for whatever position in life they would like to fill. It admits the right of every person to choose his or her environment, fight it out, and rise as high in the scale of humanity as he or she would. The Arya Samaj believes that in Vedic times there was no caste by birth in India ; though the Vedas recognized the division of humanity into four classes by virtue of their qualifications and occupations.

The following, from a book written by a learned theosophist Hindu who is not an Arya Samajist, will explain what we have written. Commenting upon the text of Manu[1], which is generally relied upon as sanctioning the caste system, he remarks :

"In those times and places in which the various parts of the human organism are very strongly and sharply differentiated from each other in the individual—as they would be in the stages of highest development of egoism, sex-difference, and the separative intelligence—in those times and places, specialization and demarcation of castes, classes, or vocations would also naturally tend to be most complete. And the passing of individuals, then, from one to the other, would be difficult, as of cells and tissues from one organ to another. But in the ages when the

[1] *Manu* i. 31.

"For the increase of the world's well-being, and not for the increase of egoism and individualism, the Creator sent forth the Brāhmanas, the Kshatriyas, the Vaishyas, and the Shudras from his face, arms, thighs, and feet."—*The Science of Social Organization* (of the Hindus), by Babu Bhagavan Das, M.A., Adyar, Madras, 1910.

constituent parts of the individual organism were, and will again be, more homogeneous, the distinction between the individuals who make up the racial organism will also be less emphatic. Then, exchange of functions and vocations was, and will be, easier.

" As by gradual selective cultivation from the same original seed containing various possibilities, two or more very dissimilar kinds of plants may be gradually raised, and then, by neglect, the progeny of both may revert, in the course of generations, back to the original type—so it must be with the human race. The verse of Manu shows that all the castes come from the same source, viz., the body of the Creator. The *Markandeya Purana* mentions expressly the gradual differentiation of the different castes out of homogeneous material. Other Puranas have similar statements. The *Vayu Purana* says, in so many words, that :

> " ' There were no " stages of life " and no castes and no " mixtures " of them, in the Krita Yuga.'

" In the *Vishnu Bhagavata* we read, not of solitary instances like those of Vishvámittra, but of many cases of whole families and tribes changing from lower to higher castes, in the earlier Yugas. The chapters on the future, contained in most of the Puranas, say that at the end of the Black Age, when the confusion of caste is complete—in other words, homogeneity reverted to—then the Avatara will re-establish castes on a higher level—out of the existing material, not by a new creation. Yudhishthira, in his conversation with Nahusha,[1] declares confusion

[1] *Mahābhārata, Vanaparva*, clxxx. See *Advanced Text-Book of Hinduism*, II., vii.

of caste to be already complete, even in his time, five thousand years ago, and that distinction is possible only by natural, internal tendencies and qualifications and character and conduct.

> " 'Nor birth, nor sacraments, nor study, nor ancestry, can decide whether a person is twice-born (and to which of the three types of the twice-born he belongs). Character and conduct only can decide.'[1]

" And Manu also says:

> " 'By the power of *tapas*-force acting selectively on the potencies of the primal seed in all, persons born into one caste may change into a higher, or, by the opposite of self-denial, by self-indulgence and selfishness, may descend into a lower. . . . The pure, the upward-aspiring, the gentle-speaking, the free from pride, who live with and like the Brahmanas and the other twice-born castes continually—even such Shudras shall attain those higher castes.'[2]

" In the earlier races, this held true in the same life. In later days, it has become a matter of generations and of new births. Rules for change of caste by gradual purification are given in *Manu*, x. 57-65."

Those who trace the caste system in the Vedas rely on *Rig-Veda*, x. 90, 11, which, literally translated, means:

> " Brahmans are the head of mankind (personified), Kshatriyas are made his arms, Vaishyas are what are his thighs, and Shudras are made his feet."

That this alone is the correct meaning of the *mantra*

[1] *Mahābhārata, Vanaparva*, cccxiii. 108.
[2] *Ibid.*, x. 42 and ix. 335.

is evident also from the context. In *mantra* 9 of this hymn mankind is spoken of as a person. *Mantra* 10 asks:

"'What is his head, what are his arms, and what are said to be his thighs and feet?' The *mantra* under consideration (No. 11) is a reply to this question. . . .

"The *mantra* does not in any way countenance the caste system, but describes the constitution of human society by means of an analogy between mankind and the human body. The Brahmans, the Kshatriyas, the Vaishyas, and the Shudras occupy the same places in society as the head, the arms, the thighs and the feet respectively do in the human body. The *Brahmans*, or those who possess learning and direct other men to discharge their duties, are properly called the Head or Brain of Humanity. The *Kshatriyas*, or those who possess strength and protect mankind, are aptly termed the Arms of mankind. The *Vaishyas*, or those who go from place to place for the purpose of trade and commerce, are spoken of as the Thighs of human society. And the *Shudras*, or those who are illiterate or otherwise unfit for the higher duties of life, are represented as the Feet of human society. This is . . . a division of mankind on the principle of 'Division of Labour.' It is based not on *birth* but on *merits*. . . . Indeed, the whole spirit and tenor of the Vedic teaching is opposed to it (*i.e.*, to the system of hereditary castes); and it would not be difficult to point out texts which show in the clearest manner that the members of the same family might pursue different professions according to their tastes and capabilities. *Rig-Veda*, IX., 112, 3 (which is put in the mouth of a worshipper), says:

" 'I am a poet, my father is a physician, my mother grinds corn on stone. Being engaged in different occupations, we seek wealth and happiness, as cows seek food in different pastures. May Thy bounties flow for our happiness, O God!' "

We need not multiply quotations, as even European scholars now unanimously hold that the hereditary castes did not exist in Vedic times. We shall quote the opinions of only two celebrated Sanskritists:

Professor Max Müller says:

"If, then, with all the documents before us, we ask the question, 'Does Caste, as we find it in Manu, and at the present day, form part of the most ancient religious teaching of the Vedas?' we can answer with a decided 'No.'" (*Chips from a German Workshop*, Vol. II., p. 807.)

Weber thus remarks about the Vedic age:

"There are no castes as yet; the people are still one united whole, and bear but one name, that of *Visas*." (*Indian Literature*, p. 38.)

Mr. R. C. Dutt also says that in the entire range of the Vedas "we have not one single passage to show that the community was cut up unto hereditary castes."[1]

As instances of non-Brahmins by birth having been raised to the dignity and status of Brahminhood in ancient India, we may refer to those of:

(*a*) *Satya Káma Jábála*, son of a low caste helot, mentioned in the *Chhandogya Upanishad*.

(*b*) *Kavasha*, mentioned in the *Aitareya Brahmana*.

[1] *The Caste System*, by Ganga Prasad, M.A., pp. 2-4.

(*c*) *Aitareya*, son of a Shudra woman, the author of the *Brahmana* and the *Upanishad* of that name.

(*d*) *Viyasa*, founder of *Vedanta* philosophy and reputed author of the *Mahabharata*, who was the son of a sailor woman.

(*e*) *Parashara*, the author of a code of Aryan laws bearing his name, who was the son of a *Chandal* woman (one of the lowest possible castes, even lower than the Shudras).

(*f*) *Vasishta*, a Vedic *Rishi* of great renown, the son of a prostitute.[1]

(*g*) *Vishwamitra*, a Kshatriya by birth.[2]

(*h*) *Arishta Shena*, *Sindhudwipa*, *Devapi*, and *Kapi*, all Kshatriyas by birth.[2]

(*i*) Two sons of *Nabhga*, a Vaishya by birth.[3]

One of the greatest services rendered by the Arya Samaj to the cause of social reform among Hindus is its championship of the rights of the depressed and untouchable classes of Hindus to be admitted into the Arya Samaj on an equal footing with persons of the highest castes. But of this we will speak in a separate chapter.

3. *The Relations of the Sexes*

It must be frankly admitted that at the time when the Arya Samaj was brought into existence the condition of Hindu women was deplorable. In certain respects it was even more deplorable than that of men. A proportion of the men (though forming only a very small percentage of the population) had

[1] (*f*) Mentioned in *Mahábhárata*.

[2] (*g*) (*h*) Mentioned in *Mahábhárata*.

[3] (*i*) Mentioned in *Harivamsha Purana*, chap. xi.

received some sort of education, in the schools and colleges opened by the Government, the Christian missionaries and other private agencies, but very little had been done in the matter of the education of Indian women. In the dark period of Hindu history the women shared the ignorance of the men. The latter, however, possessed some means of acquiring knowledge which the former had not. With the advent of the British their opportunities of receiving education increased. The system of Government introduced by the British, necessitated the education of Indian men for administrative reasons ; and though, in the course of a century and a quarter of British rule in Bengal, Bombay, and Madras, the number of males receiving education in schools and colleges did not exceed 4.35 per cent. of the total male population, in the case of females it was only ·75 per cent. of the total female population in 1911-12.[1] This was partly due to paucity of educational facilities for girls, and partly to a deeply grounded prejudice against the education of females, as also to the evil institution of child marriage. Among other agencies that have worked for improvement in this respect, the Arya Samaj occupies a high position in the Punjab and the United Provinces of Agra and Oude. It cannot be claimed that this has resulted in a great improvement in the education of Hindu women, but it can be safely said that there has taken place a very great change in the ideas of men towards women. English education and Western ideas have

[1] The figures of literacy, according to the last Census Report, stood as follows : Males, 106 per 1,000 ; females, 10 per 1,000 ; an average of 58 per 1,000 of the total population.

played an important part in bringing about this change, but an equally great, if not even greater part has been played by an appeal to ancient Hindu ideals of womanhood and to the teachings of the ancient Hindu religion in the matter of the relations of the sexes. A study of the ancient Hindu literature made it abundantly clear that the present deplorable condition of Indian womanhood was due to a fall from their old ideals and that it was only a phase, though a much regretted phase, of their general downfall. In ancient India, both in thought and practice, woman occupied a very high position in society—as high as that of man, if not higher. In any case, her position in the community was in no way affected by any assumption of inherent superiority on the part of the male sex. For the purposes of education and marriage they held an equal position. The girls were as much entitled to receive education as the boys, and no limitations at all were placed on their ambition in this direction. The life of studentship was as much enjoined for the girls as for the boys. The only difference was that, in the case of girls, their period of education expired sooner than in the case of boys. The minimum age of marriage for the girls was sixteen, as compared with twenty-five in the case of boys. This was based on Hindu ideas of the physiological differences between the sexes. It is presumed that in the matter of choice of a mate, both parties enjoyed equal freedom and equal opportunities. The ideal marriage was monogamic, and one contracted with the consent of parents on both sides. Yet, so many varieties of legal marriage are known to Hindu law as to leave no doubt as to the sensitiveness of the Hindus to the extreme difficulty, and indeed unnaturalness, of trying to impose one law upon all persons. Some forms of marriage suggest that courtship was not altogether unknown to Hindu society, and that it was not looked upon with any grave disapprobation. A study of the ancient Hindu literature leads one to conclude that the relations of the sexes in ancient India were as free as they are to-day in Europe, though as a rule subject to the control of parents. Yet, in other respects, Hindu mothers, wives, sisters and daughters occupied a higher position than they have ever done in Christian Europe before the nineteenth century A.D. In the family the position of the mother was higher than that of the father. According to Manu[1] she is entitled to a thousand times greater respect and reverence than the father. She had the supreme control of the house and the household, including the finances. Hindu law recognizes the right of the mother, of the widow, of the daughter, and of the sister to possess property in her own right, with exclusive control over the same, even when she is a member of a joint family. A mother has an equal right with the father to the guardianship of her children. On the death of the father she has an absolute right. An ideal Hindu wife is not expected to do anything in the way of earning her livelihood. She has been exonerated from this liability by virtue of the superiority of her mother-function. Males have been made responsible even for the maintenance, etc., of unmarried girls and widows, though the latter are not debarred from acquiring property

[1] *Manu* ii. 145.

by inheritance, by gift, or by their own skill. In no case have males any control over the property of females, in law.

The Hindu marriage is a sacrament, and as such, in theory, indissoluble. Says Manu:

"The whole duty, in brief, of husband and wife towards each other is that they cross not and wander not apart from each other in thought, word and deed until death. And the promise is that they who righteously discharge this duty here shall not be parted hereafter, by the death of the body, but shall be together in the worlds beyond also."[1]

Swami Dayananda interprets the ancient *Rishis* as disapproving of second or third marriages on the death of husbands and wives (Manu is supposed to lay this injunction on widows only).[2] According to the Swami the more approved opinion is that neither widows nor widowers should remarry, but he follows the ancient law-givers in sanctioning sex unions in the case of persons who, on account of their physical tendencies or for the sake of having offspring, stand in need of the same.[3] Hindu authorities and Swami Dayananda knew this doctrine by the name of *Niyoga*, and for it the latter has been very furiously attacked by both foreigners and Indians who have derived their ideas of morality from latter-day Christianity. Even in the Arya Samaj there is much divergence of opinion on the question. Some are

[1] *Manu* ix. 101; v. 165. See *The Science of Social Organization*, by Bhagavan Das, p. 211.

[2] *Ibid.*, p. 212.

[3] See *Manu* v. 158, 159, and 160. Bhagavan Das reads these texts as placing equal restrictions on men and women. See p. 213 of his book,

thoroughly in favour of second marriages ; others accept *Niyoga* in theory, but at the same time hold that it cannot be practised in modern conditions of life. Those who are in touch with advanced social thought in Europe are in a position to say that, after all, the ideas of Dayananda on *Niyoga* are not so strange as some Christian missionaries would like to make out, much less are they immoral. In any case, Dayananda does not lay down any rule for women which he does not apply to men also, and in so doing he is only following the spirit of the ancient law-givers. There are certain conditions in which they allow men to remarry even in the lifetime of another wife ; for example, if the wife be physically incapable of bearing children,[1] or has fallen into drunkenness or immorality, or even in the case of utter incompatibility of temper ; but in similar conditions the wife, too, has the liberty of remarrying in the life-time of her first husband ; for example, if the husband be impotent,[2] or if he desert his wife, or if he fall into bad habits, or is not heard of for a number of years, and so on. In special cases, Hindu law sanctions polygamy also, though only under very exceptional circumstances. What is remarkable is the spirit of fairness which underlies the ancient law of marriage and the consciousness that the sex differences are so complex and the whole question so difficult as to make legal rigidity and uniformity undesirable and unfortunate. It is such legal rigidity that has brought the sex question into the forefront of politics in Europe, with all the agitation and unrest

[1] *Manu* ix. 18, also 80 ; *Yajnavalkya*, p. 418, v. 73.
[2] *Manu* ix.

at present visible in European thought and European life with regard to the relations of men and women. Whilst we write, this is the question which dominates European social thought and which finds universal and all-absorbing expression in the various forms of European art—in fiction, in poetry; in drama, and in painting.

It follows from what we have said above that the Arya Samaj is strongly opposed to child marriage. It has carried on a most vehement crusade against this institution, and may be congratulated on the success it has met with in rallying public opinion in favour of its view. It fixes the minimum marriageable age at 16 for girls and at 25 for boys, and it encourages celibacy to later ages. In 1880, when Swami Dayananda wrote, he suggested an exchange of photographs between the contracting parties: but the times have advanced since then. In educated circles not only do the parents insist on seeing the boys and the girls, but also the contracting parties themselves prefer to make each other's acquaintance before ratifying the contract.

Nevertheless, the marriage customs of the Hindus are in a state of flux, and we cannot foresee as yet what is to be the final settlement.

CHAPTER III

ORGANIZATION OF THE ARYA SAMAJ

ज्यायस्वन्ताश्चित्तिनो मा वि यौष्ट संराधयन्तः सधुराश्च-
रन्तः । अन्यो अन्यस्मै वल्गु वदन्त एत सध्रीचीनान्वः
संमनसस्कृणोमि ॥ ५ ॥ अथ० ३ । ३० । ५

" Intelligent, submissive, rest united, friendly and kind, sharing each other's labours. Come, speaking sweetly each one to the other. I make you one-intentioned and one-minded."

—Ath. III., 30, 5.

1. *In General*

THE most striking feature in connection with the Arya Samaj, which makes it at once the most powerful and the most influential of all reform movements in the country, is its complete and wonderful organization. Every Arya Samaj is a unit in itself. Generally there is one in every city or village which has come under its influence, but in some cities there are more than one, either on account of the distances separating the different parts of the same city, or on account of some slight differences in principle. The latter distinction is mostly confined to the Punjab, the N.W. Frontier Province, Sindh and Baluchistan.

2. *Membership*

Effective membership involves (*a*) the acceptance of the Ten Principles; (*b*) the payment of one per cent. of one's income, either monthly or yearly, towards the revenues of the Samaj; (*c*) attendance at meetings; (*d*) right conduct.

Every Arya Samaj entitled to send representatives to the Provincial Assembly is supposed to consist of at least ten effective members.

3. *Weekly Services*

The Samaj meets once a week for congregational service, which consists generally of (*a*) *Homa*; (*b*) singing of hymns; (*c*) prayer and sermon; (*d*) lecture. The service can be conducted by any member, regardless of caste, whom the officers of the Samaj select for the purpose. The Samaj does not ordain ministers or priests. Any layman can officiate at the services or at ceremonies, and be asked to lecture. The weekly service meetings are open to the public, and no distinction is made between members and non-members, or between Hindus and non-Hindus. Into the Church of God anybody can come and occupy any seat he likes. No seats are reserved, excepting for the President and the Secretary.

4. *Executive Committee*

The affairs of each Arya Samaj are governed by an executive committee consisting of five elected officers and as many members as may be elected according to the size of the Samaj. Only effective members can vote in the election of officers and the committee. The officers are five: (*a*) President;

(*b*) Vice-President ; (*c*) Secretary ; (*d*) Accountant ; (*e*) Librarian. They must be effective members themselves ; that is all. They are elected for the year at an annual meeting convened for the purpose, where the voting is done by ballot. At this annual meeting the outgoing officers and the committee render to the general body an account of the income and expenditure of the Samaj during the year together with a report of the year's working : after which the meeting proceeds to elect officers and committee for the coming year. The outgoing officers and committee are eligible for re-election. In the larger Samajes, the general body of members is divided into groups of ten, for electing representatives on the committee. This is in addition to a few members, not exceeding five, who are elected by the whole body of members. The Samaj may meet monthly or less frequently for the transaction of such business as may be referred to it by the committee, or by the officers, or on the requisition of a certain number of members, for the consideration of such proposals as they wish to be considered by the general body.

For failure to pay the required one per cent. of income, or for other misconduct, the Samaj may suspend a member, or may remove his name altogether from the register of effective members. This is no bar to readmission at the discretion of the committee, from whose decisions in all matters there is, moreover, the right of appeal to the general body. Neither the committee nor the general body is empowered to make changes in the creed, or the constitution, of the Samaj.

5. *Provincial Assembly*

In each province there is a provincial assembly consisting of representatives of the Arya Samajes in the province, the number of representatives which each is entitled to return being determined by the size of the Samaj. Every Arya Samaj contributes 10 per cent. of its gross income to the funds of this assembly, but the assembly has the right to raise, and does raise, funds for general or special purposes as its governing body may determine. This assembly arranges for the dissemination of the Vedic religion by honorary and paid preachers ; sometimes maintains papers and controls the publication of official literature ; manages provincial educational institutions, and does all that is necessary in the interests of the movement. This assembly can change the rules of management by a general referendum of all the effective members in the province, but even so has no power to alter the principles or the creed. The general assembly is elected every three years, but the officers and the committee of the provincial assembly are elected every year.

6. *The All-India Assembly*

At the head comes the All-India body, which is formed by the representatives of the different provincial assemblies and forms the connecting link between the different provinces.

7. *Young Men's Arya Samajes*

Connected with the Samajes in different cities are young men's Arya Samajes, which serve as recruiting centres for the main body. The parent Samaj admits adults only. The young men's Samaj admits all, and insists on nothing more than a belief in God and the payment of a trifling monthly subscription.

8. *Meeting Places*

Every Arya Samaj has its meeting-place. In the principal cities all over India, excepting perhaps in the Deccan, it owns and possesses splendid buildings, consisting of lecture-halls, committee-rooms, etc. In smaller places it hires rooms for meetings. The young men's Arya Samajes generally use the premises of the main body, but in some places they have separate rooms of their own. In some places the premises are used for daily prayers and for club purposes as well. Every Arya Samaj is supposed to arrange for teaching Hindi and Sanskrit to such of its members as do not know those languages. In very many places the Samaj maintains boys' and girls' schools that are open to the public; in others it generally employs a Pandit to do the work of teaching on the premises of the Samaj. To its educational work, however, we propose to devote a separate chapter.

CHAPTER IV

THE ARYA SAMAJ AND POLITICS

यथाहश्चरात्री च न बिभीतो० ॥ २ ॥

यथा सूर्यश्च चन्द्रश्च० ॥ ३ ॥

यथा ब्रह्म च क्षत्रं च० ॥ ४ ॥

यथा भूतं च भव्यं च० ॥ ५ ॥ अथ० २ । १५ । १–६

"As heaven and earth are not afraid and never suffer loss or harm, even so my spirit fear not thou.

"As day and night are not afraid, nor ever suffer loss or harm, even so my spirit fear not thou.

"As sun and moon are not afraid, nor ever suffer loss or harm, even so my spirit fear not thou.

"As Brahmanhood and princely power are not afraid, nor ever suffer loss or harm, even so my spirit fear not thou.

"As what hath been and what shall be fear not, nor ever suffer loss or harm, even so my spirit fear not thou."

—Ath. II., 15, 1—6.

1. *Not a Political or Anti-British Movement*

THE foreign rulers of India have never been quite happy about the Arya Samaj. They have always disliked its independence of tone and its propaganda of self-confidence, self-help, and self-reliance. The national side of its activities has aroused their antipathy. They cannot look with favour on an indigenous movement which, according to them, can do big things without their help and guidance, and which has established a sort of Government within the Government. The progress it has made, the hold which it has established for itself on the minds of the people, the popularity which it has won in spite of its heterodoxy and its iconoclasm among the Hindus, the influence which it possesses, the immense "go" which characterizes it in all its doings, the national spirit which it has aroused and developed among the Hindus, the ready self-sacrifice of its members, the independence of their tone and the rapidity with which the movement has spread throughout India, and last, but not least, the spirit of criticism which it generates, have won for it the suspicion of the ruling bureaucracy. This suspicion has more than once brought on its members the wrath of the authorities, in the shape of deportations, prosecutions, dismissals, etc.

Nevertheless, the fact that the Arya Samaj has been able to do so much, within its short life of about thirty-five years, and has spread so extensively and rapidly, is an incontestable proof of the general fairness of British Government in India.

In order to give the reader a fair idea of both sides of the question, we intend to give somewhat copious extracts from the writings of those who have tried to discredit the Arya Samaj as a political and anti-British movement. We will begin with the writings of one who is believed to be among its most virulent and bitter critics, occupying at the same time a high position among the English publicists of the day. Sir Valentine Chirol, as a special correspondent of the London *Times*, visited India in 1907-10, and wrote a series of articles on Indian unrest, which were widely read and applauded in the British Isles. It was shortly after that their author was knighted. These articles have since been published in book form, with a dedication, by permission, to Lord Morley, the Secretary of State for India in those troublous times. One chapter deals almost exclusively with the Arya Samaj; but, before we come to his criticisms, we must inform the reader of the general conclusions formulated by Sir Valentine Chirol on the whole question of Indian unrest.

He is disposed to think "that the more dangerous forms of unrest are practically confined to the Hindu,"[1] and that, instead of calling it *Indian* unrest, it would be "more accurate" to call it "Hindu unrest," and that "its main-spring is a deep-rooted antagonism to all the principles upon which Western society, especially in a democratic country like England, has been built up." That he was entirely wrong in both these propositions has been abundantly proved by the events that have happened since he wrote.

Coming to the Arya Samaj, however, Sir Valentine Chirol thinks that "the whole drift of Dayananda's teachings is far less to reform Hinduism than to range it into active resistance to the alien influences which threatened, in his opinion, to denationalize it." In support of this assertion he relies upon a string of stray expressions (without giving the references)

[1] *Unrest in India*, p. 5.

alleged to be translations into English of those used by the Swami in his writings; refers to the useful social work done by the Samaj, and concludes: "These and many other new departures conceived in the same liberal spirit at first provoked the vehement hostility of the orthodox Hindus, who at one time stopped all social intercourse with the Arya reformer. But whereas, in other parts of India, the idea of social reform came to be associated with that of Western ascendancy, and therefore weakened and gave way before the rising tide of reaction against that ascendancy, it has been associated in the Punjab with the cry of 'Arya for the Aryans,' and the political activities of the Arya Samaj, or, at least, of a number of its most prominent members who have figured conspicuously in the anti-British agitation of the last few years, have assured for it from Hindu orthodoxy a measure of tolerance and even of goodwill which its social activities would certainly not otherwise have received. That the Arya Samaj, which shows the impress of Western influence in so much of its social work, should at the same time have associated itself so intimately with a political movement directed against British rule, is one of the many anomalies presented by the problem of Indian unrest."

2. *Sir V. Chirol versus the Arya Samaj*

The facts on which Sir Valentine Chirol has relied in respect of his conclusions may be thus enumerated:

(1) That "in the Rawalpindi riots in the year 1907 the ringleaders were Aryas."

(2) That "in the violent propaganda which for about two years preceded the actual outbreak of

violence none figured more prominently than Lala Lajpat Rai and Ajit Singh, both prominent Aryas."

(3) That in certain legal proceedings taken against another Arya, Bhai Parmananda, some letters were produced written by Lajpat Rai to Parmananda while the latter was in England in 1905, in which some political works had been asked for for the use of students and certain opinions had been expressed about political conditions in the Punjab.

(4) That this Bhai Parmananda "was found in possession of various formulæ for the manufacture of bombs."

(5) That, in Patiala, the Aryas "constituted the great majority of defendants, 76 in number . . . who were put on their trial . . . for seditious practices"; and that "so seriously were the charges felt to reflect upon the Arya Samaj as a whole that one of its leading members was briefed on its behalf for the defence."

(6) That, though "it is impossible to say . . . how far the evidence outlined by Counsel" for the prosecution "would have borne out" the "charges, one may properly assume it to have been of a very formidable character, for after the case had been opened against them the defendants hastened to send in a petition invoking the clemency of the Maharaja" and "expressed therein their deep sorrow for any conduct open to misconstruction, tendered their unqualified apology for any indiscreet acts they might have committed, and testified their 'great abhorrence and absolute detestation' of anarchists and seditionists. Whereupon His Highness ordered the prosecution to be abandoned, but banished the defendants

from his State and declared their posts to be forfeited by such as had been in his service, and only in a few cases were these punishments subsequently remitted."

(7) That Shyamji Krishna Varma, whom the founder of the Arya Samaj appointed a member of the first governing body in his lifetime, and after his death a trustee of his will, has said that " of all movements in India for the political regeneration of the country, none is so potent as the Arya Samaj," and that " the ideal of that society, as proclaimed by its founder, is an absolutely free and independent form of national Government."

Now, it is a great pity that many of these so-called facts should be either untrue or merely half-truths ; that a writer of Sir Valentine Chirol's position should have been guilty (*a*) of not giving chapter and verse for his quotations ; (*b*) of suppressing important facts which must be within his knowledge and which throw quite a different light on the incidents relied on by him ; (*c*) of having ignored evidence which shatters his case to its foundations ; and (*d*) generally of *suggestio falsi*.

3. *Reply to Sir V. Chirol's Charges*

The true facts are as follows :

(1) The so-called Arya "ringleaders" in the Rawalpindi riots were all acquitted by a European judge, a senior member of the I.C.S., who presided over their trial and who found that the evidence produced by the prosecution against them was false and fabricated. This judgment was never contested by the Government, and these facts ought to have

been known by Sir Valentine Chirol when he wrote his articles.

(2) (Sirdar) Ajit Singh's connection with the Arya Samaj was openly repudiated by the leading Arya Samajists. He never claimed to be an Arya, and it was not known that he ever became a member. In fact, it is well known that for "two years immediately preceding the outbreak of violence in 1907" he was an atheist, and made no secret of his beliefs as such. No evidence is forthcoming that before 1907 he carried on any propaganda at all, much less a violent propaganda. This fact is strongly corroborated by the further fact that no notice whatever was taken of him by the Government excepting in 1907. He was not known to the Press or to the Police, and earned his living by teaching Indian languages to English officers, civil and military, and European ladies. The charge preferred against him in 1910, after he had left the country, had nothing to do with the events of 1907 or before. These facts were all before the public at the time Sir Valentine Chirol was writing his book.

(3) As far as Lajpat Rai is concerned, it is significant that:

(*a*) He has never been put on his trial.

(*b*) That, in spite of his repeated demands to be informed of the reasons for his deportation, those reasons have not been forthcoming.

(*c*) That even Sir Valentine Chirol, with the whole machinery of the Government of India at his back, has not been able to give any quotations from Lajpat Rai's speeches or writings which justify his statements about him.

(*d*) That even Lord Morley could not do so, and that, in his revised speeches since published in book form, his lordship has considered it necessary to delete almost all accusations that he had made against Lajpat Rai in the House of Commons in justification of his policy of deportation in 1907.

(*e*) That Lajpat Rai has thoroughly vindicated his political character by obtaining judicial verdicts in his favour in the highest courts in India and in England, in suits which he launched against powerful journalists in these countries.

(*f*) That he has never concealed his political opinions, and even Sir Valentine Chirol has given him, in one place, a character for frankness.

(*g*) That Indians of the highest standing (some of them in the confidence of the Government)—men of admitted veracity and unimpeachable character—have publicly associated with him both before and after his deportation, and have spoken and written in his favour in most unambiguous terms.

(*h*) That the stray expressions culled from his letters produced in the case against Bhai Parmananda were fully explained by him on oath in the course of Bhai Parmananda's trial, and no exception whatever was taken to his statement either by the Court or by the Government Prosecutor.

(4) Bhai Parmananda has always denied that he was ever in possession of any formulæ for the manufacture of bombs, though his denial was not accepted by the Court.

(5) and (6) It is well known in the Punjab that the Patiala prosecution was due to the over-zeal of a

retired British Police Official, and instituted by the State under the impression that the British Government would be gratified thereby. As soon, however, as it was found that there was practically no evidence in support of the serious charges brought forward—that even Sir Louis Dane, the Lieutenant-Governor of the Punjab, one of the greatest enemies the Arya Samaj had, had given a sort of certificate to the Samaj exonerating the latter as a body from any charge of sedition—His Highness became anxious to stop the proceedings. The petition referred to by Sir Valentine Chirol was the outcome of certain negotiations between the State and the defendants, and contains no admission of guilt or of any truth in the charges brought against the defendants. The order of banishment was in the nature of "saving the face" of the prosecution. Several of the defendants belonged to British territory, and most of the others, if not all, were allowed to re-enter the State. Some of them are at the present moment in the service of the State that nominally banished them. In fact, we are not aware of any native of that State against whom the order still subsists. But the most significant fact is that the principal accused in the case, the President of the Patiala Arya Samaj, who was a British Indian officer of high rank (an Executive Engineer in the P.W.D.) lent to the State, is still in the service of the British Government, and in full enjoyment of his rank and salary. These facts must be known to Sir Valentine Chirol, since they were public property at the time when he brought out his book. The officer in question, we may add, received his full pay for the period during which he was under suspension pending trial, and on the administrative side his case was decided by the Viceroy in Council.

(7) With regard to Mr. Shyamji Krishna Varma, the facts are as follows:

In 1881 or 1882, when the Swami Dayananda appointed him a trustee in his will as "one of the governing body" of his Press, Mr. S. K. Varma had not expressed any political opinions. Swami Dayananda's will created no trust of the Arya Samaj. It only created a trust of the property which belonged exclusively to him in his own right, and which he had accepted in gift for public purposes and which was under his sole control. Among these trustees were a number of persons who never belonged to the Arya Samaj, as for example, the late Mr. Justice Ranade, of the Bombay High Court. Mr. Varma was then holding a high position in a native State, and for a number of years after that he enjoyed the confidence of high British officials (Political Agents of the native State where he served, Agent to the Governor-General, and others). Mr. Varma denies that he ever was a regular member of the Samaj, and it is well known that, immediately before leaving India for good, he was on exceedingly bad terms with the Arya Samajes in general, and with the leading Arya Samajists in particular. The opinions of Mr. Varma about the Arya Samaj are not the opinions of the latter, yet there is nothing in the expressions quoted which in any way justifies the conclusions of Sir Valentine Chirol. One is in the nature of a prophecy and the other talks of an "ideal" which is as different from actualities as it is remote from practical politics.

Of far greater significance, however, than the opinions we have just criticized, are those expressed by eminent Anglo-Indian officers actually engaged in the work of administration and occupying positions of trust and responsibility in the Government of British India. Of these the most significant is the letter written by the Chief Secretary of the Punjab Government in 1910, on behalf of Sir Louis Dane, the Lieutenant-Governor of the Punjab, in which he stated that the Government was not convinced that the Arya Samaj as a body was seditious or even political.

The recent utterances of Sir James Meston, the present Lieutenant-Governor of the United Provinces of Agra and Oude, are even more clear and pronounced. They leave no doubt that the Government does not consider the Arya Samaj to be a political association.

4. *Official Testimony in favour of the Arya Samaj*

We proceed to give, in their own words, and with references, a few opinions expressed by other responsible officials.

In his *Census Report for the Punjab*, for 1891, Sir Edward Maclagan (then Mr. Maclagan, I.C.S.) said: "The fact that the Aryas are mainly recruited from one class and that the Samaj possesses a very complete organization of its own has laid it open to the charge of supporting as a body the proclivities of a large section of its members; *but the Samaj as such is not a political but a religious body.*"

Mr. Burn, I.C.S., of the United Provinces of Agra and Oude, said in his *Census Report* for those

Provinces for the year 1901: "That the Aryas are would-be politicians is true, but that they are so because they are Aryas is a proposition in the highest degree doubtful."

The point has again been discussed at some length in the *Census Report* for 1911 by Mr. Blunt, I.C.S., of the same United Provinces, and we make no apology for the following somewhat voluminous extracts therefrom (page 135, etc.):

"Long ago the Samaj was charged with being a mere political society, with objects and opinions of a dubious character; and of late the charge has again been made, and with greater insistence. The heads of the charge seem to be three—firstly, that many prominent Aryas are politicians with opinions not above suspicion;[1] secondly, the Samaj strongly supports the Gaurakhshini movement; and thirdly, that the Samaj grossly attacks other religions. As regards the first allegation, it is doubtless true. The Arya Samaj has *many*[2] politicians of good and bad repute in its ranks. . . There is, of course, no doubt whatever that the Samaj doctrine has a patriotic side. . . . The Arya doctrine and the Arya education alike 'sing the glories of ancient India,' and by so doing arouse the national pride of its disciples, who are made to feel that their country's history is not a tale of continuous humiliation. Patriotism and politics are not synonymous, but the arousing of an interest in national affairs is a natural result of arousing national pride. More-

[1] In the opinion of Anglo-Indians, all nationalist politics are suspicious.

[2] It would have been more accurate to write "*some*" in place of "many."

over, the type of man to whom the Arya doctrine appeals is also the type of man to whom politics appeals, viz., the educated man who desires his country's progress, not ultra conservative with the ultra conservatism of the East, but, to a greater or less extent, *rerum novarum cupidus et capax.* It is not therefore surprising that there are politicians among the Arya Samaj. But it is impossible to deduce from this that the Arya Samaj, as a whole, is a political body. From the first the Samaj has consistently affirmed that it is not concerned with politics, has laid down this principle in various rules, has discouraged its members from taking part in them and disavowed their actions in express terms when they needed disavowal. . . . The position indeed is that the tree has been judged by its fruits, the society by the action of its members. . . . The judgment, whether right or wrong, is at all events natural, but it nevertheless seems to me to be absolutely necessary that a distinction should be drawn between the action of the Samaj as a whole and the action of its individual members —or, to go to the utmost length, of its individual *sabhas* (though the attitude of most *sabhas*, as of the central *Sabha*, has always been correct)."

Mr. Blunt then quotes the opinion of Mr. Burn, and adds :

" Ten years later, there seems no need to alter this opinion, save that one may perhaps safely put it in even less undecisive terms, and also add the rider that ' Aryaism of its very nature appeals to men to whom politics will also appeal, and turns out a stamp of man who is likely to take some interest in national affairs.' But, having said so much, no more can be said. The Samaj, as a whole, is not a political body, all Aryas are not politicians, and those Aryas that are politicians have not necessarily opinions that lead to or connote disloyalty."

As regards the second argument, Mr. Blunt begins by saying: "The connection of the Arya Samaj with the *Gaurakhshini* movement is a trifle obscure," discusses the position of the founder and the members in relation thereto, and then concludes:

"The sum of the matter is that, though the *Gaurakhshini* movement, in unscrupulous hands, is a political weapon, and too often is used as such, yet, with the majority of its Hindu adherents, it is still a religious matter pure and simple. With some Arya adherents it may be also a matter, almost unconsciously, of religion; but, whatever their reasons for supporting it, it is impossible to suppose that they are all insincere and unscrupulous in that support."

With reference to the third point, Mr. Blunt says: "That the attitude of the Arya Samaj to other religions is often objectionable cannot, unfortunately, be denied. . . . The matter touches the question of politics, however, only at one point, and that is, how far the Arya Samaj, in attacking Christianity, can be said to attack the British Government. It seems certain that the Arya Samaj do fear the spread of Christianity. There is no question that Dayananda feared it . . . in part because he considered that the adoption or adaptation of any foreign creed would endanger the national feeling he wished to foster. But no more than this can be said. There seems no reason to hold that Dayananda, in attacking Christianity, had any thoughts of attacking the British Government. And, if he and his followers attack Christianity, they attack Hinduism and Islam also."

5. *Position of the Leaders*

The position which the leaders of the Samaj take on this question of politics may be stated in several quotations from their speeches and writings, which we give. We take the first from a speech delivered by L. Munshi Ram, the acknowledged leader of the Gurukula section of the Samaj, at Lahore in November, 1907:

"The Arya Samaj is a society that promotes arts of peace. It supports educational institutions which will turn out self-respecting, good, noble and saintly men whose intellectual energies cannot but be enlisted on the side of Law and Order, and whose beneficent work can only conduce to the welfare of society. . . . I say . . . of all religions in the world the Vedic Religion alone is universal. Its doctrines are of universal applicability, without reference to geographical or ethnological limits or to the 'colour line.' . . . Revolutions, bloodshed, disorder, clannish malevolence and racial hatred are fatal to the spread of true Dharma and therefore the Arya Samaj has set its face against them."

Again: "The Arya Samaj is a self-respecting religious body whose activities are perfectly lawful and which owes duties to God as well as to man. . . . The Arya Samaj believes in four Ashramas. Politics forms a part of the duties of *Grihasthas*. The colleges, schools and universities in various parts of the world represent, however imperfectly, the *Brahmcharya* Ashrama. All philosophers and reformers who retire from the turmoil of the world and concentrate their attention upon the problems of life and death are *Banprasthas*. But who are the *Sanyasis*? Surely all *Dharma Sabhas*; for their duty it is to point out the path fearlessly. The Arya Samaj in its collective capacity is a *Sanyasi* and, therefore, cannot have anything to do with politics—for that would be encroaching upon the work of *Grihasthas*—beyond rendering unto Cæsar what is Cæsar's due."

Our second quotation is taken from a voluminous work published under the joint names of Lala Munshi Ram and Professor Ram Deva, of the Gurukula, Kangri, in 1910, and entitled, *The Arya Samaj and its Detractors* :

"The Vedic church is undoubtedly a Universal Church. It preaches that the Veda was revealed in the beginning of creation for all races. . . . It contains germs of all sciences—physical, mental and psychical. But it cannot be denied that the glorious period of the supreme achievements of the Vedic Church was the bright period of Indian history. When India was the centre of Vedic propaganda and missionaries were sent from it to different parts of the world, it was also the seat of a world-wide empire, and Indian kings exercised direct sovereignty over Afghanistan, Baluchistan, Tibet, etc., and Indian colonists colonized Egypt, Rome, Greece, Peru and Mexico. When, therefore, the Arya Samaj sings the glory of ancient India—

the land of expositors of Revealed Learning, the sacred soil where Vedic institutions flourished and put forth their choicest fruits, the holy country where Vedic Philosophy and Vedic Metaphysics attained their highest development, the sanctified clime where lived exemplars who embodied in their conduct the loftiest conceptions of Vedic ethical teachings—the health-forces of nationalism receive an impetus, and the aspirations of the young nationalist who had persistently dinned into his ear the mournful formula that Indian History recorded the lamentable tale of continuous and uninterrupted humiliation, degradation, foreign subjection, external exploitation, etc., feels that his dormant national pride is aroused and his aspirations stimulated. It is also true that the nationalism which seeks the shelter of the Vedic Church is a great agent of unification of Indian races and is least productive of racial animosity or sectarian bigotry. The Arya Samaj takes us back to a period of Indian History long anterior to the birth of Zoroastrianism, Buddhism, Christianity, and Mahomedanism. . . . Rama and Sita, Krishna and Arjuna, are national heroes and heroines of whose magnificent deeds and righteous activities all Indians—without distinction of caste, creed, or race—might well feel proud. The Upanishads and the Darshanas are in a peculiar manner the common heritage of all Indians in whose veins flows the blood of *Kapila, Jaimini, Viyasa* and *Patanjali,* no matter to what religion they belong now. If Sanskrit is wonderfully perfect in its structure and capable of infinite development, the credit is due to the remote ancestors of all

Indians who lived and taught ages before religious squabbles, which have now split up the children of India into warring sects, were even dreamt of. So patriotism, which is the handmaiden of Vedicism, is lofty, inspiring, vitalizing, unifying, tranquillizing, soothing, bracing and exhilarating. Instead of fomenting discord, it promotes love and fosters harmony. Instead of teaching Indians to hate their foreign rulers, it tends to unite the rulers and the ruled in a fraternal embrace, because it inculcates the valuable historical truth that classical culture directly and modern European culture indirectly were derived from Indian sources, and therefore Europeans, being the descendants of the disciples of our forbears, are our brothers in spirit—their traditions and arts having a common origin with ours. . . . The Vedic Church supports Indian nationalism, not only by inspiring nationalists with pride in the past and hope in the future, but also by creating reverence in minds of non-Indian Aryas for India—the birth-place, nursery, and seat of development of the system of thought which alone has given them solace of mind. If devout Buddhists all over the world regard *Kapilavastu* with feelings of profound reverence, if the mention of the very word Palestine touches untapped springs in the Christian heart, India, and especially the peninsula of Gujerat, where Dayananda was born, will become a place of pilgrimage for Aryas all over the world. Though, as we have shown above, Vedicism fosters healthy patriotism, which statesmanship like that of Morley and Minto recognizes as a force to be encouraged and enlisted on the side of law, order, evolution, orderly development and evolutionary political progress on democratic lines . . . there is yet another fruitful cause of misunderstanding. The Vedic Dharma, like all great religious movements that have left their mark in the world, is not only a creed, but a complete system of thought, a complete code for the guidance of humanity in all relations of life and all departments of human activity, a polity as well as a science of living—in short, a way of looking at things, a point of view. The Vedas teach us all about the ideals of individual and social conduct, of social governance and political philosophy. But it also teaches that the supreme rule of progress is righteousness. It is righteousness that exalteth nations. Righteous activity is the keystone to the arch of social polity and political authority. No nation can be regarded fit for the exercise of collective responsibility unless the individual units composing it have learnt to be righteous in their conduct and dealings. 'Dharma is the supreme governing authority in the world,' the Veda declares in unequivocal terms. . . . If professors in Government Colleges who teach or recommend to their boys books like Mill's *Liberty* and *Representative Government*, Bentham's *Theory of Legislation*, Bagehot's *Physics and Politics*, Spencer's *Man versus the State*, and other works too numerous to detail, are not regarded as political agitators, there is no reason why the Arya Samaj, which along with other things preaches Vedic ideals of social reconstruction and modes of social governance, and keeps studiously aloof from current politics, should be regarded as a political body. . . ."

The third of our quotations is taken from an article in which the writer, believed to be a prominent member of the other section of the Samaj, reviewed a book published in the form of a novel, by an Anglo-Indian author of very strong anti-Indian and anti-Arya Samajic views, in which it was insinuated that the Arya Samaj was a seditious body and its institutions the nurseries of seditious propaganda :

" Before we finish we want to state for the one hundredth time the position of the Arya Samaj in the clearest possible terms. The Arya Samaj and the Arya Samajists accept the *fact* of the British Government and believe that under the circumstances it is the best kind of Government that India can have. As such, it is the duty of every Arya Samajist to be a law-abiding citizen and to advance the cause of peace and order. The Arya Samaj makes no secret of its mission to make men better, morally, intellectually, spiritually, and socially. The Aryas cannot but recognize that they have special ties, religious, social and national, with all those who accept the Vedas as their Scriptures, and as such it is their duty to develop and bring about in them all those traits of character which lead to manliness, frankness, honesty, love of truth, generosity, kindness, sense of justice and fair play, in short to do everything which will contribute to their social efficiency and make them worthy descendants of worthy forbears (however remote). It is their mission to unfasten the chains of intellectual, moral, religious and social bondage. The Arya Samaj is for everything good in human nature, and, if loving one's country and one's people is good, the Samaj stands for it and is not ashamed of it. The Arya Samaj stands for progress on solid foundations and is, therefore, engaged in building up the character of its people. It believes in the ever-true principles of association, co-operation and organization. Whatever the Samaj does, it does openly. Our schools are open, our meetings are open, our services are open, and we challenge anyone to give one single proof of the Arya Samaj having ever encouraged secrecy. In fact, the complaint sometimes is that it is too outspoken and too open. Its one outstanding fault has been that it has ever hated diplomacy and has paid too little regard to expediency. It does not stab people in the dark, either by words or by deeds. It is not a body of snakes. It discourages sycophancy and double dealing of all kinds. Well, if all this leads to a desire for political freedom, it has no reason to say, 'no,' to it.

"If ever the time comes when the Arya Samaj, out of fear, or out of diplomacy, or out of expediency, or for the sake of pleasing any human being or beings, says otherwise and changes its principles and its procedure, it shall be false to its God, and His scriptures, it shall be false to its founder and his mission, and it shall deserve to die the death of a worm."[1]

It should be carefully noted that Dayananda's followers do not say that he was not a great patriot. His personal views on politics he has expounded in

[1] From an article entitled "Sri Ram, Revolutionist," published in *The Vedic Magazine and Gurukula Samachar.*

his book, called *Sattyarath Prakash.* He says, in the sixth chapter:

"Foreign Government, perfectly free from religious prejudices, impartial towards all the natives and the foreigners—kind, beneficent and just though it may be—can never render the people *perfectly* happy."

But he adds that, in the case of India, foreign rule "is due to mutual feud, differences in religion, *want of purity in life, lack of education, child-marriage, marriage in which the contracting parties have no voice in the selection of their life-partners, indulgence in carnal gratifications, untruthfulness and other evil habits, the neglect of the study of Veda, and other malpractices.*"

Elsewhere in the same work he "praises the superior social efficiency, better social institutions, self-sacrifice, public spirit, enterprise, obedience to authority and patriotism of the rulers of India, and tells his countrymen that:

"'It is the possession of such sterling qualities and the doing of such noble deeds that have contributed to the advancement of Europeans.'"

6. *A Critical Phase*

The Arya Samaj has passed through a serious crisis. For some time (1907 to 1910) it was the object of singular and not very intelligent persecution on the part of officials who should have known better. Aryas in Government service were summarily dismissed for the simple reason that they were members, or active members, of the Samaj. In the case of a regimental clerk so treated, it was admitted that "all his certificates" were "good," but that it was subsequently discovered that "he was a member of the Arya Samaj, and it was considered undesirable to have a member of that society in a Sikh regiment." In other cases men were asked to resign the membership of the Samaj. Some complied with the order, but others refused and were consequently dismissed. At one place the officer commanding a brigade issued an order to the effect that "all ranks" were "forbidden to attend the meetings of the Arya Samaj or any other political body." In another place it was proclaimed by beat of drum that "all the books belonging to the religion of the Arya Samaj have been forfeited and confiscated to His Majesty." The head of the district where this was done, however, repudiated having authorized the proclamation.

In some districts a census of the Aryas was taken, and their names entered in Police Registers as suspects. Similarly, Departments of Administration caused to be prepared special lists of Aryas in their employ, with a view to their being coerced to sever their connection with the movement. Some men were told to remove their boys from Arya schools, on pain of dismissal from their posts. The police watched every Arya and shadowed the prominent members from place to place. A vast system of espionage was introduced to discover the real sentiments of the community. One Government is known to have twice deputed special officers of great detective ability to report on the Samaj.

Eventually it was discovered that there was no

substantial reason to suspect the organization of any evil design against the Government; so it was decided to inaugurate a policy of conciliation towards them, the credit of which is due to Lord Hardinge, the present Viceroy, and to Sir James Meston.

CHAPTER V

THE EDUCATIONAL PROPAGANDA

ब्रह्मचर्येण तपसा देवा मृत्युमपाघ्नत । इन्द्रोह ब्रह्मचर्येण
देवेभ्यः स्वराभरत् ॥ ६ ॥ अथ० ११ । ५ । १९

"By Tapa and Brahmacharya the holy saints drove away death (attained salvation).

"By Brahmacharya did they receive heavenly light from God."

—Ath. XI., 5, 19.

THE eighth of the Ten Principles of the Arya Samaj points out to the Arya that he should endeavour "to diffuse knowledge and dispel ignorance." The Samaj as a body, and its members in their individual capacities, have accordingly been engaged in educational work of considerable importance. In the Punjab and the United Provinces its work, in extent and volume, is second to no other agency except the Government. Christian Missions maintain a large number of schools of all kinds, but no single mission can claim to have as many schools for boys and girls as the Arya Samaj.

On the side of boys' education it has two typical Colleges, one affiliated with the Government University, the other independent of official control.

1. *Dayananda Anglo-Vedic College at Lahore*

The educational aims of this institution may be gathered from its official reports. The first of these, now out of print, is a valuable document as giving the genesis of this important institution in the language of one of its principal founders, and we give two extracts therefrom. The following is the preamble, somewhat condensed, of a draft scheme circulated for public discussion before the institution was actually started:

" It will be conceded by all right-thinking minds that to secure the best advantages of education, it is necessary to make it national in tone and character. No doubt, speaking broadly, the primary aim of education is to develop the mental faculties, to invigorate them, and to practise them by proper and healthy exercise ; and education is said to be sound according as it achieves these ends. But, however true and incontrovertible this might be in the abstract, this single criterion of education is far from the true ideal of useful education. For it may be taken for granted, independently of theological considerations, that man lives, and ought to live, not for himself alone, but also for the good of the community in which he moves, and of which, by birth, locality, and antecedents, he is a member. This is termed his nationality. And as it is impracticable that every member of a nation should receive thorough education, it is peremptorily necessary, and absolutely desirable, that those who do receive education at the national cost, should receive it in a manner best suited to make them useful members of the community. In fact, the system of education should be

THE D.A.V. COLLEGE BUILDING.

so devised as to strengthen the ties which naturally bind individuals into a common nationality. On the other hand, it is equally clear that a process of education which tends to loosen these ties, or obstructs the beneficent influence of education from being fairly extended to, and beneficially operating upon, the uneducated, must be declared partial, and, from the public point of view, undesirable.

" A cursory view will show that the current system of education is open to this vital objection. The rush of foreign ideas, by the introduction of English literature into this country, has had, no doubt, the effect of enlightening and improving many thousand minds, of a few of whom the country may well feel proud. But foreign education has produced a schism in society which is truly deplorable. An educated class has been created—a class which moves by itself; a class incapable of materially influencing, or being influenced by, the uneducated masses; and a class without precedent in any country on the earth. This result, sad in itself, is the inevitable consequence of the one-sided policy of education imparted through a foreign agency, for whom it was simply impossible to appreciate the indigenous wants, and to apply a suitable method.

" But the mistake is not past remedy; there is still ample time to set matters right, did we but know how to use our opportunities. The reaction towards a national education is asserting itself everywhere, and the demand for the study of national literature is growing. This points out to us the remedy, namely, to make provision for the efficient study of the national language and literature, and carefully to initiate the youthful mind into habits and modes of life consistent with the national spirit and character. We are not unaware that there are at present institutions in the Punjab, as the Lahore Oriental College, which profess to give learned education in Sanskrit, but the education imparted in these institutions is as one-sided, and therefore as defective, as the education in the Government institutions which profess to give a thorough training through the medium of the English language. But, what is still more important, is that an all but exclusive attention is paid to the study of the degenerate period of Sanskrit literature. The classical period, wherein lie deep buried and crystallized the fruits of whole lives spent in secluded meditation on the nature of soul, of virtue, of creation, of matter, and, so far as can be vouchsafed to man, of the Creator, is entirely ignored in these institutions.

"Besides, no means exist at present in this country for imparting technical and practical education, which is so essential to its economic and material progress.

"Influenced by these important considerations we propose to establish an educational institution which will supply the shortcomings of the existing systems, and combine their advantages. The primary object will, therefore, be to weld together the educated and uneducated classes by encouraging the study of the national language and vernaculars; to spread a knowledge of moral and spiritual truths by insisting on the study of classical Sanskrit; to assist the formation of sound and energetic habits by a regulated mode of living; to encourage sound acquaintance with English literature; and to afford a stimulus to the material progress of the country by spreading a knowledge of the physical and applied sciences."[1]

We take the following also from the first report:

"The institutions of a nation are the best indexes and emblems of its intellectual progress. They not inaptly form so many stages along the path of a country's civilization. They are not the outcome of chance, but the deliberate consequences of intelligent causes incessantly moulding the destinies of a nation. The ways of Providence are truly said to be inscrutable; it is not within the power of every individual to trace the whole series of these causes; yet there occur events so prominent in character as to be remarked even by a superficial observer. Such an event was the appearance and public career of Swami Dayananda Saraswati. This great reformer, in the course of a few years, has revolutionized the intellectual and social thought of Hindu society. There is hardly a school of thought, hardly a social custom, which has not been affected by his preaching and writings.

"His was a power which has permeated Hindu life, and has created herein tendencies which have sprung up, and will spring up, into multitudinous institutions and movements that, in their turn, will continue to multiply, and influence the destiny of the nation for centuries onward. Important and prominent among these tendencies is the strong desire created by him in the public mind for an exploration of the treasures of classical Sanskrit. The accumulated ignorance of centuries had cast

[1] It should be remembered that this was written in 1885.

over them a thick veil of oblivion. It needed the power and persuasion of a preacher of Swami Dayananda Saraswati's calibre of mind and learning to direct public attention to this long forgotten but most precious heritage. The effect produced by this awakening was at once vehement. Partial attempts were made here and there, under the auspices of the Arya Samaj, by opening classes for teaching Sanskrit; but these were obviously inadequate and too isolated to satisfy the growing passion.

"While the agitation was daily gaining ground in the public mind, and before any practical steps could be undertaken on a sufficiently large scale, the founder was suddenly taken away from this world. His death, in 1883, cast a deep gloom over the face of hope and progress. But the interval of despair was temporary; despondency was soon dispelled by firm resolution, and his death instead of discouraging the movement, brought it redoubled vigour. It united with the movement a desire, as forcible and intense as the movement itself, for expressing public gratitude by some permanent commemoration of the great benefactor. The effect of this union of love and gratitude was irresistible. The necessity for giving practical shape to the movement for the study of the Vedas and classical Sanskrit could be no longer postponed. The result was that soon after Swamiji's death, the proposal to found the Dayananda Anglo-Vedic College Institution was simultaneously made in several places, notably at Ferozepur, Multan, and Lahore. It was publicly put forward at a meeting called by the Lahore Arya

Samaj on November 9th, 1883, and, as expected, was unanimously and enthusiastically adopted."

The following extract from the *Arya Patrika*, of June 20th, 1885, based on a contemporary published account, affords some idea of the importance of this meeting: "But the scene which presented itself in the subsequent public meeting held on November 9th (1883) was of an entirely different character. On this occasion the spirit of grief had given place to that of gratefulness, and the touch of enthusiasm seemed to reverberate through every nerve and heart. There was one united purpose that the glorious life of the departed Swami should be immortalized, and the proposal to found an Anglo-Vedic College in honour of his memory, was unanimously adopted. The sight that followed was worth observing. Though the meeting was composed mostly of middle-class men, from 7,000 to 8,000 rupees were subscribed on the spot. Women and children and even poor menials zealously came forward with their mite." The movement which was thus auspiciously and enthusiastically inaugurated at Lahore, soon spread itself throughout the Province, and identical resolutions were immediately adopted by other Samajes.

The objects of the Dayananda Anglo-Vedic College Institution, as recorded in the registered Memorandum of Association, are the following:

"1. To establish in the Punjab an Anglo-Vedic College Institution, which shall include a school, a College, and Boarding-house, as a memorial in honour of Swami Dayananda Saraswati, with the following joint purposes, viz.:

(*a*) To encourage, improve, and enforce the study of Hindu literature.

(*b*) To encourage and enforce the study of classical Sanskrit and of the Vedas.

(*c*) To encourage and enforce the study of English literature, and sciences both theoretical and applied.

"2. To provide means for giving technical education in connection with the Dayananda Anglo-Vedic College Institution as far as is not inconsistent with the proper accomplishment of the first object."

The enterprise was of an entirely novel character in this Province. At first there was cause for discouragement, not only in the apathy of the miserly and the prejudiced, but in the active counsel of those who thought the attempt impractical and destined to end in failure like other native enterprises. But it had been inaugurated to commemorate a man whose name and work could never die; and it was this auspicious connection, and the national character of the movement, which supported it at critical moments, and encouraged its promoters to tide over all difficulties.

These efforts and sacrifices might have ended in nothing but for the timely offer of a young man who agreed to give his time *free*. This young man, Lala Hansraj, had just graduated after a brilliant University career and had an equally bright future before him. The call of duty to religion and to the Motherland, however, proved too strong to be ignored, and he offered to serve the Institution as a teacher free of any remuneration, his elder brother agreeing to share his scanty salary with him. For the first two

L. HANSRAJ

years he served as Honorary Headmaster, and then for twenty-four years consecutively served as Honorary Principal.

This sacrifice made it possible for the promoters to open the first department of the College, *i.e.*, the school, in 1886. Lala Hansraj has ever since been the guiding star and mainstay of this Institution. In the interests of the College he has not spared himself in any way. His personality is unique in the history of the modern Punjab, the only other of whom we could speak in the same breath being Lala Munshi Ram, the founder of the Gurukula at Kangri. It is impossible to think of the Arya Samaj without these two names next to that of the great founder, Dayananda himself. It is equally impossible to think of the Dayananda Anglo-Vedic College without Lala Hansraj. There are other names worthy of remembrance as of those who have by their devotion and service contributed to the success of the College, one of them being the late Rai Bahadur Lala Lal Chand, once a judge of the Punjab Chief Court; but the one person among the founders, whose name will always occupy the first place in the respect of those who love the College, and whose name and life-work stands or falls with this College, is Lala Hansraj. While others have had other interests in life, professional, social, political or industrial, his sole concern has been the service of the D.A.V. College and the Arya Samaj. There may have been some others who have perhaps given the best in their life to this Institution, but he alone stands as one who has given *his all* for it. For fully twenty-eight years it has been the one object of his devotion. In his work he has met with all kinds of opposition, criticism, and misfortune. He has been misunderstood, misrepresented and maligned. His best friends have sometimes differed from him, but he has stood firm, leading a life of unique simplicity, of unostentatious poverty, of unassuming renunciation, and of singleminded devotion—a life irreproachable in private character and unique in public service.

The feeble seedling planted in 1886 by even more feeble hands, has, in the course of time, grown into a stately tree, and is at the present moment the biggest institution in Northern India, and probably the second in the whole of India, in point of numbers. The following extract from a speech delivered by the author in June last, at the Founder's Day celebration in London, will further explain the principles on which the Institution has been conducted, and its success.[1]

"I have already spoken of the main objects of the College: I wish now to say a word about the principles on which it was understood that it would be conducted. Some are embodied in the constitution, others are assumed. It was provided in the rules that the management should be in the hands of elected representatives of such Arya Samajes as contributed to its funds, with the addition of a few Hindus representing the professions and the classes; and that rule has been acted upon without exception. No non-Hindu has been associated with the management of the College.

"The second principle, nowhere recorded but

[1] We have preferred this form because of its being more impressive.—THE AUTHOR.

THE D.A.V. COLLEGE SCIENCE BLOCK.

generally accepted, was that the teaching should be exclusively done by Indians, and there has been no exception on this point. The College teaches Sanskrit, Hindi, English, Persian, Philosophy both eastern and modern, History, Political Economy, Logic, Elementary Physics, Chemistry, Elementary Botany, Elementary Biology, and Higher Mathematics. The results have been excellent. Our students have often headed the lists of ordinary passes, as well as honours passes, in Sanskrit and mathematics. They have several times headed the list in English, Political Economy, History, Philosophy, Chemistry, Persian, and other subjects. A good number of Government and University scholarships, granted on the results of University examinations, have every year been won by our students, and also medals and prizes. In the M.A. class we coach only in Sanskrit. All this has been achieved by the labours of Indian teachers, unaided by any foreign agency.

"The third principle (which also is an unwritten law) imposes on the managers the moral obligation not to seek monetary assistance from the Government. This principle has been acted upon, unless a petty grant of a few thousand rupees made by the University be considered an exception.

"The fourth principle was to aim at giving free education. The paucity of funds, and Government and University regulations, have prevented us from giving effect to this; but still our fees have generally been 50 per cent. less than those of Government schools and colleges.

"Now one word about the reasons for these principles. They were not adopted in any spirit of hostility or antagonism to the British, or the Government, or any other community. The object was firstly to try an experiment in purely indigenous enterprise; secondly, to develop a spirit of self-help and self-reliance in a community in which those qualities had, by lapse of time and want of opportunities, reached a low level. Everyone who knows the Punjab and can read the signs of the times, knows how well we have succeeded in this direction; probably no other province in India has developed private enterprise in education to the same extent and with the same success as we have in the Punjab. When I say "we" I include all classes, Hindus, Aryas, Brahmos, Sikhs, Muslims, and Indian Christians. This spirit of self-help, called exclusiveness by our critics, has cost us a great deal, because on that account we have always been under the shadow of official mistrust. No bureaucracy loves people who can do big things without their help and guidance; much less a foreign bureaucracy. They wish to keep the strings of all public activities in their own hands, or in the hands of those who can be used as tools. We set a different standard, and so we were disliked. Yet, on the whole, the attitude of the Department and the University towards us has not been unfair. They have generally given us credit for our work, and praised our public spirit, but they have never been happy with us. Once or twice when we sought their help to acquire land for a building site and playgrounds, they would not give it. Lately they have compulsorily acquired a piece of land, which we had secured with great trouble and after protracted litigation, and refused to give us one of the Government plots lying under our own walls. And this in spite of the fact that Lord Curzon's Universities Act brings all colleges, whether in receipt of Government grants or not, effectively under Government supervision. The University sends a sub-committee of its own for the annual inspection of the College, and the Government Inspectors regularly inspect the school. Their suggestions and recommendations have to be carried out almost in full, for fear of disaffiliation. But this only by the way. The general attitude of the Department and the University has been fair, though both have often been influenced in framing new regulations by the fact that our School and College were formidable rivals to the Government and aided institutions of similar nature.

"The School department was opened in June, 1886, and at once became popular. The College department was opened in June, 1889, and began with less than a dozen students. The popularity of the institution can be judged from the fact that on December 31st, 1913, we had 1,737 students in our School, and 903 in the College, besides a number in the purely Vedic department, in the faculty of Hindu medicine, in the engineering and tailoring classes.

"Yet we have managed to achieve all this with very scanty funds. The total funds of the College (including the cost value of its building property) amount to a little over a million rupees. The operations in 1886 commenced with less than forty thousand rupees, while no single donation has ever exceeded ten thousand rupees (about £700). Our success is mainly due to the spirit of self-sacrifice which has animated our workers. Until 1911, the Principal was an honorary worker. The present Principal is also practically honorary. He receives only £5 per month for his expenses, and so do some others.[1] The officers of the managing committee have always been honorary, and the investments of funds judicious. The University has, under the new regulations, compelled us to sink a large amount of our funds in buildings, which, as they stand, are splendid, stately, and adequate. For a number of years in the beginning we depended very largely on monthly subscriptions and other seasonal collections, etc., and we had to lodge ourselves in poor buildings.

"Yet I cannot help remarking that if Lord Curzon's educational policy had been in force when this College was proposed, it could not have come into existence at all. Thus we have every reason to congratulate ourselves on having started rather early and having succeeded so well. Let me add that we are not quite satisfied with what we have achieved. It is true we have popularized University education and turned out hundreds of graduates and thousands of other scholars, so much so that there is hardly any department of public and private activity in Upper India in which old D.A.V.'s are not to be found doing their part creditably and honourably. It is also true that we have given a great impetus to the study of Hindi and Sanskrit which stood very low in the Province when we started, and it is equally true that we have created an atmosphere of Hindu nationalism and developed a spirit of self-help and

[1] Lala Sain Dass, M.A. (Calcutta), B.Sc. (Cantab.), is the Principal. The others are Lala Diwan Chand, M.A. (Eng. and Philosophy, B. Ram Rattan, B.A., B.T., and Lala Mehar Chand, M.A.

THE GURUKULA BUILDING.

self-reliance among them; but when all has been said, we cannot say that we are very near the ideals that we set before us. Among the old D.A.V.'s, and men connected with the College, the Province has some of its best and most reliable public men; some of them have also done literary and journalistic work; others have been, and are, pioneering trades and industries; some hold high appointments under Government; others hold distinguished positions in the professions; yet we cannot say we have produced any high-class writers or scholars, nor have we so far been able to make any provision for original research.

"In the D.A.V. College we have a large number of resident students—697 in the College Department and an equally considerable number in the School department; but the discipline enforced and the life lived in the Gurukula at Kangri is more in accordance with genuine Hindu ideals than those in the College."

2. *The Gurukula*

This leads us directly to the other College which has been established and is being managed by the vegetarian section of the Samaj. Its origin is due to the same spirit of revolt which compelled Dayananda to leave his parental home and become a wanderer in quest of truth. The founders had originally taken part in the starting of the D.A.V. College, but within a few years they found that the system of education followed was not after their heart; that it did not come up to their ideal of Vedic education; that the managers cared more for University results than for sound national education; that the fact of its affiliation with the official University prevented them from making radical changes in the curriculum of studies, and materially interfered with their independence.

For a time they carried on an agitation aiming at radical changes in the Institution, but finding that the majority of those entrusted with the management were determined not to make such changes, they resolved to secede and go on their own way. At first they thought of concentrating all their energies on propaganda work, but soon found that the effective success of that work also required an educational seminary, embodying their ideals of education. The dominating idea was to give a good trial to the system of education propounded by Dayananda in his works. High proficiency in Vedic Sanskrit, and character building on Vedic lines were the objects of the scheme.

The following account of the aims of the Institution is in the words of the founder himself:

"The Gurukula is an educational institution founded with the avowed aim of reviving the ancient institution of Brahmacharya (continence), of rejuvenating and resuscitating ancient Indian philosophy and literature, conducting researches into the antiquities of India, of building up a Hindu literature incorporating into itself all that is best and assimilable in Occidental thought, of producing preachers of the Vedic religion and good citizens possessed of a culture compounded of the loftiest elements of the two civilizations which have made their home in this ancient land of sages and seers, and of retaining in a permanent form for the use of Humanity, the perennial features of the virile and vitalizing civilization of the ancient Aryans by moulding and shaping its institutions to suit the altered environments of the times. In an age wherein values are economic, the standard of respectability is wealth, and the tutelary goddess of worship is Worldly Success, it is difficult to understand that moral stamina cannot be strengthened, independence of character cannot be fostered, absolute rectitude and supreme righteousness cannot be made the dominant springs of action, and righteous incentives to conduct cannot be made operative in an atmosphere of luxury and bodily comfort. One cannot fight manfully the temptations that beset a man of character at every step in his progress towards the goal of life, if he has not learnt to sacrifice mere bodily comfort and luxurious living at the altar of principle. And this no one can do who has not led a hardy life in his juvenile age and who cannot at a moment's notice renounce the pleasures of the flesh without a pang or a sigh of regret."

I give an account of its history, progress, and success in the language of an American visitor, Mr. Myron Phelps of America, whose letters on the subject were published in the *Pioneer*, the most influential Anglo-Indian daily of North India, and have been republished in pamphlet form by the founder himself as containing a true account of the Institution.

About the history of the Institution, Mr. Phelps says:

"The Gurukula was established in 1902, chiefly

through the efforts of the present Principal and Governor, Mr. Munshi Ram, formerly a successful pleader of Jullundher. Mr. Munshi Ram was by nature an earnest and devout man. He became a member of the Arya Samaj in 1885. How the Gurukula came to be started will be best stated in his own words :

"'It is all suggested,' he said to me, 'in Swami Dayananda's book, *Sattyarath Prakash.* The Dayananda Anglo-Vedic College of Lahore was started in 1885 to carry out his idea. A difference of opinion arose as to whether English science, or the Vedas, should be given first place in the school. This was in 1891. Up to that time we had all worked for the College.

"'I was among those who thought that the true spirit of the religious reform which we all had at heart could only be carried out with the help of a school primarily devoted to re-establishing the principles and authority of the Vedas in the lives of men. Those who held the view that English and science were the most important, declared that the rest of us were religious fanatics and debarred us from the management of the College. Then we turned our energies into the line of preaching the religion. In time we keenly felt the necessity of a school. I wished one for the education of my two sons, and secured the co-operation of thirteen others to establish it. Our object was a school where strong religious character could be built up on the basis of pure Vedic instruction. We recognized two great wants of the people—men of character and religious unity—and we set out to do what we could to supply these wants.

MAHATMA MUNSHI RAM

Our primary aim is simply to give our boys the best moral and ethical training it is possible to give them—to make of them good citizens and religious men, and to teach them to love learning for learning's sake. Our model is the great universities of ancient India, such as that of Taxilla, near Rawalpindi, where thousands of students congregated, and which were supported, as were also the students who attended them, by the munificence of the State and wealthy citizens.

"'The managing committee of the Samaj (that is, of our section of the Samaj; there had been a split, caused not, as some have said, by questions as to meat-eating, but by the educational difference) soon after took up our scheme. They authorized the starting of a Gurukula when Rs.30,000 should be subscribed and Rs.8,000 paid in. The project hung fire for some months, then I went out myself to raise the money. I was not satisfied with Rs.8,000, and secured Rs.30,000 in cash in a short time. Then we started it.

"'I was not at that time engaged in active business, having retired a short time before from the practice of Law, finding it uncongenial, and not having yet taken any other avocation. I, therefore, had some leisure to give to the Gurukula, and found myself insensibly drawn into its permanent management.

"'While I was searching for a suitable spot we were offered the gift of a large tract of land (900 acres), chiefly jungle, three miles below Hardwar. We examined it, and found its location and character satisfactory, and it has proved all that we desired.'"

About its work and strength Mr. Phelps says:

"There are now in the Institution 274 boys,[1] of whom fourteen are in the College, and 260 in the ten classes of the school. The boys when entering are usually of the age of seven or eight years. They are taken with the understanding that they are to remain sixteen years. On entering, the boys take a vow of poverty, chastity, and obedience for sixteen years, and this vow they renew at the end of the tenth year. The pupils are not allowed to visit their homes during this long period of training, except under exceptional and urgent circumstances, nor can their relations come to the school oftener than once a month. Usually they come about twice a year. The Gurukula authorities are thus given control of all the influences tending to form the character of the boys.

"The discipline is strict, though at the same time parental, personal, and even tender in its mode of application. The boys are under constant supervision both during and outside school hours. There are, beside the teachers, thirteen superintendents who are with the boys at all times when the latter are not actually in the schoolrooms. The boys forming classes or sections of a class live together in large rooms, in each of which also lives a superintendent.

"The whole school is pervaded by an atmosphere of affectionate familiarity and mutual confidence, which characterizes the relations of the pupils with each other, and with the teachers and the superintendents. This feeling finds its strongest expression

[1] There are now over 300.

towards the Governor, Mr. Munshi Ram. All teachers, officials, and pupils alike, speak of him with special reverence and affection, and evidently feel for him the sentiments of a son for a father.

"When I first came to the Gurukula Mr. Munshi Ram outlined to me the aim of the management as regards the relations which they have sought to establish among those in the community. 'The feeling is cultivated,' he said, 'that all are members of the same family—brethren. The boys are taught to share all their pleasures with their comrades, and to seek no enjoyment that cannot be so shared. Even when their parents come here the boys will not accept individual presents from them. If an apple were offered they would say, "you must give me a box, so that they may go round." This is not merely an idea or a pious hope with us; it is an accomplished fact exemplified in the actual relations of the boys with us and with each other. They are ready to make great sacrifices for each other. If one of their number is sick, they nurse him by turns at night. They will do anything—any sort of repulsive work required by nursing—for their brothers. Except in an out of the way place like this, this idea could not have been carried out.'

"The Governor receives no pay, and has given all his property, between Rs.30,000 and Rs.40,000, to the school. Some of the best of the teachers have promised their services for life at a salary which is no more than a living allowance.[1] A resolution was taken by the Board of Control to abolish all charges for board and lodging, tuition having been free from

[1] The same as in the D.A.V. College.

the beginning, thus bringing the institution into line with the policy of the entirely free ancient universities.[1] . . .

"Taking up now in detail the discipline of the school, the rising gong is sounded at 4 a.m. for all except several of the youngest classes, which are given an hour's longer sleep. First goes a procession of white and ghost-like figures to the jungle, shortly it returns, and half an hour is then given to dumb-bell exercises and other calisthenics. Many of the younger boys take a sharp run. The next half hour, from 5 to 5.30, is allowed for bathing, either in the Ganges or the bath-house as each boy prefers, and completing the toilet. Next follows the morning worship. This consists of Sandhya, a prayer, silently and individually offered, and the agnihotra, a fire oblation made by the boys in groups. Sandhya is the mental repetition, with closed eyes, of a number of Sanskrit verses, and occupies about twelve minutes. . . .

"All the boys next assemble to listen to and take part in a conversation with the Governor on some moral or ethical subject. This occupies half or three-quarters of an hour.

"A little light food, usually milk or nuts, is then distributed. Two hours of study follow. At 8.45 the morning meal is taken. The school boys assemble in two dining-halls, the college boys and the Governor mess by themselves. The food is plain but substantial and well prepared, consisting of wheat chapaties, dal, a vegetable, and curd. About

[1] Paucity of funds has made it necessary to reimpose a small fee for board.

GURUKULA BOYS PERFORMING *HOMA*.

half an hour's rest follows the meal, frequently spent in the large garden adjoining the school buildings.

"From 9.45 to 4.15 are the school hours of the day—that is during the colder half of the year. The summer programme is not quite the same. An intermission of half an hour occurs soon after mid-day, during which the pupils are given milk or other light refreshment. From 4.15 to 4.45 the boys are left to themselves. From 4.45 to 5.30 is the play hour, when football, cricket, base-ball, and Indian games are played. Regular participation in these games is required of all students.

"Between 5.30 and 6 another bath is taken, usually in the river. The Ganges at this point is a swift flowing stream with remarkably pure and cold water. Only a portion of the river flows near the Gurukula, and of that the depth is not sufficient to occasion danger to bathers.

"From 6 to 6.30 Sandhya and agnihotra are again performed as in the morning. Then follows the evening meal, which is substantially a repetition of that in the morning. A little later comes an hour's study. All retire to rest at 9, with this exception, that the college boys are allowed lights until 10. This is the programme of every day except holidays. The latter occur four times in each lunar month. There are also about twenty other holidays during the year, and long vacation covering the months of August and September. During the vacation, and sometimes on holidays, the boys take excursions into the mountains, and are taken by the Professors on tours in various parts of India."

The following about moral and religious instruction is taken from another letter :

" Moral and ethical instruction is regular, and extends over the whole ten years of the school course. In the earlier years a large number of helpful Sanskrit verses are memorized by the student. Then follow three text-books, published by the Gurukula, made up of selections from the Manu Smriti, than which, as is well known, there is no more fruitful source of sound moral instruction. Appropriate parts of Swami Dayananda's works are also used. To these subjects three to seven periods per week are given. The ninth and tenth classes also receive daily religious instruction from the Governor, and, still more, the boys are assembled, as has been said, each morning for a talk with him on moral and ethical subjects.

" The moral and religious character of the student is further powerfully stimulated and developed by the study of the Sanskrit sacred literature, to which a large proportion of each of the sixteen years of the course is given. The atmosphere of the Gurukula may be said to be saturated with the Vedas and Upanishads."

About the scheme of studies, Mr. Phelps remarks :

" With all the attention the Gurukula gives to the Vedas and other sacred books it is the aim of the management to make it a first-class institution for the study of Western literature and modern science. The full development of this part of the scheme has, however, hitherto been impossible for want of adequate funds. But the effort has been made to keep the school up to the requirements of the pupils who are still for the most part in the lower classes, and, in this, measurable success has been attained. There is nothing antiquated or insular about the methods of instruction employed, and the range of study and reading is wide and liberal. English is begun in the sixth year and is compulsory during the following eight years, and as most of the teachers have a good command of English the boys of the college classes have acquired considerable facility in its use. They have, therefore, the mental equipment for keeping in touch with the thought and activities of the world, and it is the aim of the management to see that they do so. They have had installations of the telephone and wireless telegraphy in the laboratory. The library is fairly large and well chosen, and the reading room is supplied with a number of Anglo-Indian and Indian dailies as well as magazines. The curriculum includes Plato, Mill, Herbert Spencer, Jevons, Fowler, Stock, and Welton in logic; James and Ladd in psychology; Flint's Theism; Muirhead's Ethics; Marshall, Nicholson, Keynes, and Seligman in economics; Seeley, Gardiner, and Oman in English history; Bluntschli's State and Alston's Constitution. On the private library shelves of college students I noticed such authors as Bacon, Locke, Goethe, Emerson, Martineau, Mallock, Sir Oliver Lodge, and in these volumes work was attested by abundant underscorings.

"In science, the boys passing from the tenth class, which corresponds with the matriculation class of other institutions, have several years' advantage over the latter. They have completed Wright's and Jones' text-books of physics and

Furneaux and Jago's chemistries, and have had two years' instruction in mechanics, whereas other arts matriculants have commonly only studied these subjects in primers. For two years they have had lectures on political economy, of which the others have had nothing. Those who have wished have had instruction in carpentry and the elements of agriculture. Students in agriculture are required each to cultivate a plot of ground under the supervision of a graduate of an American agricultural college. In mathematics, the tenth year Gurukula boys are about on a par with the ordinary matriculant, having studied arithmetic, algebra up to quadratic equations, and eleven books of Euclid. In history their reading has covered a far wider range than is usual with boys of their age. They have had 1,000 to 2,000 pages of Indian and English history, whereas the usual amount read by students of their grade is 300 or 400 pages. They may fairly be said to have reached the ordinary B.A. standard in this subject. In English they are somewhat behind in the tenth class, but do not seem to be materially so in the fourteenth class, which is the highest now in the school. In Sanskrit they are far advanced. As it is the first language of the school, comparison should be made with the proficiency of other students in the first language of other schools, *i.e.*, English. It is said that tenth year boys are as well acquainted with Sanskrit as most M.A.'s are with English. They read, write, and speak Sanskrit with ease. I have myself attended these clubs, meetings, and heard Sanskrit spoken fluently by both school and college boys. This experience is quite impressive as indicating the efficiency of the instruction in this language. There are six essay and debating clubs in which Sanskrit is spoken, three in which English is spoken, and one conducted in Hindi, all of these being above the fifth class of the school. In and below the fifth class there are other language exercises of a similar character.

" Tenth year boys have also given much time to Indian philosophy and logic. As to the vernacular, that used here being Hindi, of course the Gurukula students have far better knowledge of it than those of other schools, since it is the only usual medium of instruction, both in school and college classes. I was told by a professor who has compared the language of essays and speeches given here on special occasions with that heard at Hindu Conferences, that the former is far superior to the latter. The age of the tenth year boy is 17 to 18, which is about one year higher than the average age of other matriculants.

" So far as I can gather, the boy at the end of the tenth year of the Gurukula is at least on a par in intellectual equipment with the student who has reached the F.A. standard in other colleges. This advantage is no doubt partly due to the much more favourable conditions for study which he enjoys, viz.: quiet and natural surroundings, pure air, sufficient exercise (which is here compulsory), and the greatest regularity of life. Contrast this with the cramped and congested city surroundings of most Indian college boys, their habitual neglect of exercise, and their utter irregularity of life, frequently working as they do far into the night, or all night before examinations—for Indian students really work with great intensity at times, habits which frequently so impair their health as to leave them quite unfit for the serious work of life.

"The advantage of a Gurukula student is due in a still greater degree to the fact that instruction is imparted to him in his own language, and is therefore readily understood and assimilated. The use of Hindi as a medium of instruction is one of the features of the school which is regarded as exceedingly important."

Why the Gurukula does not invite Government aid and why it is held in suspicion is further explained:

"From what has been said in previous letters it will be readily seen why it is impossible for the Gurukula to invite Government co-operation, that is, to submit to Government supervision as an aided school. This would mean, in the first place, that Sanskrit must be displaced in favour of English, as the first language of the school. Thereby the primary object of the instruction, which is to secure for the students a thorough grounding in Sanskrit and Vedic learning, would be given a secondary place. The general character of the institution in respect to the instruction which it imparts would be reversed. In the next place the use of Hindi as a medium of instruction is a feature of the school regarded as essential to sound education, but which Government rules for aided schools would not permit. Thirdly, the school to a large extent uses its own text-books, which are found essential to its work, and which the regular system would exclude in favour of standard text-books. Finally, were the school recognized, the courses of study in the work of the institution would necessarily be subject to the usual University examinations, which, for the reasons stated above, are considered destructive of good educational results.

"It ought, therefore, to cause no surprise, and should be no ground for suspicion that the school does not seek recognition or aid from the Government. Its aims and methods are so radically different from those which govern the regular educational system that it cannot do otherwise than stand alone.

"Nevertheless, since its object is one which all good men approve, since its methods are so unexceptionable, and since it does not draw upon the resources of the State, it would seem that it ought to have the encouragement and approval of the Government. These, however, it is said that it does not receive, and I have myself had reason to observe that it is regarded with suspicion.

"The complaint is also made that the Government is not open with the Gurukula. Officials assure the management, it is said, that no fault is found with it, that there is nothing against it, while from other sources reports constantly come to their ears that men high in authority speak of the institution as a breeder of anarchy and a source of danger to the State.

"It is believed that misrepresentations of the institution have been made to the Government both by Mahomedans and by Christian missionaries. The latter particularly, having ready access to those in authority, are credited on grounds more substantial than mere suspicion, it is said, with a good deal of responsibility for the false impression. I have myself known of Christian missionary statements being quoted as authority by a Government official against both the Gurukula and the Arya Samaj, which statements I am satisfied were outrageous slanders. Then there are many Mahomedans in the detective service, and it would be doing a violence to our knowledge of the characteristics of human nature to believe that their reports can be unbiassed. Some light was thrown on the character of these reports by a district official, who visited the Gurukula some little time ago, and talked freely with the staff. He said that he had been told that the school was only a blind, and that more of the time was spent there in physical exercises and military drill; but he only said this after examining the muscles of some of the boys and so satisfying himself that their development was not abnormal."

These suspicions were first articulated by Mr. (now Sir) Valentine Chirol in his articles on modern Indian unrest in the (London) *Times*. In the article on "The Punjab and the Arya Samaj," he observed:

"What makes the question of the real tendencies of the Arya Samaj one of very grave importance for the future is that it has embarked upon an educational experiment of a peculiar character which may have an immense effect upon the rising generation."

Then follows a brief account of the Gurukulas (as there are more than one) and the life lived therein, with the following conclusion:

"As the Chelas after sixteen years of the monastic training at the hands of the Gurus are to be sent out as missionaries to propagate the Arya Samaj doctrines throughout India, the influence of these institutions in the moulding of Indian character and Indian life in the future cannot fail to be considerable. Some five years more must elapse before we shall be able to judge the result by the first batch of Chelas who will then be going forth into the world."

Happily those five years have elapsed, and the first two batches of graduates of the Gurukula at Hardwar have now been before the public for some time, and nothing untoward has happened.

On the other hand the authorities have put themselves into closer touch with the institution, and the present Lieutenant-Governor of the Province, Sir James Meston, has declared it to be an "ideal educational institution." The first time he visited it, in 1913, he said (March 6th, 1913):

"The Gurukula is one of the most original and interesting experiments carried on in these provinces, in fact in the whole of India. One of the most wonderful, interesting, and stimulating institutions; we have a band of ascetics devoted to their duty, and working in the wilderness following the traditions of the ancient Rishis, combined with the most modern scientific methods, and working practically for nothing, and a set of students of strong physique, obedient, loyal, thoughtful, devoted, extraordinarily happy, and extraordinarily well fed."

In the course of his speech he explained that one of the reasons for his visit was that "he wanted to meet a community which had been described in official papers as a source of infinite, terrible, and unknown danger." The right answer to this, he added, "was to come myself." Sir James Meston has since then repeated his visit to the Gurukula, and has laid the foundation stone of a sister institution at Mathura, where in the course of his speech he paid a high tribute to Lala Munshi Ram, the founder of the Kangri Gurukula, and affirmed that the Arya Samaj was not a political body.

We do not think we need add anything further to what Mr. Phelps has said about the sacrifice and devotion of the founder of the Gurukula and his fellow workers in the cause. Lala Munshi Ram has a magnetic personality, unique in its own way, which attracts kindred souls to him, and creates an atmosphere of noble ambitions and pure disinterested service.

Besides these two colleges, the Arya Samaj have founded and are maintaining a large number of boys' schools, Primary and Secondary, *Gurukulas* and *Pátshálás*. A good many of these are high-class educational institutions, and are being carried on at a great cost, and with a great deal of self-sacrifice.

For the education of girls the Arya Samaj maintains a college, and a large number of girls' schools, both Primary and Secondary. The college is at Jullundher, Punjab, and is called the Kanya Mahávidyálá. It has a very large boarding-house attached to it where girls and lady students live in charge and under the supervision of Indian lady teachers. It is a very successful institution and a monument of the public spirit and zeal of its founder, Lala Deva Raja of Jullundher. Among the subjects taught are Music, Domestic Economy, Cooking, Needlework, English, Sanskrit, Hindi, History, Geography, Mathematics, Political Economy, etc. For the school department they have compiled their own series of readers. Hindi is the medium of instruction. The institution receives no aid from the Government.

CHAPTER VI

PHILANTHROPIC ACTIVITIES

पृणीयादिन्नाधमानाय तव्यान्द्राघीयांसमनु पश्येत पन्थाम् । ओ हि वर्तन्ते रथ्येव चक्रान्यमन्यमुप तिष्ठन्त रायः ॥ ७ ॥

ऋ० १० । ११७ । ५

"No friend is he who offers nothing to his friend and comrade who comes imploring food."

—R. X., 117, 4.

1. *Philanthropic work*

BESIDES its religious and educational propaganda the Arya Samaj engages in philanthropic work on a large scale. Outside Christian circles it was the first purely Indian Association to organize Orphanages and Widow Homes. The first Hindu orphanage was established at Ferozepur, in the Punjab, in the lifetime of the Founder of the Samaj; it still retains its position as the premier Hindu orphanage in India, has splendid and commodious buildings, all erected by private charity, and maintains schools and workshops for the training of boys and girls. There are a number of other orphanages on similar lines in Northern India, controlled and managed by the Arya Samaj; and, besides these, many Hindu institutions and orphanages spread over India bear the impress and influence of the Arya Samaj, and owe their birth and efficiency to Arya Samajists.

2. *Famine Relief in* 1897-8 *and* 1899-1900

India has been described as a land of famines. During the last twenty years alone we have had about ten famines, of which no less than five were both intense and widespread. Famines in India are due ostensibly to the failure of the rains, but in reality to the inability of the Indian ryot and labourer to purchase food at enhanced prices. In normal years India produces foodstuffs in such quantities that, were there no exportation, one year's produce would suffice to feed her population for several years. In order to get better prices, foodstuffs are largely exported every year, not only in normal years, but even in famine years. In 1899-1900, when the country was suffering from one of the severest famines of the century, millions of hundredweights of wheat were exported to foreign countries; in 1877-78, when 5,220,000 persons died of hunger, 16,000,000 cwt. of rice were exported from the Calcutta port only. The fact is that the bulk of the population lives in chronic poverty. A single year's failure of seasonal rainfall results in an abnormal rise of prices and throws millions of men out of employment. This general poverty of the people is the real cause of Indian famine and explains the frequency of famine conditions.

The Arya Samaj was the first non-Christian private agency which started a non-official movement for the relief of distress caused by famine. The writer of this book was among the first organizers, and the following facts taken from a report which he prepared after the famine of 1899-1900 may be of interest. In the first two famines dealt with by the Arya Samaj, the movement was confined to orphan relief, and was called the Hindu Orphan Relief Movement. This was started in February, 1897, for the relief of Hindu children left destitute in the famine of 1896-97. Appeals for help, issued under the auspices of the Arya Samaj, were liberally responded to by the Hindu community generally, and by the members and sympathizers of the Arya Samaj in particular. About 250 Hindu children were rescued by agents deputed by the movement and were brought into the Punjab, where four new orphanages were founded to accommodate them, in addition to that already existing at Ferozepur.

The failure of the rains in 1899 brought about another famine, which it was clear from the very outset was likely to be more disastrous than its predecessor. Moreover, the people had hardly had time to recover from the effects of the scarcity of 1897. By October, 1899, the pinch began to be felt severely in Rajputana, the Central Provinces, Bombay, Kathiawar, and portions of the Punjab. It was, therefore, resolved to revive the orphan relief movement and to push it on vigorously so as to be able to render help to as large a number of children as it might be possible to rescue. The Lahore Arya Samaj lost no time in acting upon this resolve, and deputed one of its younger members (a senior student of the Dayananda Anglo-Vedic College, and Secretary of the local Young Men's Arya Samaj) to go to Rajputana and ascertain on the spot in what way and to what extent they could render help, and whether it was possible to enlist local sympathy in their cause in the famine-stricken parts themselves. On this mission Lala Dewan Chand Chaddha travelled to Jodhpur, and stayed at many places (amongst them Kishangarh, Ajmere, Beawar, Pali, etc.) to see the famine relief camps. He spent altogether a month in Rajputana, and on his return gave a graphic and touching account of his experiences which brought tears to many eyes and moved almost the whole of Lahore to immediate and vigorous action for the help of the unfortunate Hindu waifs and orphans of Rajputana.

In several Native States our agents waited upon high officials, and tried to impress upon them their duty towards the orphans and other destitute children of their territories, explaining how necessary it was, in the interests of the States, to keep the children upon their own soil and to protect them in that trying period, not only from death by starvation, but also from being carried to distant places for conversion to alien faiths.

The missionaries were fighting a noble battle, and it was not for us to start an agitation against them in Rajputana ; nor had we the means and strength to do so even had we the mind to try. We made no secret of our concern at the conversion of a large number of our co-religionists to an alien faith, and we tried to arouse attention to it here and there ; but we soon found that this negative work alone would not suffice, and that it was not likely to bear fruit, even in Native States, much less in British territory. To save even a few hundreds, we must be prepared to bring them to the Punjab, where they were sure to find sufficient food and clothing to keep them going till the end of the famine. But the Punjab was at this time itself in need of help, as some portions of it were seriously affected by the famine, and the Punjabi children could not be neglected in favour of the little ones from Rajputana. So we called upon the Hissar Arya Samaj to organize an orphan relief movement for their own as well as the neighbouring districts. The British Government, having made fairly good provision for British subjects in these parts, much was not required of us ; but we were bound to help the Hindu orphans of our own province, because, notwithstanding the efforts of the Government, there were still some who required outside assistance to save them from starvation or conversion.

In this relief of distress in our own province, valuable work was done by the Hissar Arya Samaj and the Bhiwani Hindu Orphanage. Led by the late Lala Chandu Lal, the President, and Lala Churamani, their secretary, they relieved hundreds of children and fought a noble battle against death and misery. For Rajputana children we addressed representations and memorials to the Commissioner of Ajmere, Merwárá, to the Agent of the Governor-General, Rajputana, and to the Deputy Commissioner of Beawar ; but elicited no replies. Our agents again and again applied personally to the local officers in charge of the famine relief camps, but met with no success, although we have reason to believe that large numbers of Hindu children were, from time to time, handed over to Christian missionaries and by them sent to distant places in India. In Bombay, our agents travelled as far as Surat and Baroda, and tried to arouse the Hindu public to a sense of their duty towards the little ones of their community, who, in their distress, needed their help and sympathy. We have reason to believe that these visits of our agents, and their readiness to take charge of as many children as might be entrusted to them, had their effect ; so that although, notwithstanding repeated applications to collectors, commissioners, and other famine officials, and notwithstanding the favourable orders of some among them, we did not succeed in getting any orphans from Bombay, we had the satisfaction of knowing that we had left no stone unturned to prove as useful to Bombay as we could. The reasons for our failure to get children from Government famine relief works need not be set forth in detail, the most important being that the missionaries were everywhere too strong for us.

Similarly we carried on a successful campaign in Kathiawar, the Central Province, and parts of Bombay, and succeeded in rescuing altogether about 1,700 children. For their protection and training we opened several new orphanages in the Punjab, some of which were only temporary shelters. All classes of the Hindu community, without distinction of caste or creed, helped us in this undertaking, and the movement proved a blessing in more ways than one. It brought unity into the ranks of the Hindus. It brought the educated into touch with the masses, creating new ties of sympathy between them. It opened new problems which required the community to rely on their own energies and resources. It put them into healthy and stimulating rivalry with powerful missionary organizations working in the same field. It opened fresh and untried ground for training Hindu youths in methods of social service. And last, but not least, it enabled them to make several experiments in reviving indigenous industries by the aid of cheap time-saving machinery within reach of modest means. Some of these industries were started to give employment to the orphans. All the girls rescued in 1897-8 and 1899-1900 have been suitably married and almost invariably to men of higher castes than their own.

The movement at last received recognition from the Government, some children also were handed over to the different orphanages established under its auspices, and some small financial help was given at the end of the famine from the unused balance of the non-official famine fund.

The report ended thus :

" Thanks to the Almighty whose grace and mercy was our main support in this difficult work, and who sustained our efforts throughout this year of difficulties and misfortunes. The best acknowledgments of the Hindu community are due to those young men (most of our agents were young and honorary) who risked their lives in this noble undertaking, because it was no easy matter to travel in search of orphans in Rajputana and the Central Provinces, where not only was there a terrible scarcity of food and water, but where cholera and fever were raging. Conceive of a young Punjabi Hindu travelling on camels day and night in search of orphans in tracts devastated by famine, where neither good food nor wholesome water was to be had for miles and miles together.

Add to this the fear of pestilence and the anxiety of having left behind wives and children. Add also their anxiety to spend as little as possible on their own comfort, with the knowledge that the funds at their disposal and at the disposal of those who had deputed them were so small as to make economy a strict necessity. Yes, blessed are those who faced all these privations boldly and worked under these difficulties with a religious sense of duty to help the little ones of their community in the time of dire calamity.

"But still more blessed are those who paid for their own bread and did not spend even a pie of public money on their own food. Personally my gratefulness to them is indescribable. They have earned the everlasting gratitude of their people by setting such a good and noble example of self-sacrifice to the other members of the rising generation. Let us hope that these services are an earnest of what may be expected of them in the future. This record of their work is a magnificent ray in the sunshine of Hindu revival, to which we all look with hope and pleasure."

3. *Famine Relief in* 1908

In 1908, however, the movement was expanded and general relief was aimed at. The following extract from the *Census Report* of the United Provinces of Agra and Oude for 1911 will give some idea of the extensive scale on which work was done during the famine :—

"The emissary of a well known Arya leader came round distributing relief during the famine of 1907-8 and visited a certain village near which I had

FAMINE-STRICKEN ORPHANS SAVED BY THE ARYA SAMAJ

encamped. After his visit, *the recipients of his bounty, being not quite sure whether they were doing right in accepting private charity when Government was looking after them*, sent a deputation to ask me whether they might keep his gifts. I, of course, told them to take all they could get; and then their leader asked me who was the man (the Arya leader) who was distributing money in this wholesale way."[1]

4. *Social Service*

The philanthropic work of the Arya Samaj is not, however, confined to famine relief, but includes various kinds of *social service*. In times of pestilence it organizes medical relief, nursing the sick, and helping in the disposal of the dead. At the time of the great earthquake in the Kangra Valley in 1904 it organized relief on a large scale for the sufferers, and earned the thanks of the people and the Government. In this calamity the Arya Samajists were the first to reach the afflicted area. This example has, within recent years, been largely followed by other organizations, and there is now a network of social service agencies throughout India, due mainly to the contact of the East with the West, and to the example of Christian missionary enterprise. Ancient India had no use for these organizations, as social life was differently constituted; but modern India cannot do without them, and they have grown up to meet the need. The Arya Samaj was the pioneer in starting this social service work in an organized form and on a large scale, at least in Northern India.

[1] He evidently referred to me as the head of the Arya relief movement. The italics are mine.—L. R.

CHAPTER VII

SHUDDHI WORK OF THE ARYA SAMAJ

अर्यम्यं वरुण मित्र्यं वा सखायं वा सदमिद्भ्रातरं वा ।
वेशं वा नित्यं वरुणारणं वा यत्सीमागश्चकृमा शिश्रथस्तत्
॥ १० ॥ ऋ० ५ । ८५ । ७ ।

"If we have sinned against the man who loves us, have ever wronged a brother, friend or comrade, have ever done an injury to the neighbour who ever dwelt with us, or even to a stranger, O Lord! free us from the guilt ot this trespass."

—R. V., 85, 7.

I. *Reclamation and Conversion*

LITERALLY, *Shuddhi*[1] means purification, but when used by Arya Samajists it includes also reclamation and conversion. The Arya Samaj, being a Vedic church, and as such a Hindu organization, engages in the work of reclaiming those who have left Hindu society, and it converts everyone who is prepared to accept its religious teachings. In this work it comes

[1] "*Shuddhi* is a Sanskrit word which means purification. In religious terminology it is now applied to (1) Conversion to Hinduism of persons belonging to foreign religions, (2) Re-conversion of those who have recently, or at a remote period, adopted one of the foreign religions, and (3) Reclamation, *i.e.*, raising the status of the depressed classes." (Punjab *Census Report* for 1911, p. 148.)

into direct conflict with the proselytizing work of the Musulman *Mullah* and the Christian missionary; the Musulman fanatic and the Christian zealot hate it, but even the sober-minded moulvie and the broad-minded Christian do not like it. Yet it has met with considerable success in reclaiming Hindus converted to other faiths, and in stemming the tide of conversion. But its greatest success lies in raising the social status of the depressed classes among the Hindus and preventing them from leaving Hinduism and joining other religious denominations. About the reconversions the Census Commissioner of the United Provinces of Agra and Oude remarks: " Special efforts are directed to the reconversion of converts from Hinduism to Christianity or Islam, while persons who are Christian or Mahomedan by birth are also occasionally converted."

" . . . of such Mahomedan converts I have myself known at least one case, and others have occurred. There is a society affiliated to the Arya Samaj, which is known as the Rajput Shuddhi Sabha, which has as its chief object the reconversion of Mahomedan Rajputs to Hinduism via the Arya Samaj. On a single day 370 such Rajputs were converted to Aryaism. In three years, between 1907 and 1910, this society claims to have converted 1,052 Musulman Rajputs."[1]

2. *Ceremony of Conversion*

Another Census Commissioner of the same province (Mr. Burn, I.C.S.) says that " the ceremony of

[1] *Census Report for U.P. for* 1911, p. 134. Mr. Udey Vir Singh, Barrister-at-Law, Aligarh, is the secretary of this Sabha.

conversion is simple. The would-be Arya lives on milk alone for a period of fifteen days,[1] this being known as the *Chandrain birt.* The admission into the Samaj is made the occasion of a public meeting, at which the convert declares his adherence to the ten principles of the Samaj, a great *homa* sacrifice is performed, passages from the Vedas are recited, and the convert distributes sweetmeats to those present."[2] In some cases a certificate of *Shuddhi* is issued, which facilitates social intercourse with Hindus.

3. *Depressed Classes*

But the greatest interest is being taken in the social uplifting of the lower castes ; this reclamation is taking two distinct lines : (1) the raising of the status of castes not entitled to wear the sacred thread, by admitting them to that privilege ; and (2) raising the untouchables to the rank of touchables, and educating them to higher social ideals, with a view to eventually raising them to social equality with other Hindus. This work is done by the Arya Samajes as such, as well as by special organizations supported by the Arya Samaj and affiliated, directly or indirectly, to the latter.

Two years ago the author delivered a speech on this subject as President of a large Conference, at the anniversary of the Gurukula at Hardwar, and discussed the question from three standpoints : from the point of view of the Hindu community ; as a question of all-Indian importance ; and in its humanitarian bearing. Discussing it from the all-

[1] It has now been reduced to three days.

[2] *Census Report* for 1901, page 87.

India point of view, he said : " It is to be remembered that national decline has its origin in the oppression of others, and if we Indians desire to achieve national self-respect and dignity, we should open our arms to our unfortunate brothers and sisters of the depressed classes and help to build up in them the vital spirit of human dignity. So long as we have these large classes of the untouchables in this country we can make no real progress in our national affairs, for this requires a high moral standard ; and this is unthinkable where the weaker classes are unfairly treated. No man may build his greatness on his brother's weakness ; man shall stand or fall by his own strength."

As recently as December last the author again discussed the subject, as the President of another large Conference of the same nature at Karachi (Sindh). In the course of this speech he remarked that " the cause of the depressed classes combines in it the best of religion, the best of humanity, and the best of nationalism ; that it is a cause worthy of the best energies and the most strenuous efforts of a large number of India's daughters and sons, such as believe that ' Life is a mission and duty its highest Law,' and that the best fulfilment of that duty lies in the service and uplifting of those whom human tyranny and prejudices have put out of the pale of humanity, and who are unfortunately the victims of the idea that they deserve no better fate."

" In my opinion," continued the speaker, " no greater wrong can be done to a human being endowed with intellect than to put him into circumstances which make him believe that he is eternally doomed to a life of ignorance, servitude, and misery, and that in him any sort of ambition for his betterment is a sin.

" No slavery is more harmful than that of mind, and no sin is greater than to keep human beings in perpetual bondage. It is bad enough to enslave people, but to create and perpetuate circumstances which prevent them from breaking their chains and becoming free, is infamous. No man or number of men have a right to do this, and they deserve the severest condemnation of all who have a conscience. It is my firm conviction that injustice and oppression of fellow-men, the attempt to stifle legitimate human ambition, the desire to keep people down in order to profit by their misfortune, is sure to react on the authors and agents thereof, and that nothing can save them from a similar fate sooner or later except a timely consciousness of the gravity of their sin and a vigorous attempt to atone for it by undoing the mischief wrought.

" I am a Hindu and a firm believer in the doctrine of *Karma*. I also believe that every man makes his own *Karma*, and is thus the arbiter of his own destiny. I therefore look at the question thus: the ancestors of the Hindus (or perhaps they themselves in their previous existence), in the insolence of wealth and power maltreated people whom God had placed under them to protect and bless. The degradation of the latter reacted upon them and reduced them to the subordinate position which has been their lot for so many centuries, without in any way benefiting those who had already been degraded by them. This double degradation has resulted in the loss of the manly instincts of the race; and we find that, despite a strong and sincere desire to improve, we feel as if the wheels of progress are kept back by forces beyond our control. The highest interests of the nation therefore require that the best in us should be devoted to the undoing of the mischief wrought by us or our ancestors. We owe a heavy debt to those depressed classes; that debt must be paid, and paid as soon as possible. No amount of paper resolutions and no amount of talking on platforms will make us men unless we adopt the first principle of manhood, viz., of making the *amende honorable* to those of our own people whom we have wronged and whom we continue to wrong under an entirely mistaken idea of our dignity and social position. Living in the midst of large classes of people not conscious of their manhood, we cannot hope to progress towards a better type; a man living in an atmosphere of infectious disease has to keep up constant war lest the germs of disease get admittance into his body and destroy it. At the best, action in such circumstances can only be preventive and not operative: our work for ourselves can only be negative and not affirmative. Even if we succeed in avoiding infection, that does not mean much, as our time is spent in preventive measures without making advance. We have, therefore, to realize that the best and highest sacrifices we may put forth for our national advancement cannot come to much as long as the depressed classes remain what they are. The question then, is one of national importance, and one which deserves to be placed almost at the head of the list of reforms needed to bring about our social efficiency. It is not a question of charity or goodwill but *one of National self-preservation.* I have so far looked at it from humane and national points of view, but there is another aspect which Hindus cannot ignore. The depressed classes or the vast bulk of them, are Hindus ; they worship Hindu gods, observe Hindu custom, and follow the Hindu law. A great many of them worship the cow and obey their Brahman priests. They have no desire to go out of Hinduism unless it be impossible for them otherwise to better their position religiously, socially, and economically. Nay, they cling to Hinduism in spite of the knowledge that by giving it up and adopting other faiths they have an immediate prospect of rising both socially and economically. There are agencies prepared to receive them with open arms if only they give up their ancestral faith, of which they know little, and whose priests care so little for them. Indications are not wanting that many of them have already become conscious of the wretched position they hold in Hindu society. Some have begun to resent it, and it will be no wonder if large numbers of them leave Hindu society with thoughts of retaliation and revenge. Hindu society is in a state of transition, and is throwing off the accretions that have gathered round it in times of stress and trouble. With the advance of education and under modern influences, striking changes are taking place in the ideals and modes of life and thought of the society. The great majority of educated Hindus think that their progress, even on the most advanced modern lines, does not necessitate their giving up their religion or its forms, or even the mainsprings of their life as Hindus. If so, it is a question of paramount importance to Hindu society, that all those who call themselves Hindus should not only be properly educated, but that each member should have the consciousness that there is no position in society to which he cannot aspire if he is otherwise fitted for it by personal qualifications. No society can hold its own in these days of universal competition and education if it does not allow its members the fullest scope for progress.

" Modern societies go further; they not only allow the fullest scope to their members but they have also to find opportunities for progress. According to sound social conceptions, there cannot be much hope for a society which keeps a fourth of its total strength in perpetual bondage, doomed to dirty work, insanitary life, and intellectual starvation, and denies them opportunities of association with other members of the community. I am not prepared to admit that such a state of things forms an essential feature of Hinduism; it is enough to shame us that it should be associated with present day Hinduism. Happily there is some awakening among the leaders of orthodox Hinduism also. The famous Gait Circular proved a good tonic for the apathy of orthodox Kashi. One fine morning the learned pandits of Kashi rose to learn that their orthodoxy stood the chance of losing the allegiance of six crores of human beings who, the Government and its advisers were told, were not Hindus, in so far as other Hindus would not acknowledge them as such, and would not even touch them. The ways of Providence are strange and inscrutable. The Gait Circular had a quite unexpected effect and galvanized the dying body of orthodox Hinduism into sympathy with its untouchable population, because that was so necessary to avert its own downfall. The possibility of losing the untouchables has shaken the intelligent section of the Hindu community to its very depths, and were it not for long established prejudices and deep-rooted habits, the untouchableness would soon be a thing of the past. The danger having been removed of Hinduism being bereft of the depressed classes by the fiat of the Census Department, there is a chance of Hinduism reverting to its old apathy and indifference, and against this the leaders and well-wishers of the Hindu community have to guard. From the Hindu point of view too, then, the matter is of first-rate importance and cannot be ignored without serious loss to the body and soul of Hinduism. I would, therefore, appeal to every Hindu to be serious about it ; this is no time for trifling. The Christian missionary is gathering the harvest and no blame can attach to him for doing so. He is in this country with the message of *His God*, and if the Hindus forsake their own people, he, in any case, will not fail them. The depressed classes, as I have said, have no desire to leave Hinduism, if the latter make it possible for them to progress on humane lines ; but if in its stupidity it hesitates and hesitates, they are not willing to follow in its train any longer."

The following extract gives an account of what has so far been done by the Arya Samaj in this connection :

" . . . in the Punjab and the United Provinces substantial work is being done by the Arya Samaj.

In my eyes the chief merit of this work lies in forcing or persuading Hindu society to assimilate these classes and raise them to a respectable position in the social scale. From that point of view the methods of the Arya Samaj are much more effective than those adopted in other parts of India. The Arya Samajists occupy an admittedly good position in Hindu society. The orthodox party often threatens to outcaste them, but eventually find that it is not in their power to do so. In fact they cannot afford to lose them : Hinduism in Northern India cannot be thought of without the Arya Samaj. It is not only a source of strength to Hinduism and Hindus, but is the principal effective agency, always and everywhere present, to defend them, to save them, and to serve them. It is the Arya Samajists who open and maintain schools, colleges, Vidyalas, and Gurukulas for the education of their boys and girls ; it is they who fight their religious and denominational battles, who defend their Shastras, who serve them in times of famine or distress, who look after their womanhood, and who spend money, time, and energy in reclaiming those who would otherwise be lost to them. The orthodox are angry with the Arya Samaj on account of their audacity in admitting some of the depressed classes and untouchables into Hindu society. They threaten to excommunicate and in some cases they carry out their threats, but eventually find it is useless to break their heads against rocks. In their despair, they pour out the vials of their wrath upon the untouchables and persecute them, but at this stage the law steps in and they have to submit to the inevitable.

"The Arya Samajists reclaim these depressed classes by admitting them to the privileges of the *Dwijas*. They administer Gayatri to a select number, invest them with the sacred thread, confer on them the privilege of performing Homa, and start inter-dining and in a few cases even inter-marriage with them. This startles the Hindus. The whole country where such a thing is done for the first time is thrown into convulsions. People begin to think and talk. Occasionally they resort to violence which in some cases leads to litigation, but eventually truth, justice and perseverance triumph. In the territories of the Maharaja of Jammu and Kashmere the whole strength of one of these castes (in one pargana), about 10,000 souls, has been admitted into the Arya Samaj. This is the result of about three years' work. The agitation is now subsiding and things are resuming their normal condition. In another district (Sialkote) over 36,000 of another caste have been similarly raised. A special organization has been formed to look after their education, etc., called the *Megh Udhar Sabha* (a society for the uplift of Meghs), which maintains a Central School and several primary schools. The Central School has a splendid building of its own, the foundation stone of which was laid by the Collector of the District, and on which they have spent some forty thousand rupees. In another district (Gurdaspur) Pandit Ram Bhaj Dat has reclaimed several thousands within the last two years. The orthodox party is still agitated there, and no organization has yet been formed to look after those reclaimed. In another district (Hoshiarpur), thousands have been reclaimed and there is a regular organization looking after their educational and other needs. In Lahore itself good work is being done among Hindu sweepers and Chamars. In July, I purchased a large plot of land at Lahore on the other side of the Ravi, at a cost of Rs.21,000, to build a Central Home and a Central School for the Depressed Classes Mission. We have used a portion of the balance of the famine fund, raised by me in 1908, towards the uplift of the depressed classes, and are maintaining some Primary Schools scattered over the province for the benefit of these classes. Some of these are receiving Government grants and others will soon earn them. The funds thus released will then be available for other schools. There is hardly a district in the province where some work in connection with the uplift of the depressed classes is not being done, though in most cases it only forms part of the general programme of the Arya Samaj. But the best and most cheering part of this work is that in some places the orthodox party have become conscious of their duty towards the depressed classes and are in full sympathy with the Arya Samaj. At the last session of the Punjab Hindu Conference, at the suggestion of a Hindu Sadhu of the orthodox party, a resolution was unanimously passed to invite the depressed classes to send representatives to the Conference in future. In Lahore and some other places we find that high caste Hindus have no scruples in sending their children to the schools which we maintain mainly for the depressed classes. The children mix quite freely and on equal terms. In the U. P., the home of Hindu Orthodoxy, the work is more difficult; but last year I succeeded in making a big hole in the orthodox fortress by reclaiming a number of *Domes* (one of the lowest untouchable castes in the U.P.) and admitting them into the Arya Samaj. I went to their house in the interior of the hills and along with a number of high caste Arya Samajists ate food cooked by them and drank water brought by them. Last year I went to Benares and in that very centre of Hindu orthodoxy addressed a huge meeting on this question, and challenged the pandits to outcaste me and others working with me. I did the same only lately at Muradabad and Bareilly. The Arya Samajists in these districts are maintaining a number of schools for the Chamar boys, who alone number 60 lacs in the United Provinces. The untouchables in the U. P. number about a crore and a quarter in a total Hindu population of about four crores, and the problem there is gigantic. The great need in those provinces is a mission solely devoted to the work, consisting of good Hindus, who really believe in the Hindu Shastras and have a genuine respect for Hindu life and thought."

These extracts give a fair idea of the influence of the Arya Samaj in the sphere of social uplift. It is a magnificent work, of which any single Indian organization may well be proud. But no one feels more than we do how little has yet been achieved in this line. We are yet only on the fringe of the area to be conquered, and many a battle will have to be fought before the victory is achieved. The Arya Samaj as a body is, however, conscious of the magnitude as well as of the importance of the work, and their success is, humanly speaking, almost certain.

Their feeling may well be expressed in the words of the poet:

> It may be that the gulfs will wash us down:
> It may be we shall touch the Happy Isles,
> . . . but something ere the end,
> Some work of noble note, may yet be done.
>
> —TENNYSON, *Ulysses.*

PART III

THE ARYA SAMAJ—*(continued)*

CHAPTER I

RELIGIOUS IDEALS AND AIMS

समानी प्रपा सह वोन्नभाग:समाने योक्त्रे सह वो युनज्मि।
सम्यञ्चो ऽग्निं सपर्यतारा नाभि मिवाभितः ॥ ६ ॥
अथ० ३ । ३० । ६

सध्रीचीनान् वःसंमनसस्कृणोम्येकश्नुष्टीन्त्संवननेन सर्वान्
॥ ७ ॥ अथ० ३ । ३० । ७ ॥

"Let what you drink, your share of food be common, together with one common bond I bind you. Serve Agni, gathered round Him like the spokes about the chariot's nave.

"With binding charm I make you all united, obeying one sole leader, and one-minded."

—Ath. III., 30, 6, 7.

1. *The Christianizing of India*

AT the birth of Dayananda, in A.D. 1824, British rule in India was in its preliminary stages. Large tracts of what now is known as British India were still under native government. The whole of the Punjab, Sindh, and the Central Provinces required about another quarter of a century to be brought under British sway. Even in parts in the immediate occupancy of "John Company," British rule was more or less in a fluid state, and British institutions yet in their infancy. The facilities for education were few and far between. "The very scanty encouragement originally given to education by the East India Company was confined to promoting the study of oriental languages still used at that time in the Indian Courts of Law in order to qualify young Indians for Government employment and chiefly in the subordinate posts of the judicial service."[1] Missionary propaganda, however, seems to have been in full swing, at least in the Presidency towns of Calcutta, Bombay, and Madras. By an easy effort of imagination we can see Raja Ram Mohan Roy discussing the merits of Christian religion with Mr. Arnot or Mr. Adam, in his garden house at Calcutta in the summer of 1818, about six years before Dayananda was born. The missionaries had opened some schools also, though it is not clear whether they taught English or vernacular only. We are told by Sir Valentine Chirol that "it was in direct opposition to Carey and other earlier missionaries" that Dr. Alexander Duff made up his mind to establish "the supremacy of the English language over the vernacular" as a preliminary to the Christianization of India, and that it was Dr. Duff's influence, as much as that of Macaulay, which enabled Lord William Bentinck's government to decide that "the great object of the British Government ought to be the promotion of English literature and science."[2]

[1] *Indian Unrest,* by V. Chirol, p. 208.
[2] *Ibid.,* p. 209.

A study of Raja Ram Mohan Roy's life, and of the tracts published by him between 1820 and 1830, gives some idea of the fierce controversy then raging between the Christian missionary and the champions of the Hindu religion led by the Raja. It appears that no effort was spared to convert the Raja to Christianity. We have it on the authority of Professor Max Müller, who quotes one Mr. Adam, an American missionary, a contemporary and a friend of Raja Ram Mohan Roy, that "Dr. Middleton, the first Bishop of Calcutta, thought it his duty to endeavour to convert Ram Mohan Roy to Christianity, and, in doing so, he dwelt not only on the truth and excellence of his own religion, but spoke of the honour and repute, the influence and usefulness he would acquire by becoming the Apostle of India," and that Raja Ram Mohan Roy expressed his bitter indignation that he should have been deemed capable of being influenced by any consideration but the love of truth and goodness, and he never afterwards visited the Bishop again."[1]

It is well known in historical circles that the early Christian missionaries wielded a vast political influence in the early days of the East India Company's administration—an influence which they still exercise and which varies only in different epochs and different provinces by the amount and kind of interest shown by the Viceroys and Governors and other high State dignitaries in the spread of the Christian doctrine. Sir Valentine Chirol tells us that it was Dr. Alexander Duff "who inspired the prohibition of *Suttee* and other measures which marked the withdrawal of the

[1] *Biographical Essays*, by Max Müller, 1884, p. 24.

countenance originally given by the East India Company to religious practices incompatible, in the opinion of earnest Christians, with the sovereignty of a Christian Power," and who influenced the decision of the Government in favour of English education.[1] It is added that Dr. Duff's authority was "great both at home and in India, and was reflected equally in Lord Hardinge's Educational Order of 1844, which threw a large number of posts in the public service open to English-speaking Indians."

It is thus clear that between 1824, the year of Swami Dayananda's birth, and 1845, the year of his flight from home, the Christian missionary exercised a great influence over Government policy. Dr. Duff himself opened an English school in 1830, and succeeded in converting some of his most brilliant pupils to Christianity. By the time Swami Dayananda started his public life, Christianity had made great progress in India. The country was simply studded with Christian schools and colleges and covered with a network of Christian agencies. The voice of the Brahmo Samaj was a mere wail in the wilderness. The Brahmo leaders' chief weapon was rationalism, which could appeal but to a few. Even in the case of these few, the Brahmo Samaj at that time was condesired to be a kind of reformed or refined Christianity, resembling more the Unitarian Church than the Monotheism of the Vedas or the Vedicism of Ram Mohan Roy. Whatever little of Hinduism it con-

[1] *Indian Unrest,* p. 209. It would be more accurate to say: "who inspired the policy of the East India Company to interfere with such religious practices of the Hindus as in the opinion of earnest Christians were incompatible with the sovereignty of a Christian Power."

tained in its original form gradually dropped off, as the leadership passed into hands which had grown strong on English food and English thought. This phase of Brahmo teaching reached its zenith in the Christian rhapsodies of Babu Keshub Chunder Sen, whose teachings on Christ and Christianity left only a thin partition between orthodox Christianity and Brahmoism. Max Müller, in one of his letters to the *Times* (November 24th, 1880), makes one of Keshub's critics, the Rev. Charles Voysey, say that "Believers in Keshub Chunder Sen have forfeited the name of Theists because this leader has more and more inclined to the doctrines of Christianity."[1] Keshub Babu's "earliest profession of faith in Christ" was made so far back as 1866. In a letter addressed to Professor Max Müller by Babu W. N. Gupta, on behalf of the Brahmo Missionary Conference in 1880, the writer added that "one of the main causes of irritation" was "the Minister's (*i.e.*, Keshub's) allegiance to Christ."[2]

Another Christian writer, Mr. Frank Lillington, in his book entitled *The Brahmo Samaj and Arya Samaj, in their Bearing on Christianity*, published in 1901, refers to "the Christianity of the Brahmo Samaj of India." It is true that the Brahmo Samaj never accepted the divinity of the historical Christ in the same sense in which orthodox Christianity accepts it, but it cannot be denied that it went perilously near doing so, and the Sadharan Brahmo Samaj was a protest against Keshub's interpretation of Christianity and his exposition of the New Dispensation started

[1] *Biographical Essays*, p. 89.
[2] *Biographical Essays*, p. 98.

by him. Torn by internal dissensions of this character, the Brahmo Samaj had ceased to be an effective shield for the protection of Hindu Theism from the assaults of Christians when Swami Dayananda completed his education with Virjananda about 1860.

Raja Ram Mohan Roy's teaching was a denial of the superiority of the West in matters of spirit. He maintained that Hindu Theism was as good as, if not better than, Christian Theism taken at its best. Maharishi Debendranath Tagore was also firm on that point to the last, although he had repudiated the infallibility of the Vedas on the testimony of four young men sent to Benares to study and to pronounce upon their teaching. But Babu Keshub Chunder Sen's development was in a way a confession of Hindu inferiority, which once more strengthened the hands of the Christian missionary who at that moment was engaged in a most bitter campaign against Hinduism based on the opinions of Western scholars of Sanskrit.

The movement inaugurated by Sir William Jones and his colleagues had affected India in two ways. On the one hand it brought to light the immensity and variety of Indian literature and made known to the European world that Indians had produced immortal works in religion, philosophy, poetry, mathematics, etc., and were not quite the unlettered barbarians which the early English settlers had thought them to be. On the other hand it placed a strong weapon in the hands of the Christian missionary against Hinduism and what it stood for. Thus, by the time Swami Dayananda entered the field, "India had witnessed a change," the like of which had never been known before, viz., " the intellectual and moral conquest of the people by Englishmen." The picture has been so well drawn by an acknowledged leader of the Arya Samaj, Lala Hansraj, that I cannot do better than quote his words. Speaking at the anniversary of the Lahore Arya Samaj, he said :

" . . . During the palmiest days of Mahomedan rule, the Hindus had never acknowledged themselves beaten by their masters in intellectual and moral progress. A Mahomedan *Babar* might defeat a Hindu *Sangá* and dispossess him of a portion of his territory, but even he had to bend before a Hindu *Nanak. Akbar, Faizi, Jehangir,* and *Dara Shikoh* had to bear testimony to the learning and saintliness of Hindu devotees. But with the advent of the English the case has become different. Hardly a day passes when we are not reminded of our inferiority. The railway, the telegraph and the factory speak in unmistakeable terms both to the educated and the uneducated that Englishmen are far superior to them in the knowledge of natural laws and their application to the conveniences of human life. The wonderfully complex machine of administration which regulates our affairs displays to us high powers of organization in the nation that bears rule over us. The dramas of Shakespeare, the poems of Milton, and the writings of Bacon attest the intellectual eminence of the ruling people. The perseverance, truthfulness, courage, patriotism, and self-sacrifice of Englishmen excite feelings of respect and admiration in our minds. What wonder is then that in their company we feel ourselves conquered and humiliated?

" Just at this moment of weakness, the missionary

comes to us and whispers that the superiority of the European over the Indian is the gift of the Son of God whom he has acknowledged as his King and Saviour, and that your countrymen can really become great if they come under His banner. The idea thus insinuated is daily fed and strengthened by the education that he imparts to us through a large number of Mission Schools and Colleges that cover the country with their network. The missionary criticizes the evils that have of late corrupted our society, and proudly points to his own community as entirely free from those curses. He compares our sacred books with Christian Scriptures, and proves to the satisfaction of many misguided people that the latter are infinitely superior to the former. He is also encouraged in his proselytizing work by the apathy of the Hindus towards religious instruction. They send their children to schools for secular education without making any provision for religious training at home or at school, with the result that our boys grow up utterly ignorant of the religious principles of their Shastras. No Christian father will ever entrust his sons to the care of him whom he believes inimical to his faith, but we do it daily, only to bewail the result of our folly when some mishap befalls us. The godless education of Government Schools and Colleges has increased our indifference to religion, and we have been so completely won over to the world that we are ready to sacrifice our highest religious interests for the slightest worldly advantage to ourselves.

"The labours of the Sanskrit scholars of Europe have also facilitated, though unconsciously, the path of the missionary. Accustomed to receive secular truths from the West without the slightest hesitation, our young men, unacquainted with the sublime truths of their Scriptures, are led to put implicit faith in the opinions of Western scholars on the subject of Hindu religion. . . . I do not mean to blame such distinguished savants as Professors Max Müller and Monier Williams, or cast a slur on the world-wide reputation which they have deservedly won after years of toil in the sacred field of Sanskrit literature. European savants . . . have been misled by the commentaries of native Sanskrit scholars whom they have closely followed, and it is no fault of theirs if they have failed in fields where men more favourably situated than themselves had shared the same fate. . . .

"The Hindu religion, which could well withstand the steel of Mahomedan bigotry for hundreds of years, has been brought face to face with European science and criticism, wielded by the hands of men who are either indifferent to our interests or interested in converting us to their faith. Our situation demands that we brace our nerves to defend our religion, if we believe it to be true, against the attacks of its assailants; but, alas! we ourselves have misgivings in our hearts. The vast and insensate majority of our conservative countrymen is so much steeped in idolatry and superstition, that it is well-nigh unconscious of its own wretchedness. It is, moreover, divided into rival sects giving nominal allegiance to the Vedas but passionately clinging to the various books composed by their founders for the benefit of their followers. Whenever any section of the community has kept itself aloof from contending factions, it has, with an inconsistency characteristic of our race, outwardly recognized the sovereignty of all, but, inwardly ignoring the claims of religion altogether, yielded its heart to none. A few meaningless ceremonies excepted, there is no common tie that unites the Hindu masses, no common link that fastens them to each other, no one principle which all of them may be moved to defend. As for the people who call themselves educated, they are beset with greater difficulties and less provided for against danger. Education has deprived them of the ignorant pride which, in the case of common people, is the source of dogged pertinacity and tenacious adherence to their own views. Light has reached them only to reveal the hideous situation they are in. The godless education of our Schools and Colleges has sapped the foundations of faith in God and His revealed Will; our boys are taught to despise their own religious books and prize those of the foreigner; above all, the conviction has been brought home to us by the writings of European savants that, although we possess some philosophical works of inestimable value, our religious books contain a great deal of rubbish and nonsense along with a few gems of truth that lie embedded in it. We are told that the Vedas, which are the basis of our religion and science, embody the child-like utterances of the primeval man, that they teach the worship of the elements, and enjoin the practice of foolish rites that could please children but are disgusting to civilized man. Some of these opinions derive countenance even from the opinions of our priests, the natural guides of our people, who, devoting themselves exclusively to the study of works composed in the mythological period, remain ignorant of the knowledge of Divine Revelation and, in their zeal to defend the present corruptions of society, lend a helping hand to the enemies of their faith. Thus the ancient religion of the Hindus, deserted by those who ought to have proved its best defenders, seems doomed to destruction by the blows dealt to it by its young adversaries. It seeks safety in concealment; it is afraid to come out and measure swords with its opponents in the field of debate and discussion; it confesses itself humbled and beaten by its enemies. It seems impossible to defend, without a blush on the face, the faith of the *Rishis* who at one time gave law and learning to the whole civilized world."

The speaker then paid a tribute to Raja Ram Mohan Roy and deplored the fall of the Brahmo Samaj from its original ideals, and continued:

"Thus the Hindu faith, assailed on all sides by its vigorous opponents, had put forward one defender, but he also deserted it in time of need. The faith of the *Rishis* was in danger of being swept out of the land where it had flourished from immemorial times. Even the Vedas, the expression of the Divine Will, entrusted to the care of the Brahmins, were threatened with oblivion. Men had despaired of finding unity in the chaos of conflicting opinions which the Hindus erroneously believed to be their religion, and had given up the task as hopeless. Everything portended utter confusion and dire destruction to our faith when Swami Dayananda Saraswati, the great Seer of the age, appeared among us.

"I have called Swami Dayananda the great Seer because, like *Rishis* of yore, he saw the Truth face to face. . . . There are some who call Swami Dayananda an impostor, a liar, a false interpreter of the Vedas. I do not quarrel with them, because, in the search after truth, these slanderers have never wandered in the mazes of Hindu Shastras, never felt the difficulties that lie in the way of Vedic students, and never realized the importance of the discovery made by Swami Dayananda. The great Swami stands on a pedestal so high that the eyes of those who look at him from below are dazed, and they find nothing substantial in his place. . . . I admit that the truth discovered by him is the only bond which can unite us as a nation and that the movement inaugurated by him will, like the famous cow of the Hindu mythology, yield us all that is desirable in social and religious matters ; but these collateral benefits should not weigh in our minds as proofs of the ulterior motives of the Swami. They are rather an index of the importance of his discovery and work. The brightness of the truth, discovered by him, would have been the same without these additional lights. Nor should we be swayed in our judgment against him by what has been miscalled the unanimous voice of the pandits. Had truth been judged by numbers, no reform would have ever succeeded. Weigh him not by the votes of those who are the devoted followers of the mythological school, but by the evidence which he can bring forward to establish the existence of the school which he has followed."

2. The Forces against Dayananda

The forces, then, that Dayananda had to face, may briefly be summed up as follows:

1. The host of Brahmins, learned and unlearned, who had established for themselves a supreme position in the Hindu hierarchy and whose interests were vitally involved in the proposed reform movement. Their strongest citadel was the established caste system, and they were backed by all the forces of ignorance, superstition, prejudice, custom and conservatism.

2. The organized forces of Christianity, backed on the one side by all the resources of civilization, moral, intellectual and political; on the other by an endless and inexhaustible supply of men and money—men who had consecrated their lives to the cause of their religion and had made it their sacred duty to defend and to disseminate it at all costs; and money which could establish a network of philanthropic activity, many-sided and hydra-headed, ungrudging in sympathy and unstinted in flow.

3. The analytic tendencies of modern science, which denied God, revelation and religion, and established secularism and materialism on the throne formerly occupied by God.

4. The collapse of the prevailing Hindu system of thought, religion and life before 2 and 3.

5. The pessimism and inertia which had been engendered by centuries of political and intellectual decline; the apathy and indifference of the Hindus and their conviction that they had been hopelessly beaten, perhaps never to rise again; and the shame

and fatalism which are born of intellectual and moral subjugation and stagnation.

6. The ever-active propaganda of Islam, which claimed its victories in every nook and corner of the land, almost every day of the year, without the Hindus realizing the extent to which it was gaining ground.

3. *His Fitness for his Task*

All his life, Dayananda had studied Hindu religion only. All its forms and manifestations were thoroughly well known to him. Of Christianity and Islam, however, he knew nothing when he entered upon his work in 1860, excepting what he might have observed during his long travels in the practices of his Muslim and Christian countrymen. But, so soon as he took up the idea of bringing about a radical reform in Hindu thought, Hindu religion and Hindu life, he found that in Christianity and Islam Hinduism had formidable rivals, which threatened its very existence, if left unchecked and unresisted in their systematic efforts to displace Hinduism from the position it occupied in India. He concluded that a movement directed against current Hinduism alone might reform it away altogether, unless at the same time he could dislodge its opponents from the positions of vantage they occupied against it. He therefore absorbed himself in a critical study of both these alien religions, with the assistance of friends who knew English and Arabic, and with the help of such literature as was available to him in the vernacular of the country. By this study he attained the reasoned conviction that Vedic Theism was in many respects superior to even the Theism of Islam, and very much superior to dogmatic Christianity. Having reached this conclusion, it did not take him long to decide that his movement must aim not only at a defence of Vedic Hinduism, but must go further and establish a new era of propaganda and conversion; or, in other words, that he must take the offensive also. What he aimed at was nothing short of a complete revolution in the mental and spiritual outlook of the Hindus. He believed that, although other religions contained some truth, the religion of the Vedas was the only absolutely true religion; that it was for all mankind; and that it was their duty to give it to mankind, irrespective of caste, colour, or country.

Dayananda had thus at the outset the idea of a universal mission, but at the same time he never forgot the prior claim of the nation in which he was born and to which he had the honour to belong. He aimed at world-conquest in the domain of spirit; but he knew that this mighty task must be begun at home, and that his first converts must be won from among his own people, who stood in greater need of his light than any other: therefore he decided that he must not only first restore Hinduism to the Hindus, but that also he must teach them to defend it against all aggressors. He also decided that the best interests of an effective defence required that the defender should be prepared at every opening to take the offensive against his assailants, throwing upon them, in turn, the onus of defence. In plainer language, that he should be ready not only to meet criticism at all points, but also, in turn, to criticize his critics and compel them to see the beams in their own eyes.

He wanted the Hindu mind to turn from passiveness to activity ; to exchange the standard of weakness for the standard of strength ; " in place of a steadily yielding defence " to take " the ringing cheer of the invading host."

Islam and Christianity, the rivals of Hinduism in India, were both proselytizing religions ; it was therefore necessary to give the same character to Hinduism. Hinduism had made conversions in the past ; it was quietly and unconsciously making conversions every day[1] ; all that was needed was to create a conscious, active, proselytizing spirit, which would take pride in its work. This, in brief, was the Swami's attitude towards other religions. If one come across some mistakes in his statements concerning other religions, they may be the mistakes of his informants, or of those on whose authority they have been taken and criticized. Mr. Blunt, in his *Census Report for the United Provinces* (p. 136), complains that the Aryas study a religion *only* in the works of its opponents. If this charge is true—which we do not admit—we have only to reply that in that respect the Arya is perhaps a too apt disciple of the Christian missionary ; and, if evidence be required of this, such evidence will be found in abundance in the tracts against Hinduism, the Arya Samaj and Islam issued by the Christian Literary Society of Madras. We do not admire

[1] See Census Reports ; also Sir H. Risley's learned work on *The Peoples of India.*

this spirit, but it is impossible to separate it altogether from proselytizing zeal. It should not be forgotten that the Christian Missionary was the first in the field of controversy: he opened war upon Hinduism, and in doing so used the strongest possible language, calling the greatest of Hindu heroes, like Krishna, adulterers, fornicators, and what not.

Dayananda's attitude towards other religions was a necessity of the times in which he lived, and partly due also to his ignorance of the languages in which the best literature of these religions was to be found. But, in our opinion, there is no justification for his followers to continue to hold that attitude, and the sooner the Arya Samajists come to this conclusion, the better for them and for their cause. The other religions of the world, including those of India, must be studied in the writings of their best exponents, and always spoken of in terms of respect and consideration, even if one is unable to accept them as true in their entirety.

4. *The Arya Samaj as the Parent of Unrest*

The Lieutenant-Governor of the Punjab, in replying to a deputation of the leading Arya Samajists, who in 1907 waited upon him to assure him that the Samaj had no hand in the political or agrarian disturbances of the year, is reported to have said that his officers informed him that wherever there was an Arya Samaj, it was the centre of unrest. We wonder if he realized that in that verdict he was paying the greatest compliment to the work and to the spirit of the Arya Samaj that its illustrious founder could have wished. Mental unrest is holy. There can be no progress without unrest. But, to be quite just, the Arya Samaj is not the only source of unrest in India. The Government itself, with its educational policy and its Western methods of administration, has contributed materially towards that same unrest. The Arya Samaj may quite logically be pronounced an outcome of the conditions imported into India from the West, and, as such, it has absolutely no reason to repent or be ashamed of the share it has had in adding to the volume or modifying the character of the unrest that was the inevitable consequence of modern conditions of life in India. That the Arya Samaj is one of the most potent nationalizing forces, no one should or need deny. The Arya Samaj aims at radical changes in the thought and life of the people. It aims at the formation of a new national character, on the fundamental basis of Vedic thought and Vedic life. It was essential for it to create dissatisfaction with the existing conditions in Hindu society; to create an ambition for better thought and better life—an ambition that was bound to bring about unrest. The Arya Samaj began its work by recalling the greatness of ancient India, and impressed upon the Hindus that the land of Vedas and *Shastras* had no right "to sink into the *rôle* of mere critic or imitator of European letters" or European life. Yet that was at best the condition of the Indian mind at the beginning of Dayananda's apostolic career. The Hindu mind which, till then, could not get out of the vicious circle of mere forms or mere habits—and to some extent is even now in bondage—had to be broadened. So it had to be told that habit was only a factor in the evolution of character and not character itself; that mere personal refinement could not take the place of active ends and ideals, which are the elixir of life of all social organisms as of individuals; that mere "quietness, docility, resignation, and obedience" could not form a national character; and that it was necessary to foster also "strength, initiative, sense of responsibility, and *power of rebellion.*" The whole idea is expressed so beautifully by the late Sister Nivedita (Miss Noble), who had so completely identified herself with the Hindu cause and than whom no truer friend of Hinduism ever was born in the British Isles, that no apology is necessary for giving a long quotation from one of her essays on aggressive Hinduism. Looking on Hinduism "no longer as the preserver of Hindu custom, but *as the creator of Hindu character,*" she observes:

"It is surprising to think how radical a change is entailed in many directions by this conception. We are no longer oppressed with jealousy or fear when we contemplate encroachments on our social and religious consciousness. Indeed, the idea of encroachment has ceased because OUR WORK IS NOT NOW TO PROTECT OURSELVES BUT TO CONVERT OTHERS. Point by point, we are determined, not merely to keep what we had, but to win what we never had before. The question is no longer of other people's attitude to us, but, rather, of what we think of them. It is not, how much have we left? but, how much have we annexed? We cannot afford, now, to lose, because we are sworn to carry the battle far beyond our remotest frontiers. We no longer dream of submission, because struggle itself has become only the first step towards a distant victory to be won.

"No other religion in the world is so capable of this dynamic transformation as Hinduism. To Nagarjuna and Buddhaghosh the many was real, and the Ego unreal. To Shankaracharya, the one was real and the many unreal. To Ramakrishna and Vivekananda, the many and the one were the same reality—perceived differently and at different times by the human consciousness. Do we realize what this means? It means that CHARACTER IS SPIRITUALITY. It means that laziness and defeat are not renunciation. It means that to protect another is infinitely greater than to attain salvation. It means that *Mukti* lies in overcoming the thirst for *Mukti* (salvation). It means that conquest may be the highest form of *Sannyas* (renunciation). It means, in short, that Hinduism is become aggressive, that the trumpet of *Kalki* is sounded already in our midst, and that it calls all that is noble, all that is lovely, all that is strenuous and heroic amongst us to a battlefield on which the bugle of retreat shall never more be heard."[1]

In our judgment this represents the spirit of Dayananda's ideas, and it is his spirit which is working in the Arya Samaj.

5. *Dayananda's Claims for the Vedas*

It is often said by way of reproach that Dayananda

[1] *Aggressive Hinduism,* by Sister Nivedita, pp. 10, 11, 12; Nateson & Co., Madras.

made extravagant and absurd claims for the Vedas in trying to show that in them was to be found every scientific truth. For the examination of these claims in detail this is not the proper place, but it may be said here that :

(1) Dayananda does claim, and rightly, that in matters of religion and in the domain of spirit the Western mind has not reached either the depths or the heights commanded by the ancient Indian mind ; and in such matters it has still much to learn from the ancient Indian sages.

(2) In matters social the Indian solutions arrived at in ancient times are as good, as sound and as effective, at least, as are those arrived at in the West by the best modern thought.

(3) In the domain of philosophy India has nothing to learn from the West. The best of European thought does not yet come up to the level of the best of Hindu thought. The latest German thought is as if still groping in the dark and trying to scale the heights reached by Indians centuries ago.

(4) In the realm of physical science, the Europeans are far in advance of the ancient Indians, though it may fairly and justly be claimed that most of the fundamental truths on which the superstructure of European science is raised, were known to the Indians. For example, it was known to the Indians that the earth was round and that the earth, the sun, the moon and the stars were in motion ; they had made great progress in military science ; they were the inventors of algebra, of decimals, and so on. For centuries have the Hindus believed that plants were essentially as much to be regarded as living

things as were animals : and it stands to their credit that the latest discovery in the same line of research —that every particle of matter has life—has been discovered and demonstrated by one of their descendants, namely, Professor J. C. Bose, of Calcutta. That the Hindus were well acquainted with anatomy and surgery, and were chemists besides of no mean order, has been amply proved and is freely admitted by European scholars.

Dayananda's claims, therefore, rest upon a substantial foundation. His object in making them was not to give the Hindu matter and occasion for boasting, but to lift him from that slough of despondency into which he had fallen, and to give him leverage for the removal of the great burden that lay on his mind. He wanted to inspire him with just pride, and with confidence in the great value of his heritage, so that he might consider it worth all the sacrifices which he might be called upon to make for the preservation of that heritage and for making himself worthy to possess it. Dayananda dreamed of a regenerated India, as spiritual, as wise, as noble, as learned, as chivalrous, and as great in every way as in its most glorious past, if not more so, and he wanted his countrymen to proceed to the realization of that ideal with confidence and fervour. He had no objection to their learning from the West whatever the West might be able to teach them, but with the desire only of rendering it again to the West with double interest, if possible. He wanted them to aspire to a *rôle* of honour in the comity of nations ; to become once more the teachers of Humanity and the upholders of high and magnificent ideals before mankind. He wanted them to achieve all this in the spirit of their past, in a spirit of devotion to truth for the sake of truth, of altruism, and of humility. This great programme he thought could not be realized by mere imitation, by mere dependence on the West, by despising their ancestors and by borrowing exotic manners and habits. Not on such shifting foundations, but on the primal rock of self-respect and self-help did he desire them to build up their future nationalism, and to rear it thereon in the true spirit of *Swajati* and *Swadharma*. Yet, in spite of the greatness of the end, he countenanced no unworthy means for its attainment. He wanted the Hindus to win the whole world—but by righteousness and Dharma only. He warned them against the indulgences, the *Bhoga* doctrines of the West, and he protested against their floating with the current as unworthy of the blood of their vigorous and enterprising ancestors.

Time will show whether Dayananda was right or wrong in his ideas, but indications are not wanting that his countrymen are appreciating and imbibing his spirit. His followers do not, nor did he, care very much for the verdict of the foreigner, though not meaning ill to him in any way. To an Indian even animals, and still more plants, rivers and mountains, are all friends, but much more so are men and women, whatsoever their nationality or creed. It is not in his nature to cherish spite or hatred. The difficulty with him, in fact, is not that he is too hard, too dour, or too inflexible, but that he is, on the contrary, rather too soft, too pliable, and at times too kind and selfless, even to the degree of sacrificing the best interests of his nation and his country on the altar of chivalrous generosity.

The ideals and aims of Dayananda are the ideals and aims of the Arya Samaj, and to what we have said above about the former nothing need be added.

CHAPTER II

CONCLUSION

ईजे यज्ञेभिः शशमे शमीभिर्ऋधद्वारायाग्नये ददाश ।
एवा चन तं यशसामजुष्टिर्नांहो मर्तं नशते न प्रदृप्तिः ॥८॥
ऋ० ६।३।२।

"Thine, Thine, O Lord, is this Thy worshipper, he hath no other friends, O Mighty Lord!"

—R. V., 142, 1.

"Minds may doubt and hearts may fail when called to face new modes of thought or points of view; but the time must come when what is false in all things will fade, and what is true will no more seem strange."—Dr. Illingworth's *Reason and Revelation.*

1. *Will the Arya Samaj become Christian?*

FRIEND and foe alike are agreed that the Arya Samaj is a great movement and wields a great influence—at least in Northern India. Mr. Blunt, I.C.S., of the United Provinces of Agra and Oude, writing in 1912, called it "the greatest religious movement in India of the past half century."[1] Sir Herbert Risley con-

[1] *Census Report for U.P. for* 1911, p. 129.

siders it to be the "most conspicuous movement" of the times.[1] Writing in 1902, Mr. Burn, I.C.S., of the United Provinces, thought it was "the most important" of the Hindu movements in those Provinces."[2] Sir Edward Maclagan (then Mr. Maclagan), in writing his Census Report in 1891, described it as the "most important of the modern sects" in the Punjab. Sir Henry Cotton, in his book *New India*, characterizes the history of the movement as "one of the most important and interesting chapters of modern Hindu thought."[3]

In the opinion of Sir Herbert Risley, "it is a notable fact that the Hindu sectarian movement which appeals most strongly to the educated classes is bitterly opposed to Christianity and lays itself out not merely to counteract the efforts of missionaries but to reconvert to Hinduism high caste men who have become Christians." Further in his book, he adds: ". . . It (*i.e.*, the Arya Samaj) offers to the educated Hindu a comprehensive body of doctrines purporting to be derived from Indian documents and traditions and embodying schemes of social and educational advancement, without which no real progress is possible. In this revival of Hinduism, touched by reforming zeal and animated by patriotic enthusiasm, Christianity is likely to find a formidable obstacle to its spread among the educated classes."[4]

It is not unnatural, then, that the Arya Samaj should meet with the most merciless criticism and

[1] *The Peoples of India*, p. 245.
[2] *Census Report for U.P. for* 1901, p. 82.
[3] *New India*, Sir H. Cotton, p. 278.
[4] *The Peoples of India*, pp. 244-5.

the bitterest opposition from the Christian missionaries. In a paper read before the World Missionary Conference held at Edinburgh in 1910, it is described as " chief among the modern Neo-Hindu movements, both in point of activity and influence. . . . which hinder the spread of Christianity in India."[1] This explains the psychology of the minds that predict an early dissolution of the movement and accept anything and everything which may be said against it, without stopping to examine the data for such opinions or the motives that underlie them. There are others, however, also missionaries, who think that the movement is only preparing the way for Christianity. One of them, the Rev. —— Holland, of Allahabad, is reported to have said that " the ideas which the Arya Samaj raises without ability to satisfy them and the manifest contradictions of its system mean a not remote collapse into the arms of Christianity."[2] Another Christian writer, Mr. Frank Lillington, M.A., says :

" The Arya Samaj, out of patriotic antagonism to Christianity, has assumed a position which is becoming more and more clearly untenable. There seems good reason to believe that as Christianity is shown to be a universal and not merely a national faith, the prejudices which have given birth to the Arya Samaj will die, and its antagonism to Christianity will cease." The slender foundations on which opinions like these are based may be gathered from the following references which Mr. Frank Lillington gives as foot-notes on page 112 of his

[1] *Report of the Conference*, Vol. I., p. 17.

[2] *Ibid.*, p. 17.

book. The first is from page 37 of the Delhi Mission Report for 1898, and runs thus: "They (*i.e.*, the Arya Samajists) openly declare themselves to be enemies of ours, but they acknowledge, more frankly than most, the sinfulness of men and the need of strenuous efforts to obtain salvation." On pp. 38-39 of the same Report it is said that "in ——— a branch of the Arya Samaj has been established which I cannot help looking upon as an indirect result of our work. . . . I believe that it is a real move forward and an attempt to accept Christianity without the 'offence of the Cross.'"

To one who knows the actual position of affairs in India and the real sentiments of the Indian people, the statements just quoted have no value. They are efforts of the imagination, and represent merely the pious wishes of their authors. Perhaps they serve as a prop to their authors' faith and to hearten their supporters at home. Strengthened by these and similar hopeful declarations of the Delhi Mission, Mr. Lillington goes on to urge his Christian friends to "gently and tactfully break down the barrier of ignorant prejudice, both by making themselves acquainted with Indian literature and by coming, directly or through their representatives, the Missionaries, into sympathetic touch with these men." In his concluding chapter he adds that "in the Arya Samaj the Christian Missionary has an avowed enemy, but one who appears to be susceptible to courtesy and likely to become Christian when the increase of knowledge and a brotherly love of the Christians has warmed their hearts and enlightened their minds." Mr. Burn examines these statements and these hopes rather closely and says that "there is nothing improbable in the view that Christianity has had an effect on the doctrines of the Samaj . . . but it is necessary to state clearly the nature of its influence. . . . During the nineteenth century Christianity has advanced in India and its tenets have become better known; its success may have had some influence as far as causing an inquiry into the reasons for belief and forms of dogma . . . is concerned, but I find no trace of any doctrine directly borrowed or imitated, such as has been noticed in other reforming movements. . . . Their attitude towards it (Christianity) is far more iconoclastic than eclectic. For this . . . the success of Christianity with the lowest castes, and the fear of its influence spreading, are probably responsible." Mr. Burn then compares the Arya Samaj with the Brahmo Samaj and concludes as follows: "I am, however, unable to see in its history or principles any warrant for the belief held by many missionaries that the Aryas will end by becoming Christian."[1]

2. *The Future of the Arya Samaj*

The conditions in India are so mutable and the influences at work so complex, varied and numerous, that it is impossible to see very far ahead. The Christian missionary is not merely hopeful but even positive that India will be Christian in the near future. Independent testimony of varying weight is opposed to this view. We have no qualifications for the *rôle* of prophet, and we do not think highly

[1] *Census Report for U.P. for* 1901, pp. 89-90.

of persons who assume that *rôle* without such qualifications. In our personal capacity as Indian, as Hindu and especially as Arya Samajist, we hope that the Hindus will be true to the faith of their forefathers, and will not change their national character so completely as would be involved by their becoming Christians. But we know that powerful influences are at work in favour of Christianity. Europe and America alike are eager propagandists, and their resources in men and money are practically inexhaustible. It would be futile to deny that Christianity is gaining ground; every decade sees a large accession to its numbers; Christian institutions, religious, educational, and philanthropic, are being multiplied. It is no satisfaction to be told that "the work of conversion to Christianity is now limited mainly to the depressed classes."[1]

The apologists say, and rightly, too, that "it is not at all surprising that low caste converts should be many, and high class converts few, because this was always the course that Christianity took."[2] Consequently they see no reason for reproach in the fact that "certain missions converted chiefly the lowest of the low and did not demand of them a high standard of belief." The simple truth is: "they could get no other than low class converts."[3] It is further admitted that their greatest weapon is the ample provision they can afford to make for the *corpus sanum* of their converts. In a poverty-stricken country like India, with its recurring

[1] *Punjab Census Report for* 1911, p. 191.
[2] *Census Report for U.P. for* 1911, p. 145.
[3] *Ibid.*

famines, earthquakes, floods and other visitations, that is the most effective argument any propagandist can advance in support of the superiority of his or her religion. This is all true, but what the Hindu reformer dreads most is the political argument.

We have already noticed that one of the reasons why the Arya Samaj is considered anti-British is that it is anti-Christian. Mr. Blunt has considered that argument at some length, and we have reproduced his conclusion. But the very fact of this argument requiring so much serious consideration is significant of the political importance of Christianity. In the *U.P. Census Report for* 1901, Mr. Burn also said that the "future of Christianity was of some importance apart from its spiritual aspect."

We ourselves have heard Indians expressing themselves in favour of the wholesale conversion of India to Christianity for the sake of political unity and political progress. It is true they do not care a brass farthing for religion, or for the spiritual aspect of the question : all that they have in view is the political gain. One may deplore the Machiavellian *naïveté* of the suggestion, but it is impossible to overlook its significance. Those who make these suggestions, however, know very little of their country and their people. They have seen them only through the eyes of foreign writers. They forget that even Islam could not conquer Hinduism. Much less is the chance for Christianity to succeed where Islam failed. Nor must the significance of the fact be ignored that no sooner had Christianity started its work in India than Hinduism prepared to fight it with its own weapons. The Brahmo Samaj was the first defence of Hinduism against the Christian invasion. And, immediately the Brahmo Samaj showed signs of weakness, the more formidable Arya Samaj sprang into being. In parts or circles of the country which the Arya Samaj did not reach, or failed to impress, the Hinduism of Mrs. Besant and the Vivekananda Mission stepped in. Moreover, Hinduism still has vitality enough to throw out further defensive "*isms*" if by any combination of circumstances the movements we have named fail to protect it from the attacks of aggressive, proselytizing Christianity. Christianity is bound to progress, as we have stated before. It may claim millions more of converts in the near future ; but, so far as mere human foresight will serve us, we can see no ground to fear that the bulk of Hindus or Musulmans will ever become Christians.

So critical an observer and scholar as Sir Herbert Risley has said that, "The supremacy of Hinduism as the characteristic religion of India is not as yet seriously threatened. The Animistic hem of the garment may, indeed, be rent off, and its fragments be parted among rival faiths. But the garment itself, woven of many threads and glowing with various colours will remain intact and continue to satisfy the craving for spiritual raiment of a loose and elastic texture which possesses the Indian mind."

"It has often been said," proceeds Sir H. Risley, "that the advance of English education, and more especially the teaching of physical science, will make short work of the Hindu religion, and that the rising generation of Hindus is doomed to wander without guidance in the wilderness of agnosticism. This opinion seems to lose sight of some material considerations. Science, no doubt, is a powerful solvent of mythology and tradition, and the 'seas of treacle and seas of butter' over which Macaulay made merry in his famous Minute are not likely to resist its destructive influence. But the human mind is hospitable and the Indian intellect has always revelled in the subtleties of a logic which undertakes to reconcile the most manifestly contradictory propositions. Men whose social and family relations compel them to lead a double life, will find little difficulty in keeping their religious beliefs and their scientific convictions in separate mental compartments. Putting aside, however, casuistry of this kind, an inevitable feature of a period of transition, it may fairly be said, in justice to the adaptability of Hinduism, that a religion which has succeeded in absorbing Animism is not likely to strain at swallowing Science. The doctrine of Karma, which in one of its aspects may be regarded as a sort of moral totalisator infallibly recording the good and bad actions of men, admits of being represented, in another aspect, as an ethical anticipation of the modern determinist doctrine that character and circumstance are the lords of life; that the one is a matter of heredity and the other a matter of accident, and that the idea of man being master of his fate is no better than a pleasing fiction conjured up by a human fantasy to flatter human egotism. Nor is this the last refuge of Hinduism. If it appeals to the intellect by its metaphysical teaching, it also touches the emotions by the beatific vision which it offers to the heart and the imagination. Dr. Grierson may or may not be right in holding that the doctrine of *bhakti*, or ecstatic devotion, which has played so large a part in the later developments of Hinduism, was borrowed by Chaitanya from Christian sources. To some minds the evidence in support of this view may appear rather conjectural. But, whatever may have been its origin, the idea has now taken its place among the characteristic teachings of Hinduism; it has been absorbed in the fullest sense of the word. And a religion which rests both on philosophy and on sentiment is likely to hold its ground until the Indian temperament itself undergoes some essential change."[1]

Mr. Burn also points out that the belief that the Aryas will end by becoming Christians "starts out with the assumption that Hinduism is a moribund faith, an assumption which was strongly contested by Sir A. C. Lyall. It further seems to ignore the fundamental difference between the attitude of East and West towards philosophy, which is often considered by Christians as an intellectual study of no great importance, as far as religion is concerned, but which in India is a very vital part of religion. The faith of the Arya Samaj appeals strongly to the intellectual Hindu by its adherence to the philosophy and cosmogony which are familiar to him, and by its maintenance of the inspired nature of the Vedas, while even its position with regard to Pantheism and image-worship is not unfamiliar. Further, while the attitude of the orthodox Hindu

[1] *The Peoples of India*, pp. 245-6

towards Christianity is for the most part one of indifference, probably based on a supreme belief in the superiority of his own faith, and the impossibility of Christianity supplanting it, the Arya Samaj has taken up an attitude of active hostility, and directs special efforts towards the conversion of persons who have embraced Christianity or Islam. For these reasons the Arya Samaj appears to me to contain the elements of a certain success as a religious movement."[1]

But what is most significant is that some Christian thinkers and writers do not hesitate to confess that, so far, all the missionary labours have resulted in "a comparative failure, when viewed from the standpoint of conversion of India to the Christian faith."[2]

All competent and impartial observers are thus agreed that in the immediate future there is no fear of Christianity dislodging Hinduism from its predominant position among the religions of India. On the other hand, the greater the activities of the Christian missionaries to convert India to Christianity, the greater the chance of the Arya Samaj to work, to struggle and to thrive. The Arya Samaj is not afraid of struggle. In the words of the Rev. C. F. Andrews, the Arya Samaj has been from the first "decidedly militant in spirit and policy"; for the simple reason that it has two militant Churches to counteract, viz., Islam and Christianity. Any increase in the activities of the latter is its chance and from its past history we may safely conclude that it is not likely to miss it.

[1] *Census Report for U.P. for* 1901, p. 90.

[2] *Our Task in India*, by Bernard Lucas, p. 45; Macmillan, 1914.

It must be remembered that the spirit of militancy in the Arya Samaj does not aim at destruction. "To-day it is by far the most powerful indigenous reforming movement in the North of India."[1] Its opposition to Christianity and Islam is by no means its principal work. In fact, much of its vitality lies in active constructive propaganda. It has a complete social programme and is always active. In the minds of some of its adherents, the fear is not that it may collapse by inactivity, but that it may suffer from over-activity. This is an aspect with which we propose to deal later. Here it should be noted, however, that every time the Arya Samaj has been in trouble, it has come out of it the stronger. The greatest crisis in its history came in 1907, when its existence was in danger at the hands of the Government. This crisis lasted until the end of 1910, but, in the census of 1911, it was found that its numbers had more than doubled within the preceding ten years.

The Arya Samaj is militant, not only externally —*i.e.*, in its attitude towards other religions—but it is equally militant internally. Its members do not spare one another. It is not unfrequently the case that the Press and the platform are both vigorously engaged in internal warfare. The two parties are often at loggerheads, and on such occasions they do not leave any weapon unused which they have ever wielded against outsiders. The less educated members do not always use refined language in their criticisms of the opposite party, or even in their inter-party criticism. We have often deprecated

[1] Rev. C. F. Andrews, in *The Indian Renaissance*, p. 122.

this spirit of hyper-criticism, but at the same time we have always maintained that we would rather have this spirit than the indifference and stagnation that characterized the Hinduism of pre-Arya Samaj days. The one gratifying and hopeful feature that stands out pre-eminently in the history of the Arya Samaj is that its members know how to close their ranks whenever there is an attack on them from outside. Every time a serious crisis had to be faced, the Arya Samaj has been ready to face it. Against dangers from without, the Arya Samajists have always shown a united front. It was so in 1902, when the Christians proposed to give them a crushing blow by prosecuting one of their Presidents for kidnapping an orphan Hindu girl, of whom they had taken charge in famine days. The girl had a husband. In the days of scarcity their home had been broken, and in search of food they had strayed away from each other. The girl was taken charge of by one of the Christian agents, and was eventually transferred to a lady hotel-keeper at Simla, who, the girl alleged, sweated and ill-treated her. She ran away and took refuge in the house of the President of the local Arya Samaj. The lady appealed to the police, who arrested the President, and for several days kept him in custody, refusing bail. After a costly trial, however, the case ended favourably to the Arya Samaj. Both sections made a united stand. Again, in the troubles of 1907 and 1910, the same thing happened.

The mutual recriminations in which the Arya Samajists indulge against one another are not at all a pleasant feature of their activities, especially when we see the same spirit exhibited in their dealings with Hinduism and Hindu movements. For some time they would have nothing to do with purely Hindu movements. Happily, that phase has disappeared, and we shall find testimony enough on that point in the following paragraphs.

3. *The Future of Hinduism bound up with the Arya Samaj*

In the opinion of many, the future of the Arya Samaj is practically the future of Hinduism, and there is no reason to think that the latter is in any way seriously threatened. The Arya Samaj teaches the true and genuine Hinduism of the Vedas, it works in the interests of the Hindus, and it protects the Hindu community from the aggressions of other alien religions. It does not aim at any future, outside and beyond the pale of Hinduism.

For a short time in the history of the Arya Samaj there was a tendency to break away from Hinduism altogether, but that was due principally to the dislike which the Aryas have to the word "*Hindu*," which they think is of foreign origin and means "a slave."

On this point we have the incontestable testimony of the Census Commissioner of the Punjab. Referring to Mr. Maclagan's remark in the *Report* of 1910 that "the stricter Aryas" had "a prejudice against being classed as Hindus," he observes: "But this objection was, and still is, based upon the contemptuous meaning which the foreign term, Hindu, acquired during the Mahomedan period." Yet when, "at the time of issuing instructions to enumerators, the chief authorities at the headquarters of the Arya Samaj were consulted as to whether they should be returned as professing a separate religion or not, although taking exception to the term 'Hindu,' they did not wish to be treated as separate from the Hindu society, and consequently decided that the Aryas should return themselves as Hindu by religion and Arya or Vedic Dharm by sect. Of course the Aryas do not regard their faith as a sect. . . . A part cannot, however, be larger than the whole, and, considering that the term 'Hindu' has come to be universally accepted as representing the religious and social practices of people known as Hindus, no course was open but to treat the Arya Samaj as a sect." It should be noted as a fact of some importance that the writer of this report is himself a Hindu of the highest caste (a Kashmiri Pandit) who is not an Arya, and throughout this chapter he takes pains to explain that the Arya Samaj is not a separate religion and that the Aryas are Hindus.

It is true, as Mr. Blunt says, that "the Brahmin priest hates and fears the Samaj," but it is not correct to add that "the educated among the orthodox abhor their teachings." It is a pity that a generally fair critic like Mr. Blunt should have been misled by a few stray facts so far as to say that "the educated Hindu hates and fears and is seldom unready to speak evil of them."[1] He admits, however, that "a great majority of Arya converts belong to the educated classes," and that, on the whole, "Aryaism appeals rather to the educated

[1] *Census Report for U.P. for* 1911, pp. 137-8

and to the higher castes than to the illiterate and the lower castes."[1] The statement that "the stricter members of the orthodox Hinduism would never regard Aryas as true Hindus" and that "no one would think of taking water from them"[2] are so transparently extravagant that no one need seriously refute them. Even Mr. Blunt has to add that "there is some evidence that Aryas are beginning to gain a footing with the orthodox" and also that "the orthodox Hindus are willing enough to claim the Aryas as a Hindu sect when it happens to suit their political aspirations."[3]

Pandit Hari Keshan Kaul's description of the present situation is much more accurate in this respect. He says: "Owing to the lapse of time the opposition of the Sanatanists (the orthodox) to the Arya Samaj has become feeble, and, with the marked change in the ideas of the majority of educated Hindus, a great many of the Arya Samaj propaganda have been accepted by the Hindu community, while, on the other hand, the Arya Samaj have moderated their tone of criticism and begun to show more respect to some of the orthodox Hindu institutions. The result is that a greater harmony now prevails between the Arya Samajists and the orthodox Hindus. . . . and the two communities work together in several lines, such as the revival of ancient festivals, the promotion of the study of Sanskrit and Hindi, the spread of female education and the introduction of social reforms."[4]

[1] *Ibid.*, p. 139.
[2] *Ibid.*, p. 139.
[3] *Ibid.*, p. 140.
[4] *Punjab Census Report for* 1911, p. 134.

In the opinion of the present writer, the Arya Samaj can have no higher or nobler ambition than that the whole of its teachings, or at least its spirit, may be adopted by Hinduism as its own, thus obviating the necessity of a separate propaganda. Be that as it may, however, the *rapprochement* of the orthodox and the reformers is a hopeful sign of the times.

In this increasing friendliness with orthodox Hinduism lies the strength of the Arya Samaj, but therein also lurks the danger of a lowering of the standards of reform. We earnestly desire, of course, that the Arya Samaj should effectually serve both Hinduism and the Hindu community: which service is, has been, and shall ever be, its guiding nature and very *raison d'être*: but, nevertheless, we should not like the Arya Samaj to be lost in the vast sea of Hinduism. We should like it to exist for Hinduism first and for the rest of the world afterwards; but we should deplore its being merged in Hinduism or in any other *ism*. Its independence is the charter of its existence and of its usefulness. It is a champion of Hinduism in more senses than one. Its members are proud of Hinduism. They have no hesitation, and will never have any, in staking everything they possess in the defence of the Hindu community; but the strength of the advocate lies in maintaining his independence in spite of his identifying himself with the cause of his client. This peril to its independence is one against which we would seriously warn the Arya Samaj, and we say so in the best interests of the Hindu community and of Hinduism.

Another danger against which we would warn

the Arya Samaj is the multiplication of institutions beyond its immediate resources. We have it on the testimony of the Rev. C. F. Andrews that "its powers of expansion have not yet reached their limit," but the best interests of expansion on safe and sound lines require a certain amount of concentration. Having "too many irons in the fire," without the capacity and power to manage them efficiently, might prove a grave source of weakness in times of crisis. It might seriously hamper the singleness of purpose, the homogeneity of motive and the devotion to principle which have enabled the Samaj to maintain its powerful advance. It matters little if material results are slow in coming. What is of most account is that the spirit remains unchanged, unbroken, unimpaired. Too great a diffusion of energy, with an easy-going conscience and a desire to reconcile all the conflicting interests to which unrestricted expansion gives rise, has in the past brought ruin to empires, and, to compare small things with great, the same defective organization might, if not properly guarded against, bring the yet tiny bark of the Arya Samaj to hopeless wreck. We are in favour of decentralization on principle, but what we should aim at is co-ordinated decentralization. The Arya Samaj should devote its best energies to putting its house in order, before it founds new institutions and undertakes new responsibilities: and to this end it is necessary to curb the spirit of mutual recrimination and acrimony which finds ugly expression as soon as the enemy from without has been, for the time being, pushed back. The enemies of the Arya Samaj are very wise in war, and, instead of making a frontal attack, they may aim to destroy or at least to weaken the Samaj by outflanking movements. We have seen something of this in the past and may see more in the future. Mutual confidence, mutual respect and regard, make up the bed-rock upon which the edifice of the Samaj has been built. The underminer of this rock is the greatest enemy of the Samaj, whether within or without its walls. Compromise in details, in methods, in points of view, in procedure and even in measures, is the first principle of ordered public life, and this the Indians must learn from the West, no less than they must learn from Westerners how to defeat tyranny, injustice and high-handedness. Discipline, obedience to authority properly constituted and to the constitution itself, is fully as necessary to the success of an organization as is the spirit of independent criticism and of rebellion against oppression to save it from immobility, stagnation and death.

A certain amount of conservatism also is absolutely necessary for orderly progress. It gives steadiness to the movement and saves it from the evil consequences of sudden, ill-conceived and ill-organized upheavals. What the Arya Samaj should aim at is mobility tempered with conservatism, well-considered and well-conceived progress, steady though slow. In the confidence that we have a mission in life, that we have a task to fulfil which is at once noble, grand and high ; in the faith that we have the will and the capacity to reach the goal ; in the determination to reach that goal, in spite of difficulties, obstacles, and maybe persecution also;

in the hope that we are always ready, in the future as in the past, to suffer for our convictions and to prove the strength of our faith by our sufferings, we should march on with a sure step, taking every risk which cannot be avoided without sacrifice of principle so far as individuals are concerned, but jealously and zealously guarding the corporate life of the organization that was raised by holy hands for holy purposes and from the holiest of motives.

The life of the Samaj is dearer to us than the life of any member or members thereof, but what is still more dear to us is the character of the Samaj—the character given to it, the character bequeathed to it, by its founder. The founder of the Arya Samaj had many opportunities of possessing large estates, of becoming rich as the head of great and wealthy religious institutions, or as leader of different religious orders existing in the country. But he spurned all. If he was indifferent to hate and malice he was also unaffected by love and sympathy. What he avoided most was the sympathy of his enemies. Let the Arya Samaj never forget that institutions are only means to ends. The Hindus made a mistake in confounding the two. Up to a certain stage, means are no doubt ends in themselves, but not always, and not absolutely. Let not the Arya Samaj repeat the mistake of Hinduism.

Hinduism had vitality enough to survive that grievous mistake; Hinduism created the Arya Samaj; Hinduism has vitality enough to save itself by other means if the Arya Samaj should fail it: but the death of the Arya Samaj would be an everlasting shame to those on whom the mantle of

Dayananda has fallen. He extorted admiration even from the enemy. It was of him that a broad-minded missionary has said:

"For Dayananda's personality and character there may well be almost unqualified admiration. He was a puritan to the backbone, and lived up to his creed. He was a fighter, strong, virile, independent, if somewhat imperious in behaviour. . . . . *His courage in facing his own countrymen through years of contumely and persecution was nothing less than heroic. He was a passionate lover of truth.*"[1]

Dayananda stamped the Arya Samaj with his own character. It is for his followers to efface it or to perpetuate it. Ever since he left his parental roof, he never slept on a bed of feathers; did not barter his independence even for life; and once more taught the Hindus how to create, how to assert and how to build. Let the managers of the Dayananda Anglo-Vedic College, which bears his honoured name, and also the founders and managers of the Gurukula, which aims to follow his footsteps more closely, remember that and be true to their ideals. If they do so, we can have no fears for the future of the Arya Samaj. If not, Hinduism will know how to use the creative energy generated by the Arya Samaj.

The Arya Samaj and its institutions are doing only what the British Government also is doing by its Educational Department, its Universities, its Railways, its Telegraphs, its Post Offices, its Courts, and—last, but far from least—what the British Nation is doing by allowing us to share its Press

[1] Rev. C. F. Andrews in *The Indian Renaissance.*

and its Literature. British rule in India has opened for us, so to say, the flood-gates of the ocean of thought, of culture and of liberalism ; it has materially helped in bringing back to us the consciousness of the fact that we were great and mighty in the realms both of thought and action, and that our national self-respect and honour demand that we should put forth our very best efforts to regain that proud position for our beloved country.

It is useless gloating over our past unless we can work out a future to be worthy of that past. We cannot exist on the bones of our forefathers. The memory of their achievements can stimulate us, can fill our souls with mingled pride and shame (pride in their greatness and shame of our meanness) : the record of past glories may legitimately elate us : but, in order to be alive, and alive with honour, we must live in the present (as did our ancestors in theirs), armed with the armoury of present-day institutions and present-day culture.

If our motives are pure and lofty, if our weapons are those of high character, self-sacrifice and noble deeds, and if in our march onward we are guided by that single-minded devotion to duty which alone can bring success to our arms, we need fear no failure, no repulses, no mishaps. Our opponents may employ all measures to defeat us, but in their heart of hearts they must respect us. The harder the fight, the greater the opportunities of showing the strength which our forefathers have bequeathed to us. These Samajes, Colleges, Sabhas, Leagues, Associations, Congresses and Conferences are all means to an end. They mark the various stages in our onward march to nationhood. They are the tools with which we are forging our national greatness, and by their fitness to help us in the achievement of that end, and by what they contribute to the consummation of that end, they will be judged.

One word more before we close. The Arya Samaj has to remember that the India of to-day is not exclusively Hindu. Its prosperity and future depends upon the reconciliation of Hinduism with that greater *ism*— Indian Nationalism—which alone can secure for India its rightful place in the comity of nations. Anything that may prevent, or even hinder, that consummation is a sin for which there can be no expiation.

THE END

BIBLIOGRAPHY

(*Italic figures indicate pages where cited in this book*)

I.—In English, by Indians

1. *The Teachings of the Arya Samaj*, by Bawa Chhajju Singh (1908). Arya Samaj, Anarkali, Lahore. —*xxiii, xxv.*
2. *The Life and Teachings of Swami Dayananda Saraswati*, by Bawa Chhajju Singh (1903). Arya Samaj, Anarkali, Lahore.
3. *The Works of Pandit Gurudatta Vidyarthi, M.A.*, including his Terminology of the Vedas, his Translation and Exposition of the Upanishads, and his Criticism of Western Scholars, etc. Arya Samaj, Lahore; Punjab Printing Co., Lahore; or Lala Jiwan Dass, Pensioner, Lahore.—*76, 77, 95.*
4. *The Message of the Vedas*, by Dr. Gokal Chand, M.A., Ph.D. (1906), Lahore.—*xxv.*
5. *The Sattyarath Prakasha of Swami Dayananda*, by Dr. Chiranjeva Bharadwaja. Arya Samaj, Wachchowali, Lahore.—*176.*
6. Ditto, by Master Durga Prasad. Virjananda Press, Lahore.
7. *Life of Pandit Gurudatta Vidyarthi*, by Lajpat Rai. Virjananda Press, Lahore.
8. *Handbook of the Arya Samaj*, by Pandit Vishnu Lal Sharma, M.A. Tract Department of the Arya Pratinishi Sabha, Mathura, U.P.—*xxiii.*

9. *A Lecture on the Arya Samaj*, by L. Mulraj, M.A., Premchand Roychand Student, Lahore.—*108, 109.*

10. *The Great Seer*, by L. Hansraj, B.A. Arya Samaj, Anarkali, Lahore.—*243.*

11. *Lectures on the Arya Samaj*, by L. Munshi Rama. Arya Samaj, Wachchowali, Lahore. —*xxiii.*

12. *The Arya Samaj*, by Professor Ram Deva, Editor of *The Vedic Magazine.*

13. *Swamiji on the Vedas.* Young Men's Arya Samaj, Lahore.

14. *Conception of Godhead in the Vedas.* Young Men's Arya Samaj, Lahore.

15. *A Speech on the Depressed Classes*, by Lajpat Rai, Lahore.

16. *The Depressed Classes*, by Lajpat Rai. Ishwar Chandra, Arya Tract Society, Lahore.

17. *Luther of India* (Swami Dayananda), by Dr. Gokal Chand, M.A., Ph.D. Arya Tract Society, Lahore.

18. *The Arya Samaj and its Detractors*, by Mahatma Munshi Ram and Professor Ram Deva. Gurukula, Kangri, Haridwar.—*170.*

19. *The Reports of the Gurukula.* Gurukula, Kangri, Haridwar.

20. *The Gurukula with European Eyes.* Ditto.

21. *The Vedic Magazine and Gurukula Samachar* (a monthly periodical). Ditto.—*175.*

22. *The Gurukula System of Education and its Critics*, by Prof. Balkrishna, M.A. Ditto.

23. *Ideal of Education, Ancient and Modern*, by Rama Deva. Ditto.

24. *The Fountain-head of Religion,* by Ganga Parshad. M.A. Arya Tract Society, Moradabad, U,P., India.

25. *Vedic Text, No.* 1, by Ganga Parshad, M.A. Arya Tract Society, Moradabad, U.P., India.

26. „ „ No. 2. Ditto.

27. *The Dayananda Anglo-Vedic College Reports.* D. A. V. Managing Committee's Office, Lahore. —*183.*

28. *The D.A.V. College Magazine.* Office of the D.A.V. College Union, Lahore.

29. *The Gurukula Magazine* (odd volumes). Gurukula, Gajranwala.

30. *Swami Dayananda* (Eminent Men of India Series). Nateson, Madras.

31. *Nation Builders of India.* Ganesh & Co., Madras.

32. *The Arya Samaj,* by Lajpat Rai. An article in *The Contemporary Review*, London, 1909.

II.—Official Publications and Appreciations, Criticisms, etc., by non-Indians

Punjab Census Report for 1891 (Maclagan).—*165, 262, 266, 274.*

Ditto for 1911 (Pandit Hari Keshan Kaul).—*220, 274, 276.*

U.P. Census Report for 1901 (Burn).—*165, 167, 221, 262, 265, 267, 270.*

Ditto for 1911 (Blunt).—*114, 116, 131, 135, 166-169, 218, 221, 225, 261, 266, 275-6.*

All India Census Report for 1901 and 1911.

Peoples of India, by Sir Herbert Risley.—*116, 252 262, 268.*

The New Spirit in India, by H. W. Nevinson.

The Awakening of India, by J. Ramsay MacDonald, M.P.

Round Table, London, for September, 1913.

Scenes of India, by J. A. Spender.

The Indian Renaissance, by the Rev. C. F. Andrews. —*272, 281.*

The Brahmo Samaj and the Arya Samaj, by F. Lillington, 1901.—*241.*

The Puritans of India. An article in *The New Statesman*, London, for June 20th, 1914.

The New India, by Sir Henry Cotton.—*262.*

Encyclopædia of Religions, by Hastings.

INDEX

GARDEN CITY PRESS LIMITED, PRINTERS, LETCHWORTH.